How
Christianity
Came to Britain
and Ireland

For fellow travellers on the road,
and those who have gone ahead.

How Christianity Came to Britain and Ireland

MICHELLE P. BROWN

LION

A Lion Book
an imprint of
Lion Hudson plc
Mayfield House, 256 Banbury Road,
Oxford OX2 7DH, England
www.lionhudson.com
ISBN 978 0 7459 5153 9
ISBN 0 7459 5153 8

First edition 2006
10 9 8 7 6 5 4 3 2 1 0

Typeset in 10.5/14 Original Garamond BT
Printed and bound in Singapore

Text acknowledgments
Every effort has been made to trace and
acknowledge copyright holders of all the quotations
included. We apologize for any errors or omissions
that may remain, and would ask those concerned to
contact the publishers, who will ensure that full
acknowledgment is made in the future.

pp. 68 & 70 (*St Patrick's Creed*), 97 (*Blackbird*), 98
(*Writing out of doors, Forever Cold*), 99 (*The Dawn*),
104 (*The Vikings*), 106 (*Colum Cille's Exile*), 112
(*Columbanus to his monks*), 114 (*Tears*), 115
(*Pilgrimage to Rome*), 116 (*Confession*): extracts
taken from *Mediaeval Irish Lyrics with The Irish
Bardic Poet*, Carney (1985). By permission of Colin
Smythe Limited on behalf of Paul Carney.
pp. 91 (*There is an island…*), 94 (*The Monk's
Mistress*), 100 (*The Wind*), 100–101 (*The Hermit*),
101 (*I Should Like to Have a Great Ale Feast*), 102
(*Suibne the Wild Man in the Forest*), 108 (*The Boorish
Patron, Finn's Generosity*), 109 (*Sunshine Through the
Window*, On Mael Mhuru the Poet): extracts taken
from A Celtic Miscellany by Kenneth Hurlstone
Jackson (1972), Routledge publishers. Reproduced
with permission.
pp. 121 & 122–123 (Beowulf), 146 (Cædmon's
Hymn), 149–150 (Riddles): reprinted by permission
of Boydell & Brewer Ltd from The Anglo-Saxon
World: An Anthology by Kevin Crossley-Holland
(Oxford Paperbacks 1984) pp. 74–5, 130, 131, 134;
197; 248, 241 respectively).

The Lindisfarne Gospels, British Library. Chi-rho page, opening with the sacred name of Christ in abbreviated Greek form. Lindisfarne, c.715–20.

CONTENTS

Britain, Ireland and Anglo-Saxon England

ORKNEYS

HEBRIDES

Tarbat

Burghead
Craig Phadraig

PICTS

DALRIADA

Iona

Dunadd

Dumbarton

Edinburgh

STRATHCLYDE

GODDODIN

Norham
Holy Island (Lindisfarne)

RHEGED

NORTHUMBRIA

Fahan

Deer Parks Farm

Jarrow
Monkwearmouth

Dooey

Moylarg Crannog

Chester-le-Street
Durham

Donegal

DALRIADA

Bangor

Whithorn

Lough Derg

Nendrum

Whitby

Armagh

MAN

DEIRA

Donore

Moynagh Lough

York

Kells

Newgrange

Elmet

Galway

Athlone

Tara
Lagore

Dublin

LINDSEY

ARAN ISLES

Clonmacnoise

Durrow

Glendalough

Penmon

MERCIA

Ballinderry

Dinas Emrys

GWYNED

Repton
Breedon

Burgh Castle

Limerick

Derrynaflan

Wroxeter

Peterborough

Gallarus Oratory

Ardagh

Cashel

Lichfield

Brixworth

EAST ANGLIA

Dunwich

Ahenny

Waterford

Wexford

POWYS

Sutton Hoo

Ring of Kerry

Nevern

Llandeilo Fawr

Llangorse

HWICCE

Chedworth

Colchester

Skelligs

Cork

St David's

DYFED

Caerleon

Uley

St Albans

ESSEX

Bradwell

London

Reculver

Llantwit Major

Dinas Powys

Lullingstone

KENT

Canterbury

Glastonbury

Winchester

Minster-in-Thanet

Athelney

WESSEX

SUSSEX

S. Cadbury

Sherborne

Southampton

Tintagel

CORNOVIA

Castle Dore

Carn Euny

St Michael's Mount

Northumbria in the eighth century

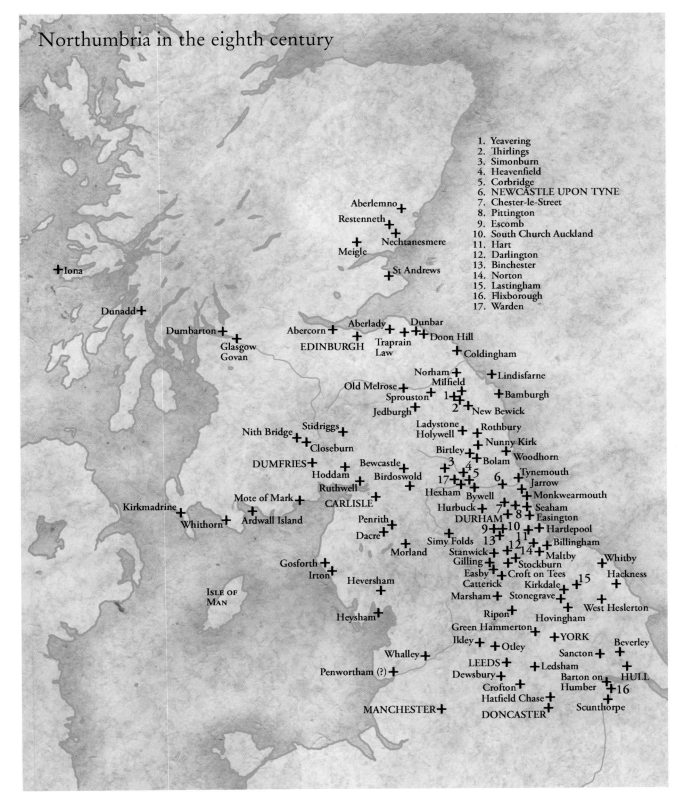

1. Yeavering
2. Thirlings
3. Simonburn
4. Heavenfield
5. Corbridge
6. NEWCASTLE UPON TYNE
7. Chester-le-Street
8. Pittington
9. Escomb
10. South Church Auckland
11. Hart
12. Darlington
13. Binchester
14. Norton
15. Lastingham
16. Flixborough
17. Warden

Iona

Dunadd

Dumbarton
Glasgow
Govan

Aberlemno
Restenneth
Nechtanesmere
Meigle
St Andrews

Abercorn Aberlady Dunbar
EDINBURGH Traprain Doon Hill
Law
Coldingham

Norham Lindisfarne
Old Melrose Milfield
Sprouston 1 Bamburgh
Jedburgh 2 New Bewick

Nith Bridge Stidriggs
Closeburn

Ladystone Rothbury
Holywell Nunny Kirk
Birtley
DUMFRIES 3 Bolam Woodhorn
Hoddam Bewcastle 4
Ruthwell Birdoswold 17 5 Tynemouth
Mote of Mark Hexham 6 Jarrow
CARLISLE Bywell Monkwearmouth
Hurbuck 7 Seaham
Penrith DURHAM 8 Easington
Dacre 9 10 Hartlepool
Simy Folds 13 11 Billingham
Morland 12
Stanwick 14 Maltby Whitby
Gilling Stockburn Hackness
Gosforth Easby Croft on Tees 15
Irton Catterick Kirkdale
Heversham Marsham Stonegrave West Heslerton

Kirkmadrine
Whithorn Ardwall Island

ISLE OF
MAN

Ripon Hovingham
Green Hammerton YORK
Heysham Ikley Otley Beverley
Sancton
Whalley LEEDS Ledsham
Penwortham (?) Dewsbury Barton on HULL
Crofton Humber 16
Hatfield Chase
MANCHESTER Scunthorpe
DONCASTER

7

Sowing the Seeds of Faith

The first millennium of the Christian faith sorely tested its radical nature. These first thousand years saw Christianity encountering and transforming the existing beliefs and structures of the world of Classical Antiquity and prehistoric northern Europe. They witnessed the demise of a superpower – the mighty Roman Empire – and the building of new relationships between the many people who came to occupy its territories and the frontier zones beyond. During this protracted tempering process, the Middle Ages were forged, with religion and the mutual support-structures of church and state at their core. What ultimately made this possible, however, was the extent to which the Christian ethos inspired men and women, from all walks of life, to embrace, enact and share its teachings.

This was a turbulent time in the history of the 'old world'. The Americas and Australasia were still undiscovered (except, of course, by their indigenous inhabitants, who had no idea that they had been 'lost'). They had long since been cut loose by continental drift to sail on the edge of the known world – which, according to medieval thought, radiated outwards from Jerusalem. It was an age of violence and uncertainty, pestilence and famine, and of competition for resources and power. In the vacuum left by imperialism a multitude of smaller states and sects emerged, and disappeared, as big fish swallowed smaller fish in the attempt to regain the myth of empire. Byzantine, Carolingian and Ottonian Christian rulers clad themselves in the imperial purple of ancient Rome and consumed their neighbours.

Religion was a powerful force. Territorial alignments were often based on ethnicity and religion, and the effects this had on the political landscape still fill our News programmes today. From the moment Jesus Christ left this earth, his teachings were supplemented by the man-made trappings of religion, as people sought both consciously and unconsciously to mould the divine to the service of human agendas. Other faiths, such as Judaism, Islam, Hinduism and Buddhism, went through similar processes of formalization and localized or sectarian adaptation. Around the time Augustine was reintroducing Christianity to the pagan court of a Germanic king, Ethelberht of Kent, Prince Shitoku was introducing Buddhism to Japan from China, building a monastery in Horyuji in 610. It is fascinating to see the parallels between these two distant groups of islands as they framed their new faiths and redefined their societies and their international relations. Each lay at the extreme edges of the then-known world, and each sat within a web of pilgrimage and trade routes that converged upon the Middle East.

Christ's command to his followers to carry the gospel to the farthest edges of the known world ensured Christianity's diffusion, initially within the territories governed by Rome and ultimately far beyond. Christianity originated in the Middle East, but its character evolved and was enriched both by the varied cultures of the Roman provinces, within an empire that stretched from Syria to the Atlantic seaboard, and by the successor states that rose to fill the vacuum left when the empire fragmented. The early Christian kingdoms of Britain, Ireland and Anglo-Saxon England were significant among the heirs of Rome, and this book will consider their distinctive contributions and background.

Christianity reached the British Isles during its earliest centuries, as new ideas were transported along with trade goods and with those who colonized this province of the Roman Empire. The megalithic monuments, sacred springs and oak groves which distinguished the landscape already spoke of the depth of faith that had existed in these isles since humankind first made its mark. By the time Rome withdrew at the start of the fifth century, the British church was flourishing, and was a participant in the life of the wider international Christian ecumen. This soon fractured, as the international edifice of Rome's authority crumbled and fragmented into East and West. Ireland had escaped absorption, but its crucial situation on the age-old trade routes of the Atlantic seaboard ensured that it too received the teachings of Christianity. By 431, the Pope was to send Palladius as bishop to those in the south-eastern coastal areas of Ireland who already believed.

Over the next 650 years more new peoples came to the isles, in the wake of their many prehistoric forerunners, as mercenaries, invaders, traders, settlers and economic migrants. There came Angles, Saxons, Frisians, Jutes, Vikings and Normans. They brought, and retained, their own cultural traditions, but Christianity helped to ease the processes of integration and assimilation, adapting its own local character to reflect and welcome the newcomer. And yet a distinctive 'insular' spirit was retained – ever of the islands. It was not inward-looking as we have come to interpret the term, but expansive and outward-looking, exchanging influences via the busy seaways, ever-conscious of ties to the land and to the encircling oceans. The landscape was a physically demanding rocky western desert, like that inhabited by the monastic fathers and hermits of the eastern deserts of Palestine, Syria and Egypt: a place where the individual could explore solitude in the wilderness places as well as life within community, taking time to listen and to empty the vessel of self in order to be filled with the spirit to recommit.

This was a time when faith was shaped not only by prophets, prelates and princes. Ordinary men, women and children opened their hearts and minds to it and placed their lives at the service of something much bigger than themselves. There is much to inspire us here as we move into the third millennium after the birth of Christ. Motivated people made a difference. They dared to think the unthinkable. In early Christian Britain and Ireland, Christianity was a radical social force. It could lead seasoned warriors to embrace pacifism and, if forced into battle, to go armed only with a wooden staff. It could lead kings to free slaves, thereby threatening to overthrow the whole social order – often at risk of their own assassination or forced abdication. Whole families, as well as individuals, chose to live God-centred lives, in innovative monastic communities that did not turn away from the world and its ills, but rather sought to address and transform it by committed service and by the positive energy of prayer. Relationship with the natural world was acknowledged and celebrated, and responsibilities to it recognized. And in response to the overwhelming beauty and bounty of creation, the impulse to create was given full rein, resulting in some of the world's most remarkable and beautiful works of art and literature, made as acts of prayer in the service of faith. Some of these – such as the Lindisfarne Gospels, the Book of Kells, the 'Dream of the Rood' and the Irish high-crosses – have survived against all the odds and continue to inspire us today.

In this misnamed 'Dark Age' there were new dreams to be dreamed, of how society could be, of how the individual related to the whole, and of the eternal relationship between creation and the creating force – God. The story of this remarkable transformation begins with the religious landscape of prehistory, before the coming of Christianity.

CHAPTER I

Sun, Stars and Standing Stones: Faith in Prehistoric Britain and Ireland

Humans first came to these islands more than 500,000 years ago, and yet it is only from around 4,500 BC that we can really begin to discern anything meaningful of their beliefs, from the physical remains they have left behind. That is not to say that they did not concern themselves before this with anything beyond subsistence, following their food in a seasonally shifting migration and seeking shelter and the tools necessary for survival; but rather that as they developed ties to the land, farming and mining it and putting down roots, they began to erect focal points to symbolize relationships across time and space. The perception of past, present and future had crystallized. From the late Mesolithic, or Middle Stone Age onwards (c.10,000–4,000 BC), we see a heightened preoccupation with ritual and burial sites. This predisposition may have helped to mould the more formal religion of the Iron-Age Celts, who began to arrive from the continent from around 650 BC and integrated with the indigenous Bronze Age (c.2,000–650 BC) population. By the time Julius Caesar came to Gaul and Britain during the 50s BC, the islands were the seat of Celtic druidism, with Mon – the island of Anglesey – its major university training ground. Many Celtic pagan beliefs may have predisposed its people to the Christian faith and indeed shaped Christianity's distinctive local form. In some ways the origins of British and Irish Christianity lie not only within the Middle East and the churches of Constantinople and Rome, but also within the cradle of local collective memory and in the shaping of the very land itself.

And it is you who say that the shades of the dead seek not the silent land of Erebus, and the pale halls of Pluto; rather, you tell us that the same spirit has a body again elsewhere, and that death, if what you sing is true, is but the mid-point of long life.

LUCAN, TO THE DRUIDS, *PHARSALIA*, BOOK I

RITUAL LANDSCAPES AND MEGALITHIC MONUMENTS

The Ring of Brodgar (see following spread) stands at the heart of the Orcadian mainland, the largest of the Orkney Islands. Its sweeping circle of stones (of which only 27 of the original 60 remain) hugs the brackened contour of a ribbon mound of land, the back of which rises like a sea-serpent from the lakes on either side – one salt water, the other fresh. At the eastern end of this isthmus stands a guardian watch stone, and beyond it the elegant, thin profiles of the Stones of Stennes, erected around 2,900 BC. A ritual pit for cremations or burial feasts lies at their feet. They frame a mound on the adjacent plain, the turfed emerald tumulus of Maes Howe which dates from before 2,700 BC. Crawl through its stone-lined entrance passage into the central chamber and you are in a perfectly corbelled vault. This was designed to enshrine the relics of the dead, and the stones once used to seal them now lie on the floor. This hall of the dead is graced by four large upright stones that recall the columns of ancient Crete and Egypt. Yet these pillars offer more than mere structural support. They are designed to align the entrance passage with the sun of the winter solstice as it rises between the far-off crags of Hoy, its rays penetrating to awaken the dead from their slumber. Leaving Brodgar towards the west, the road leads to the Atlantic, to Skaill Bay in the sands of which nestles the Neolithic settlement of Skara Brae, begun around 3,100 BC.

This is a ritual landscape, one of many to be found around the western seaboard of Europe. Humans had settled in this region before the glaciers retreated in around 9,000 BC, and had crossed to Ireland in around 7,000 BC, shortly after the last remaining land-bridges were swamped by rising seas, leaving the pattern of the isles. As they settled down to farm the land, graze their beasts, mine the ores and flints and fish the shores, during what are called the Mesolithic (c.10,000–4,000 BC), Neolithic (c.4,000–2,000 BC) and Bronze Ages (c.2,000–650 BC), these peoples marked the burials of their dead. Ancestors, they believed, bestowed identity and affirmed their ties to the land. They were signals of owning and belonging. The enduring ties between the living and the dead and hopes for reunion in times to come were the first to be enshrined in ritual. The dolmens ('table stones', cromlechs

or quoits), Neolithic long barrows and Bronze-Age circular mounds that still mark the promontories, rising ground and plains of the British Isles, Ireland, Scandinavia, Brittany and Iberia, acted as focal points within early societies, and show the great efforts these people made in the service of their beliefs. The same can be said for the circles, lines or single standing stones (menhirs), so many of which are carefully aligned to observe the course of the heavens. Others, particularly the standing and holed stones with their phallic and feminine connotations, reveal a more immediate preoccupation with fertility.

Such megalithic monuments began to be built from around 4,500 BC. They can be found around the world and date from widely different periods, despite their technical and design similarities. Such similarities have led some archaeologists to assume that those on the Atlantic coasts were modelled on those found in the eastern Mediterranean, such as in Malta. But radiocarbon dating has now shown that the earliest such monuments were built in Portugal and western France. Those found in Britain and Ireland may have been influenced by trade links with these areas, or have evolved in parallel. All such monuments share one thing in common: they contain group burials and were built through group endeavour. Some were used for centuries, serving as charnel houses for bones exposed or initially deposited elsewhere, or as the equivalents of the family mausolea of later times. Whether they were erected to contain the remains of the most powerful and wealthy, or held the communal burials of people from a more egalitarian society, they represent the formal acknowledgement of collective identity and the origins of genealogy.

Generations after they ceased to be used, they still dominate the landscape and

Men-an-Tol, a stone alignment associated with a fertility cult, sited on the Tinner's Way, an important trade route during the Bronze Age. West Penwith, Cornwall.

Ring of Brodgar, a late Neolithic observatory, Orkneys.

the imagination. Viking warriors took shelter in Maes Howe during a storm in the tenth century. They spent their time seeking the treasure they assumed was buried there and idly scratching graffiti on the walls.

For the Celts, and the subsequent folklorists, these prehistoric monuments were the portals to the otherworld, the dwelling place of the *Tuatha dé Danann* (the tribe of the goddess Dana), the immortals who left the world of men to become the *Sidhe*, the fairy folk or 'little people' (the term 'leprachaun' deriving from the

nickname for the god Lugh who became stooped when he joined the *Sidhe* in their mounds). On the Celtic festival of Samhain, which fell on 31 October (1 November marked the end of the pastoral year which was later Christianized as All Saints/All Hallows; 31 October is still celebrated as Halloween), these monuments were thought to become permeable barriers between worlds, enabling communion between humans and spirits. The other major festival of the Celtic year was Beltaine, which fell on May Eve and 1 May (May Day, Christianized as the feast of St John the Baptist) and marked the start of summer. At this festival, the fires of Bel, the life-giver represented by the sun, were lit. Fires were

Skara Brae, a Neolithic village first occupied from c.3,100 BC, perhaps by the sages who designed the astronomically-orientated standing stones and tombs of the Orkneys.

extinguished throughout Celtic lands and were rekindled from druidic pyres. The sacred fire of Bel – the sun's rays – symbolized purification and a new start. This practice was Christianized by St Patrick in the fifth century when he extinguished King Laoghaire's sacred bonfire and replaced it with the Paschal (Easter) flame.

PREHISTORIC PRESERVERS OF KNOWLEDGE

Such rituals and beliefs had their genesis in the age-old links to the land and the origin myths circulated by the professional priesthood of the Celtic Iron Age. It is possible that such specialist preservers of knowledge existed earlier in prehistory. (The term 'prehistory' refers to the period before written records were kept in any given society, which in the case of Britain was prior to its absorption into the Roman Empire in the first century AD, and in Ireland was prior to the conversion to Christianity during the fifth and sixth centuries.) Some authors have claimed that the high status and unusual nature of the village of Skara Brae suggest that it functioned as something of a proto-monastery, occupied at the height of its development by an intellectual elite engaged in divination and astronomical observation. Other prehistorians, however, prefer a more prosaic interpretation of the settlement as a secular village, if a remarkably well-appointed one. We are only now beginning to realize the level of mathematical and astronomical expertise possessed by such prehistoric sages, wherever they lived. We will never fully comprehend the true significance of their great temples of stone. But we should not let that blind us to the depth of faith and the quest for knowledge that they represent. Our Neolithic and Bronze-Age ancestors clearly concerned themselves greatly with the questions how and why, seeking to understand their place in the bigger picture and to imbue it with meaning.

Nowhere is this more evident than within the greatest prehistoric monuments of them all: Carnac, Newgrange, Callanish, Avebury, Silbury, Stonehenge and their surrounding landscapes. Some of the massive stones used at Stonehenge had to be rolled and rafted over two hundred miles from the Preselli Hills of West Wales to Salisbury Plain when construction began around 2,200 BC. Stonehenge was a modern addition to a sacred landscape of earthworks and burial mounds that was already over 1,000 years old, made by people who had just begun using gold to denote their status. Although bearing little resemblance to modern celebrations, Stonehenge undoubtedly had a religious and ceremonial focus. It was probably centred on mediation between humankind and nature, through astronomical observation based on the phases of sun and moon and the summer and winter solstices. Many of the most important people of the day would have been buried within its vicinity, as in a Christian cathedral. At Newgrange the constellations may be mapped in the spiraliform carvings that adorn the entrance stones, depicting a celestial landscape as do some Native American rock carvings. The labyrinth or maze also has its origins in prehistory, engraved upon boulders by Bronze-Age and Iron-Age carvers and described in the oral epics composed by Homer. It has been perpetuated in the Christian prayer labyrinth, such as the one delineated on the flagstone floor of Chartres Cathedral during the thirteenth century. Interestingly, prayer labyrinths are becoming increasingly popular today.

Studies suggest that animism was often prevalent during the early stages of religious development. The manifestations of nature – water, rock, trees, plants and creatures – were imbued with the attributes of deities and demons which needed to

Newgrange, entrance to the most famous of the Neolithic barrows of the Boyne Valley in Ireland. Such barrows were later thought to be entrances into the otherworld inhabited by the *Sidhe* or 'little people'.

be appeased to ensure good fortune. Vestiges of such practices can be seen in the subsequent emphasis on sacred springs, wells and groves in ancient Celtic and Germanic religion and also in their continued use today as focal points for Christian and pagan alike. The ribbons and bandages tied to the twigs of trees and the coins in the fountain or wishing-well have symbolized the hopes, fears and aspirations of ordinary people through the ages. Divination, charms and magic all find their roots here too.

RITES OF PASSAGE

Rites of passage have always been important focuses of faith. These are the times when we call out to something, or someone, to help us take the big steps on our own individual journey. The most common shared experiences are nonetheless the most uniquely personal of them all – birth, adolescence, marriage and mating, illness and death. Amongst the earliest ritual artefacts to survive from prehistory are effigies of the fertile, pregnant, female form. For our ancestors, the mystery of conception and childbirth was initially associated with the visible role of the woman in giving birth. This led to an association of the fertility of the soil and of nature with a feminine person – the earth mother, Mother Nature. Only later was the role of man celebrated by images of the phallus. Linked with this may be the identification of solar and lunar observation and worship with male and female manifestations of divinity. This has been preserved in a Christian context in the lyrical references to St Francis of Assisi and his follower, Clare, as 'brother sun and sister moon'. Similarly, grave goods accompanying burials from the earliest times show a symbolic need to signal the ongoing life of the deceased and to provide for them in the afterlife.

THE ORIGINS OF THE CELTS

The beautiful, complex art and artefacts of the pagan Celts allow us to penetrate further into their minds. The two main phases of Celtic cultural development have been named after two important archaeological sites in Austria and Switzerland:

Ogam stone with parallel Latin inscription, carved in the sixth century to commemorate Maglocunus. Nevern Church, Pembrokeshire, Wales.

Hallstatt (c.650–450 BC) and La Tène (c.450 BC until incorporation into the Roman Empire from the 50s BC in the cases of Britain and Gaul; or until the conversion to Christianity – from the fifth century AD – in the case of Ireland).

Traditionally it is believed that the Celts originated in the Steppes and, through their mastery of iron technology and the horse, spread into central Europe. From there they advanced throughout the continent and even into parts of Asia Minor, becoming the dominant element in late prehistoric society

Celtic myths

The Celtic vision of the otherworld, most popularly portrayed as *Tír na nÓg*, Land of the Young, was equivalent to that of the classical Elysian Fields wherein the blessed were forever young and blissfully happy. Its other Celtic forms included *Tír fo Thuinn* (Land under the Waves – an Atlantis equivalent), *Tír na mBan* (Land of Women) and *Tír Tairnigiri* (Land of Promise). Celtic myths abound with tales of water sprites, merpeople, submerged dwellings and water as the source of life, and these beliefs are reinforced by the votive deposits found in so many springs, rivers and lakes and the dedications of wells to the nymph Coventina.

The gateway to the otherworld was the Cave of Cruachan, guarded by Cruithne the cat, a Celtic version of the classical guard dog, Cerberus. *Tír na nÓg* was to be found floating in the Atlantic, to the west of the world against the backdrop of the setting sun. This motif was continued in the Christian literature of the Celts, the yearning to attain it characterized by Singe as the 'westwardness of things'. Cruachan was sometimes interpreted by Christian scribes as the mouth of hell. Thus Celtic beliefs may already have engendered an inclination towards Christian concepts of creation, baptism, afterlife, heaven and hell.

The legends of Ireland, and to a lesser extent Wales, exhibit an attempt – as with Germanic mythology – to encapsulate folk memory and allegorical explanation of the origins of life. The Irish Mythological Cycle, with its 'Book of Invasions' (*Lebor Gabála*), tells of an early race that perished in the biblical flood and was replaced by a band of 24 male and 24 female settlers, led by the Greek, Partholón. They started clearing the plains, adding to the lakes, farming and grazing the land, and they introduced gold working, beer brewing, the cauldron, law-giving and ritual before being wiped out by plague. They were the first to fight the demonic supernatural Fomorians. The next settlers were the Nemed, who further worked the land. They were defeated by the Fomorians, became their vassals and eventually fled. Next came the Fir Bolg, the Fir Gaileion and the Fir Domnann, their names recalling those of incoming tribes from the continent – the Belgae, the Gauls and the Dumnonii. These groups were ousted by the godlike *Tuatha Dé Danann* who attempted to co-exist with the Fir Bolg and the indigenous Fomorians, but who were dispossessed, became gods and retreated to the burial grounds as the otherworldly *Sidhe*. Finally came the human Milesians, the Sons of Mil from Iberia, from whom the historic Christianized inhabitants of Ireland claimed descent.

However, some historians and archaeologists have recently begun to question whether the 'Celts' actually existed as a distinct ethnic group. They base their doubts on the similarities between aspects of Celtic material culture and those of the Germanic peoples of the North, and on the continuity of pre-existing Urnfielder society resident throughout much of Europe, who buried their dead in urns in cemetery fields.

If 'Celtic' denotes anything it is a linguistic group, an Indo-European language, of which two branches have survived even to the present day. Goidelic (Q Celtic) and Brythonic (P Celtic) can be separated by a phonetic distinction demonstrated, for example, by the Goidelic word *cenn* and the Brythonic word *pen* for 'head'. Goidelic, the basis of Irish and Scots Gaelic and that of the Isle of Man, was probably the older branch. Brythonic was the source of Welsh, Cornish and Breton, and was probably the result of phonetic shift and contact with the Latin of the Roman Empire. Some pre-Indo-European linguistic pockets have survived, notably Finnish and Basque, and it has been suggested that the Pictish inhabitants of Scotland (named the 'Picti', or 'painted ones' by Roman authors on account of their practice of personal tattooing and painting with woad) may also have spoken a pre-Indo-European tongue. The success of Celtic linguistic and cultural imposition does not necessarily mean that mass migration and the disruption of indigenous communities occurred. It may have taken the form of the expansion of a warrior elite who took control of the existing societies they encountered and whose practices and fashions were gradually adopted by the native populace, the Celts in turn becoming influenced by local custom and circumstance. Whatever the ethnic composition of European Iron-Age society, it is clear that a distinctive form of social organization, art and religion emerged and enjoyed widespread currency. We see the first signs of the impact of such incoming groups in Scotland from around 650 BC. Soon afterwards they are evident in Ireland and then elsewhere in Britain.

THE DRUIDS

From around 400 BC more Celtic immigrants are thought to have arrived from the continent – the La Tène Celts, characterized by their beautiful organic style of art. These were followed by yet more, from the Belgic tribes of Gaul in the second and first centuries BC. They brought with them a more sophisticated hierarchical structure, headed by a chariot-borne warrior elite with numerous kings and a privileged intelligentsia consisting of craftspeople and the *druides*.

The druids were a class of professional priests, jurists, doctors and bards, both male and female, who undertook a gruelling programme of studies for 12–20 years before qualifying and achieving the accompanying high legal status. They were the preservers of group memory and culture, which they transmitted orally from generation to generation. There is evidence that they knew of the art of

... they do not think it proper to commit these utterances to writing, although... in their public and private accounts, they make use of Greek letters... they do not wish the rule to become public property, nor... to rely on writing and so neglect the cultivation of the memory.

JULIUS CAESAR ON DRUIDIC TEACHING IN *THE CONQUEST OF GAUL*, BOOK VI writing from an early date and were familiar both with Greek and Latin, as the Celts traded widely with the Mediterranean world through ports such as Marseilles. However, like Plato they feared that reliance upon writing would destroy the discipline of memory. Throughout Antiquity and the Middle Ages authors would generally compose their texts mentally for oral recitation, often dictating to a scribe who would take notes. By at least the first century BC druids had devised a proto-script, ogham or ogam (named after Ogma/Ogmios, god of eloquence and literature, who was equated by Lucian with Heracles), which survives in commemorative inscriptions on stone in Ireland and areas of Irish settlement in Britain. Some Latin bilinguals serve as a Celtic version of the Rosetta stone, giving the key to decipherment. The surviving ogham stones date from around 300 AD until the eighth century. However, the majority of such inscriptions would have been on wood, perhaps dating from much earlier, and have not been preserved. The names of heroes were carved in ogham on aspen twigs and placed in their tombs, and the tale of *Baile Mac Buain* speaks of a library of sagas and poems inscribed on the 'rods of the Filí'. In the great Irish epic the *Táin Bó Cuailnge* ('The Cattle Raid of Cooley') – an Iron-Age composition first committed to writing in the Christian period during the seventh century AD by Senchan Torpeist, chief poet of Ireland – an ogham inscription carved upon a tree by the hero Cúchulainn is imbued with such symbolic power that it can stop a whole hosting army. Ogham was only used for short talismanic and memorial inscriptions. It represents, in essence, an exploded linear response to the Latin alphabet and consists of groups of parallel or diagonal lines placed in relation to a base-line such as the edge of a stick or stone. A treatise on ogham is preserved in the Book of Ballymote, compiled in County Sligo during the fourteenth century but thought linguistically to have drawn on ninth-century texts. It refers to ogham as the 'Tree Alphabet' as each letter is named after a tree (*ailim* – elm; *beithe* – birch, and so forth).

> *Cúchulainn cut down an oak tree in their path and cut an ogam message into its side... that no-one was to pass that oak until a warrior had leaped it in his chariot in his first attempt.*
>
> THE TÁIN

DEITIES

The Celtic and Germanic peoples each had their pantheons of deities. Like those of ancient Greece, Rome and Egypt, the gods had specific attributes and powers, and were often seen as the heroic or semi-mythical ancestors of the societies that worshipped them. In each of these pantheons the most important deity was the originating father god. For the Egyptians it was Amun Ra, the creator sun-god; for the Greeks, Zeus; for the Romans, Jupiter; for the Germanic tribes, Thor, god of thunder. And for the Celts it was the Dagda (pronounced 'dada'), the 'good god', 'fire', 'All Father' or 'Lord of Great Knowledge'. With his club he could destroy or restore to life and health, and his cauldron sent no one away hungry. In Irish legend he eventually resigns as leader of the gods, declining into senility like the Egyptian Ra.

Other leading Celtic gods included the antlered Cernunnos – symbolized by the ram-headed serpent, the stag and the bull, and associated with water, fertility, hunting and warfare – who later became the folkloric Herne the Hunter. Nodens was the wealth-bringer and cloud-maker, sometimes symbolized by the dog. Goibhniu was the smith-god, and Lugh/Lud (after whom London was named) was a solar god of splendid countenance and subtle magic who was patron of the arts and crafts. His festival, Lughnasadh, celebrated harvest and became the Christian feast of first fruits – Lammas.

The mother goddess for the Celts was Dana, mother of the Dagda and, according to Brythonic tradition, wife of Bilé, god of death. Another important Celtic goddess was Brigid, the 'High One', who in her various guises was the goddess of healing, fertility, poetry and smiths. Her pastoral festival, Imbolc, was held on 1 February and has been perpetuated as the Christian feast of St Brigid of Kildare, whose life and legend came to include features originally associated with the pagan goddess. Another prominent female deity was Epona, the Celtic fertility goddess symbolized by the horse. The Celtic war deities were also female: Badh, Macha and Mórrigán, signified by crows or ravens. This sacred triad was balanced by a trio of mother-goddesses of fertility, the Deae Matres or Deae Nutrices. Furthermore, in the epic *Táin* it was the druidess Fedelm who taught the hero Cúchulainn his unsurpassed martial prowess, reflecting the actual participation of women in warfare, government and religion.

The Celtic hunter / healer god Cernunnos, with beasts partaking of the river of plenty that flows from his throne (prefiguring the Christian iconography of the fountain of Life). He is flanked by the Roman deities Apollo and Mercury, an example of cultural assimilation and adaptation. Second century AD, Reims, Gaul.

The German pantheon took a similar form. Germanic origin myths seek to explain prehistory by reference to Ymir, the giant, under whose left arm man and woman were created and suckled by a cow. The cow itself survived by licking the salt from ice, and then went on to lick into being Buri, the progenitor of the gods. The gods were initially divided into the belligerent divine race of the Aesir (represented by Donar/Thor the storm-god, Woden/Odin the god of fury, heroism and magic and Tiw/Tyr the sky-god); and the benevolent divine race of the Vanir who were associated with fertility and farming (represented by Njörd, the earth-mother Nerthus, Frey and Freyja). Others include Weyland the Smith and Loki, the mischief-maker. Their names still mark the days in the English language, along with the sun and the moon – Sunday, Moonday, Tiw'sday, Woden'sday, Thor'sday, Freyday – and can be detected in English place-names such as Wednesbury (Woden's fort) and Thundersley (Thor's clearing in the wood).

In Germanic legend, the ageing Ymir was killed by Odin and the other gods. From his body they fashioned Middle Earth, Midgard, which lay between the mist-world of the dead, Niflheim – the underworld domain of the goddess Hel, guarded

Pagan Germanic Religion

A system of proto-literacy was also adopted by the Germanic peoples of Germany, the Netherlands and Scandinavia following their contact with Rome, producing the runes used in divination. Runes were also indebted to the Latin alphabet and assumed an angular form because they were carved on wood and initially composed of twigs. At the heart of pagan Germanic religion was Irmensul ('giant column') or Yggdrasil ('the world tree'), a giant ash that was thought to form the world itself. Its roots penetrated the subterranean world and its boughs supported the heavens. At one root, which penetrated the underworld, was the fountain Hvergelmir that fed the rivers. By another root, piercing the land of giants, lay another fountain, Mimir, the source of wisdom from which Odin himself wished to drink at the cost of one of his eyes. And at the third root, lying in the heavens, was the fountain of Urd, from which the wise Norns fed the great great tree itself. In its branches perched a golden cockerel that warned the gods of attack and at its foot was buried the trumpet that would sound the final battle. The sacred space at its base was where the gods dispensed justice, while the serpent of evil gnawed ceaselessly at its roots (there are many elements of these myths, such as the tree of knowledge and the serpent of evil, which found an echo in Christian belief). In recollection of this, the Teutonic tribes would set up pillars of wood, one of which was felled by the Christian emperor Charlemagne in Westphalia in 772 as part of his subjection of the Saxons, the world tree making way for the Christian rood. The Celts too had sacred trees, which were often sited within individual settlements and were a prized focal point. Oak groves were sacred to pagan Germanic peoples and Celts alike, successors to the wooden and stone henges of the Neolithic and Bronze Ages.

by the monstrous dog Garm – and the heavenly Asgard. They also fashioned Mupellsheim, the kingdom of fire. From the inert trunks of the ash tree and the vine they created man and woman and from the maggots that fed on Ymir's body they made the subterranean race of dwarfs. A rainbow bridge linked Midgard to Asgard, the celestial dwelling place of the gods. The world was circled by oceans and beyond them lay an abyss in which dwelt the World Serpent. Gods were joined by humans in their fight against the World Serpent. Again it was women, the Valkyrie, who governed the battlefield and escorted the slaughtered heroes to the otherworldly mead hall of Valhalla. The struggle against evil was continued there, the serpent ultimately destined to consume all.

The Germanic peoples sought to explain in words and allegorical myth the nature of their universe and their origins within it. Their layering of the worlds of the gods, humans and the dead was undoubtedly influenced by Greek and Oriental views of the cosmos; and there are overtones of Christianization too, for such thoughts were mostly committed to writing after conversion to Christianity, even if the Norse, Icelandic and Orkney sagas do preserve a pagan flavour. This order was not eternal: the enemies of the gods – giants, demons and the serpent of evil – would ultimately overthrow it, causing the twilight of the gods and the collapse of the universe.

INTERACTION AND ASSIMILATION

There were undoubtedly religious and other cultural distinctions between the Celtic and Germanic tribes. However, there also appears to have been a measure of interaction between them, as well as some influence from earlier prehistoric communities and a degree of international communication. This has tended to blur ethnic distinctions and has led to such categorization being challenged by many modern archaeologists and anthropologists.

An illustration of this is the famous Gundestrup Cauldron, which has long been revered as an iconic example of Celtic art. And yet this massive silver-gilt vessel, perhaps symbolizing the vat from which the supreme god fed his people, was excavated in Denmark (Germanic territory) and its Celtic craftsmanship has even been challenged. Some researchers argue that it may have been made in India and exported in pieces, to be assembled upon arrival in the far north. Its complex iconography features a variety of beasts, some of distinctly oriental character, as well as the Celtic horned god, Cernunnos, wearing a torc, seated in traditional lotus position and holding his ram-headed serpent. It also includes the bust of a large mother goddess, a giant tree and a large, ritually dressed figure with a pony-tail who is about to immerse a smaller figure in a cauldron. This scene is usually interpreted as a human sacrifice, but it may represent ritual immersion or feeding from the

The Gundestrup Cauldron, Jutland, an example of the excellence of Celtic art from the second century BC to the first century AD.

ABOVE: detail of a ritual scene from the Gundestrup Cauldron, depicting either a human sacrifice or a pagan rite prefiguring baptism.

vat. This compelling artefact remains an anomaly, redolent of the complexity of prehistoric societies and their interaction with each other. It also serves as a reminder of the shared Indo-European roots of the Celtic, Germanic, Greek and Roman peoples.

However, lest we become too sentimental about the harmonious relationship between the early inhabitants of northern Europe and their environment, we should recall that both man and nature could be red of tooth and claw, and the over-exploitation of the land following the Neolithic agrarian revolution has left our moorlands as unusable wilderness. Survival seems artificially remote to those of us in the present developed world – the stuff of outward-bound courses or of the undercurrent of poverty and struggling humanity in the Third World. For early societies the labour of winning a living from the land was borne by all, whether as workforce, organizers or as priestly intercessors.

INTERMEDIARIES BETWEEN THE HUMAN AND THE DIVINE

The need for intermediaries between humankind, the divine and its manifestation in nature can be seen in early kingship rituals. Here, theoretically, the most powerful and responsible member of society served as guarantor of harmony and contact between them. The Ulster Cycle, composed in Iron-Age Ireland and transmitted orally across the generations until it was written down by Christian monks, tells of the symbolic mating of the king and a white mare. This represented the union of the tribe and the natural world.

The role of the shaman has also, since time immemorial, been perceived as that of intermediary between worlds and dimensions. During European prehistory, these precursors of the priestly function would probably have dressed in the guise of animal spirits on occasion, as shape-changing and the ability to assume the skills of certain animals were considered desirable. Blood sacrifice was also sometimes deemed necessary to appease the gods and nature. Innocent creatures were usually used as the sacrificial victims, a practice observed not only during prehistory but in more formal historic religions such as Mithraism (the Persian cult of the redemptive slaying of the bull) and early Judaism.

In times of particular danger human sacrifice was also called for, although not, thankfully, in anything like the quantities of the mass bloodbaths of the Aztecs. The ritual slaughter of humans – many of whose bodies have been preserved by the peat bogs of northern Europe – bears witness to the fear engendered by the encroaching waters that threatened to submerge the life-sustaining land during the Bronze and Iron Ages. One such victim was Lindow Man, whose well-preserved remains allow us to surmise that he was an aristocratic man in the vigour of his youth, his hands unused to manual labour. He was fed a last meal before being pole-axed, garroted and his body thrown to the spirits inhabiting the bog pools of Somerset. We know less of the woman who joined him there, for her remains were mangled by the mechanical digger that disturbed them both.

CAESAR AND THE CELTS

In his account of the Gallic Wars Julius Caesar gives us one of the fullest contemporary accounts of the Celts. He was contributing to a tradition of one-sided ethnic propaganda, to which the Celts were subjected from the second century BC onwards by authors such as the Greek Posidonius and the Romans Diodorus Siculus and Tacitus. To get a more rounded picture of Celtic belief we have to rely on archaeology and on the recollection of earlier beliefs contained in actual Celtic sources written down by later Christian scribes, such as the Irish cycles of tales (preserved in important collections such as the Book of Leinster, the Book of Ballymote and the Book of the Dun Cow) and the Welsh *Mabinogion* (preserved in the White Book of Rhydderch and the Red Book of Hergest).

Caesar dwells on sacrifice and cruelty, including the shocking account of the burning of live human and animal sacrifices in the effigy of a wicker man. This role, reprised by Edward Woodward in the film 'The Wicker Man', exerts a primordial terror and has come to symbolize the primitive nature of prehistoric man. Yet even Caesar notes that this was a form of capital punishment, the humans burned being felons. It is appalling to think how recently heads were displayed on poles in these islands. The pyres of Smithfield burned and prisoners were hung, drawn and quartered as late as the eighteenth century, when Sheridan wrote his plays on social mores and Hepplewhite turned his exquisite chairs. Capital punishment may be primitive, but it is alas not confined to the early stages of social development, chronologically at least.

Caesar's account was written to shock. It took the form of reports home from the front, in war-correspondent fashion, and was designed to boost his own reputation by terrifying the Roman populace with accounts of an evil, barbaric enemy – a tool for controlling public opinion which is seen all too often today. The druids had been instrumental in mobilizing political and military resistance to Roman rule and were therefore presented by their adversaries in the worst possible light. A particularly graphic account provided by Tacitus details the Roman commander Paulinus's attack on Anglesey, the heart of druidism, in AD 61. His troops had to face the fury of the frenzied display of aggression by male and female druids on the shores of the island before they could destroy their blood-soaked groves. For the Celts, conflict would often be settled by such displays, or by a game of chess or a fight between two champions representing either party, rather than by actual battle.

The cache of metalwork from Llyn Cerrig Bach, Anglesey, may have been hidden at this time by one of the druids facing annihilation. To later Christian authors the druids were usually magicians like Merlin. The chief druid of the king of Ireland is described, in the Irish tales, as wearing shamanistic dress (a bull's hide, bird headdress and wings) and, on another occasion, a colourful cloak and golden earrings. The *Life of St Columba* tells of the saint's encounter with a Scottish druid, Broichan, in the late sixth century. Druidism had evidently survived beyond Roman rule.

THE CELTIC CULT OF THE HUMAN HEAD

One aspect of Celtic belief that the Romans found particularly repulsive was the practice of head-taking. Fear of such a fate haunted the legionary as much as that of scalping did the US cavalryman centuries later. The Roman authorities banned the bearing of arms by civilians and the practice of human sacrifice – although they continued to employ the ritual blood-letting of the arena as a means of controlling the populace by 'entertaining' it, and as one means of disposing of the untamed. For the Celts, the head – the nexus of the intellect and the senses – was the seat of the self and of the soul. The commonest form of Celtic effigy and talismanic offering is that of the human head, and when full figures are depicted they often have enlarged heads with heavy-lidded eyes that seem to be seeing beyond this world. These are reminiscent of the heightened spirituality that pervades the sculpture of the reign of the first Christian Roman emperor, Constantine.

Another feature of Celtic iconography was the *Janus bifrons* or the 'tricephalos' figure, which has two or three faces. This is thought to represent the ability to see the past and the future, as well as the present, since the role of seer (*filí*) was important to the Celts.

The Celtic heads often wear torcs, twisted necklets that signified the god or hero. One Celtic shrine at Roquepertuse at the mouth of the Rhone in Gaul even features human skulls set into niches in its portals, and many a river and well received such gory tribute. Yet this was accolade not atrocity. The worst fate that might befall a Celt was that they should fall in battle and their heads not be valued enough to be retrieved by kin or taken by foe. Severed heads were venerated trophies and memorials. They were often carefully embalmed and adorned, and were brought out to grace festivities and to enable the deceased to be recalled. In one ancient Irish epic, the 'Voyage of Bran', the head of the war-leader Bran is carried by his compatriots, inspiring and leading them still, in a literal as well as a symbolic sense, and regaling them with tales at the feasting board.

Whatever the extent or perceived rationale of such ritualized blood-letting, its presence in many early societies and its inclusion within their religions prepared the way for the innovative approach of Christianity, with the belief that God sacrificed himself for humanity. For Christians, the sacrifice of Christ ended the need for any offerings of blood, achieving empathy for the human condition and reconciliation between Creator and creation.

We have seen that in northern and western Europe, the fourth and third millennia BC witnessed an agricultural revolution that impacted profoundly on humanity. It impacted on ties to the land and on a sense of community and self, and led to increased questions about the place of humans within the bigger picture. The metallurgical technology that developed in the second and first millennia of prehistory escalated these trends, leading to a proliferation of ritual sites, the emergence of professional priesthoods with distinct religious practices, and an evolving symbolism. New mythologies were formed to account for the origins of life, to reconcile different dimensions of being and to encompass a sense of conflict between good and evil. International communications had long been a part of this, and interaction with the cultures of Greece, Rome and the Middle East was already being experienced. The following chapters will explore the impact of closer contact with the faiths and philosophies of the Mediterranean and will chart how indigenous experience and memory helped to shape the Christian culture that developed in Britain and Ireland during the first millennium after Christ's birth. This was a process that went on to underpin the accelerating agricultural, industrial and technological revolutions of the second millennium.

CHAPTER 2

Merchants, Military and Tax Collectors: The Impact of the Roman World

THE COMING OF ROME

The exploratory expeditions to Britain launched by Julius Caesar in 55 and 54 BC were designed to enhance his reputation and power and to defuse British support for the Celtic resistance movement in Gaul. They also drew Britain further into the orbit of continental politics and served to stimulate the trade with the Mediterranean territories, which had already flourished for over two thousand years. The very name of the islands, which subsequently became the Roman province of 'Britannia', was derived from the name by which they were known in Classical Antiquity: the 'Pretanic' or 'tin-bearing' Isles. This perhaps stemmed from the Bronze Age when Phoenicians bartered for Cornish tin on the offshore trading enclave of the Scilly Isles.

Caesar used this nominal 'conquest' to strengthen his political power base in Rome, establishing some clientage relationships with Celtic rulers in the South East but recognizing that military occupation would overstretch his resources. Full conquest and absorption into the Roman empire had to wait for the Emperor Claudius, who in AD 43 dispatched his fleet in order to boost his otherwise unglamorous reputation. The major symbol of the imposition of Roman beliefs upon the new province was the massive classical temple devoted to the worship of the emperor, at Colchester. Its foundations can still be observed in the undercroft of the Norman Castle, along with the vestiges of its destruction in AD 61 by the rebellious Celtic forces led by Boudicca (Boadicea). The exorbitant taxation required for its construction, along with other abuses of power including the infamous rape of Boudicca's daughters, may have contributed to the revolt that led to the razing of Colchester and London.

Such edifices were new to the Celts of Britain, except those who had themselves travelled to Mediterranean climes, and the concept of worshipping within them must have seemed alien to them. They were used to venerating divinity through the forces

> *All the Britons dye their bodies with woad, which produces a blue colour, and this gives them a more terrifying appearance in battle. They wear their hair long, and shave the whole of their bodies except for the head and the upper lip. Wives are shared between groups of ten or twelve men...*
>
> JULIUS CAESAR, *THE CONQUEST OF GAUL*, BOOK V

Mithraeum, Carrawbrough, beside the Roman supply road on the south side of Hadrian's Wall. A shrine of one of the mystery religions, the cult of Mithras from Persia, that became popular in the third century AD.

of nature, focusing upon the borderline territories between this world and the next – which were to become known in Christian spirituality as 'thin places', where eternity and unity with the Spirit can best be glimpsed from this earthly dimension. These borderline territories included: the limitless ocean and the islands that floated westwards within it; wells, springs and lakes which sprang from the depths of the earth; prehistoric barrows and henges through which the otherworld could be accessed; and trees whose roots penetrated deep into the land and whose branches supported the heavens.

Yet Iron-Age shrines could also take the form of buildings within enclosures. The imposing Hayling Island Temple, discovered through aerial photography, replaced a more modest Celtic shrine. This had taken the form of a circular thatched-timber hut, resembling a domestic dwelling, approached via a fenced square courtyard and set within a rectangular wooden palisade atop an earthwork ditch and bank. Before AD 60 the shrine had been replaced by a temple complex, built on a massive scale and made of stone. At its heart was a circular *cella* 13.9 m (46 ft) in diameter. The local limestone that formed its walls was covered in plaster that was multi-coloured inside and red outside. The temple sat within a rectangular courtyard, its walls colonnaded on the inner face. It included five rooms set into the thickness of its eastern side, providing a formal entrance hall and offices. Parallels for such large-scale circular temples are to be found in central and western France, as at Perigueux, and it was probably constructed by Gaulish masons for Rome's client, Cogidubnus, along with his nearby princely palace of Fishbourne. French comparisons suggest that it may have been dedicated to the Roman god of war, Mars. Yet while it was a visible symbol of *romanitas* and of the material benefits of alliance with Rome, the ground-plan of the temple essentially preserved that of the earlier Celtic shrine, emphasizing an element of continuity with existing local ritual practices and improvement upon them. For the Roman authorities generally adopted a rather flexible approach to individual belief, as long as people adhered to the state religion (in this period, worship of the deified emperor), and paid their taxes. Their primary concern was the stability of the establishment and the status quo.

The new Roman towns and *civitas* capitals – centres of local administration,

Romano-Celtic Temples and Shrines

Many Celtic shrines were associated with settlements and this trend was maintained under the Romans, with around 40 per cent occurring in towns, forts and other settlements, including villas such as Chedworth and Winterton. However, a high proportion of Romano-British religious sites remained in isolated rural locations, especially in the fourth century when there was a corresponding drift amongst the better-off away from the towns to rural villas and country life. This picture may be somewhat distorted by the difficulties of locating and excavating sites within still occupied towns. At Silchester, for example, the medieval church of St Mary overlies two Romano-Celtic temples. However, many temples lay on territorial boundaries, suggesting a role in facilitating relations and trade between neighbouring tribes. This is supported by archaeological evidence for significant mercantile activity at the shrines of Gosbecks and Woodeaton and in similar temple sites in Gaul. Over half of these rural foci were reused locations, and over a third of the Romano-British temples located to date were erected on top of Iron-Age sites, many of them prehistoric shrines. Some were set inside or adjacent to hillforts, as at Maiden Castle, Danebury and South Cadbury; some were centred upon Neolithic or Bronze-Age barrows, as at Maiden Castle again and Brean Down; and some were masonry rebuilds of earlier timber shrines, as at Hayling Island and Harlow.

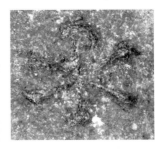

Chi-rho inscribed upon one of the nymphaeum rim-stones, perhaps in the fourth century AD.

The Celtic round, square or rectangular timber shrine was often replaced by the usual Romano-British temple plan – which favoured a square or rectangular stone building with an ambulatory wrapped around it – in classical Mediterranean fashion, but usually with closed walls rather than colonnades because of the weather. The rebuilding of shrines in Iron-Age hill-top forts is perhaps surprising, given the Roman policy of relocating sizeable populations so that their fortifications could not be maintained and provide refuge for insurgents. This initial precaution seems, however, to have lapsed, and the value of such defensive positions was to be proven during times of political and economic instability, when they were periodically reoccupied. At Maiden Castle, site of strenuous resistance to the early Roman occupation, the defences were repaired during the late Roman period to form a *temenos*, or sacred enclave. This formed part of the reconstructed temple that occupied part of the site hallowed since antiquity by a Neolithic long barrow and an Iron-Age shrine.

The pagan Nymphaeum, perhaps turned into a Christian baptistery, at Chedworth Roman villa, Gloucester.

sometimes based on existing settlements and in other cases consciously relocated to disrupt any resistance – would have been equipped with small temples or shrines. But the bulk of the citizenry of Roman Britain would have continued to worship the groves and springs venerated by their ancestors, the most prominent of which were accompanied by rural shrines.

One of the most popular and complex of native British cults was that of Nodens, and one of the most important of the late Romano-Celtic rural shrines was that devoted to his veneration at Lydney on the western bank of the River Severn. Careful excavation gave an unprecedented insight into the beliefs of the period. Nodens, like many Celtic deities, was multi-functional. He was sometimes equated with Mars, but in his guise as healer. The oculist's stamp and the numerous votive effigies of dogs at Lydney may be significant in this respect, for at some ancient Greek shrines dogs were kept for their therapeutic qualities, demonstrated by licking the wounds of the sick. (Modern medicine acknowledges the ability of some dogs to scent the presence of certain cancers, which they signal by licking and trying to bite off surface growths.) Numerous pins – associated with prayers for conception or safe delivery in childbirth – were also found along with an accompanying effigy of a goddess of plenty, to which they had probably been offered. Nodens is sometimes described as 'silver hand' and a small bronze arm discovered on site may relate to this, as may the siting of his shrine on the Severn Estuary which stretches like a silver limb into the sea. The attribute seems to have been inherited by the Cornish St Melor of the silver hand and foot. A mosaic and a bronze relief at Lydney depict a sea deity, fishermen, shells, fish, sea monsters and anchors; these, and the riverside situation, suggest association with water and a Neptune-like governance of the seas.

Inscriptions from Lydney associate Nodens with Mars and Silvanus, god of the hunt. The precinct of the shrine itself was large and complex. It was set on an escarpment terrace which had been fortified during the Iron Age, and contained a rectangular temple with an ambulatory running around it, set within a walled enclave with a corridor of rooms along one side. Adjacent to the temple was a quadrangle of buildings, resembling a monastic cloister, for administration and the lodging of religious personnel and guests, along with a well and a suite of baths.

At Uley the traditional sacred site lay in a special enclave outside the fort which has yielded flints, indicating occupation since the late Stone Age, and numerous Celtic coins. Here the Romano-British temple overlay its timber Celtic predecessor exactly and was surrounded by a Neolithic U-shaped ditch and holes to carry standing stones or wooden posts. It also lay close to a round barrow and a nearby major Neolithic burial mound known as 'Hetty Pegler's Tump'. The Iron-Age structure was found to have several infant burials beneath its foundations, a practice repeated at Maiden Castle and Springhead in Kent and also found elsewhere underlying some Romano-Celtic dwellings. Evidence for possible Celtic human sacrifice is, however, rare and we cannot be certain that the children were killed. It may be that the remains of the most innocent members of the community's dead were honoured by such ritual burial, in the same way that saints and other respected Christians were buried near to altars, at the east end or western portal of a church. As if in recollection of celtic ritual, when the late Roman temple on the site was demolished and a post-Roman Christian church constructed, the dismembered head and limbs of a classical marble statue of Mercury were buried at key points beneath the foundations. Similarly, at some point in the fourth century the fine marble sculptures of the Mithraeum at Walbrook, London (see page 36), were dismembered and buried at salient points beneath a new, probably Christian, church. The shrines of Lydney, Maiden Castle and Uley were all to be maintained after the withdrawal of Roman authority in the early fifth century, perpetuating their role as the focus of worship from prehistory into the Christian period.

BURYING THE DEAD

Veneration of the dead continued and, as in prehistory, Romano-British burial practices varied over time, fluctuating between inhumation and cremation according to prevailing fashion. In the course of the Iron Age, the communal barrows and individual cist burials of the past had already largely given way to flat cemeteries in which people were buried singly or in family clusters, often still accompanied by jewellery, weapons or other cherished possessions – if they were wealthy enough to have owned them. Some regional variations can be discerned, such as the late Celtic burials in the Yorkshire Wolds, marked by square ditches and barrows covering bodies, male and female, accompanied by the remains of chariots. This practice was also found in the Marne region of Gaul, but with the bodies crouched as in earlier local tradition. Old-fashioned crouched cist burials also continued in Cornwall. By contrast the Aylesford Culture of Kent (densely populated even then) interred its cremated dead in pottery vessels in small cemetery plots. Iron-Age cremation burials might also be accompanied by grave goods, especially those associated with feasting, and this remained the norm in early Roman Britain. There are indications that funerary feasts or wakes were held and that libations continued to be offered to the loved one after death. However, accompanied inhumations could also still be the burial practice of choice, as demonstrated by the excavation, a few years ago, of a richly attired young female Roman citizen buried along with her cosmetics and jewellery in a lead coffin in the City of London. The goods are displayed, along with her forensically reconstructed head, in the Museum of London.

Demographic analysis of some late Iron-Age and early Romano-British cemeteries, such as that of the Durotriges of Dorset at Poundbury, indicates that men were more often or more fully provided with grave goods than women, and infant burials were generally unfurnished. This reflects the differing status of the dead. It might also suggest that the goods accompanying the dead were increasingly symbolic, and that those who believed in an afterlife no longer assumed the dead would have need of all the trappings of a human lifestyle, such as food and drink.

Sometimes the dead had to be buried where they fell, with no ceremony or tribute except for the tears of their loved ones. In the war cemetery at the great Iron-Age fort of Maiden Castle, where an initial resistance to Rome was mounted, the remains of the largely male defending force found in its ditches bore the visible scars of their challenge to the Roman military machine.

Roman cemeteries, unlike their prehistoric counterparts, were generally located outside of towns and substantial settlements, flanking the approaching roads. On the continent the graves of important Christian figures, including those martyred for their faith, would later be marked by an oratory chapel (*martyrium*) that might grow into a major church or monastery, such as that of Sant' Ambrogio in Milan. But persecution was not as widely implemented in Britain and few such graves survive, other than the famous example of the shrine of St Alban. This was sited on the hilltop

St Martin's Church, Canterbury. The masonry on the right is part of a Roman chapel where Queen Bertha and her chaplain, Liudhard, worshipped and where St Augustine based his mission in 597.

above the Roman town of Verulamium where Alban was martyred, and is now marked by the great abbey and the existing town, which turned its back on its Roman origins and migrated to join its new Christian focus. Another may be Old St Pancras Church – now dwarfed by St Pancras station, the new Eurostar terminal and the British Library – which was founded by St Augustine around 600, although its site and dedication might suggest that it overlay an earlier roadside cemetery. The Roman brick-built funerary chapels of St Pancras, which now stand in the enclave of St Augustine's Abbey in Canterbury where Augustine and his Germanic royal patrons, King Ethelberht and Queen Bertha, lie buried, may also be of similar origin. Again, nearby St Martin's Church where Bertha and her chaplain worshipped and where Augustine and his followers first established the base for their mission, was adapted in this way. Some of the fabric of these Roman chapels still survives, as does that of a small Roman building now encased in the chancel of a ruined early and later medieval chapel at Stone by Faversham in Kent. Evidence for Christian churches springing from the sites of Romano-Christian martyries and mausolea in extramural cemeteries has also been found at Fordington (outside Dorchester), Poundbury, Butt Road (outside Colchester) and Northover (outside Ilchester) where a mound next to the remains of a chapel became the site of a major Anglo-Saxon Minster (a missionary church to the locality).

By the late Roman period burial practices became more standardized, favouring cremations and supine inhumations (where the body was placed flat on its back in the grave, shrouded and often within a stone or lead coffin). Burials were arranged in rows or occasionally around focal graves. Some grave goods – jewellery, knives, tools, foodstuffs, coins – still accompanied the dead: whether the burials were Christian is usually shown by the absence of such goods, as the Christian risen dead would have no need of earthly things. However, the compulsion to bury treasured items or meaningful tokens with the beloved can be a part of the grieving process for the living, not just the dead. Christians are still buried with their wedding rings, for example, even though Christ said that in the hereafter men and women are not given in marriage. Christian saints certainly continued to be buried with significant grave goods, as demonstrated by the rich array of objects found within the coffin of St Cuthbert of Holy Island and now displayed in the Treasury of Durham Cathedral. These objects were imbued with the status of relics by association with the saint.

Another feature usually taken to indicate Christian burial is a west-east alignment. The head of the deceased lay at the western end of the grave so that when Christ came from the east at the second coming, they could rise to face him. The entrances to prehistoric burial mounds were often orientated towards the rising sun in the same way. This orientation, the unfurnished state of the burials and, by way of contradiction, the presence of items bearing Christian symbols within the grave – such as the Shepton Mallet chi-rho pendant, the earliest Christian artefact to be found in a late Roman burial, and a possible chi-rho incised inside a dish from a burial at Lankhills – have been taken to betoken Christian cemeteries, the best candidates for which include Poundbury, Lankshills and Northover (near Ilchester). Inhumation became the Christian norm, for it was believed that the presence of the skull and long bones (the origin of the piratical ensign, the 'Jolly Roger') facilitated the resurrection of the body at Christ's second coming. But pragmatic considerations, not least overcrowding, ensured that cremations were also accepted. In actual fact, most late Roman cemeteries probably contained people of various faiths, including Christians.

The shrine of Coventina's well stands at Carrawbrough (Brocolitia). Within the well many pins were found, an offering traditionally associated with childbirth. (Over 14,000 coins were also discovered, along with brooches, glass, pottery, shrine bells, a bronze dog and horse, votive bronze heads and the more literal offering of a human skull.) Next to it was another well with a shrine edifice containing an altar dedicated to the nymphs and the *Genio Loci*, or 'spirit of the place'. No chances were being taken in this attempt to court the goodwill of whatever spirit presided in this watery, womb-like dell, which lay adjacent to the military supply road below Hadrian's Wall. It lies close to the Roman fort of Vindolanda, where cohorts from a far-off part of

The wooden coffin of St Cuthbert, Durham Cathedral Treasury.

the Germanic *limes* of the empire were posted to defend another remote and vulnerable border, and gives a glimpse into other aspects of life in this military frontier zone, with all its hopes and fears. The fort also contained a massive archive of wooden writing tablets, recording everything from requests home for new socks and underwear, to settlement of gaming debts in the officers' mess and a birthday party invitation from an army wife in one camp to her female friend in another.

THE EASTERN MYSTERY CULTS: MITHRAS AND ISIS

A little further along the supply road for Hadrian's Wall lay another religious focal point: the Mithraeum devoted to the male military cult of Mithras. Mithras was the bull-slayer, a Persian deity descended from the Indian and Iranian gods of light – the Mitra-Varuna of the Vedas and the Mazda of Zoroaster – who, upon passing into

Romano-Celtic Deities

Remembering one's ancestors was important, but they alone could not assist or intervene in the fates of man. For this the gods needed to be courted and appeased. The Roman pantheon had derived largely from that of the Greeks. Gods with new Latin names assumed the attributes of their Greek counterparts: Zeus became Jupiter, Athena became Minerva and so forth. This fluidity of godly function was the result of centuries of refinement of the basic roles that humans expected their gods to fulfill, and it extended to the gods of the Celts. The equations could be extremely fluid, as in the case of Mars, the Roman god of both warfare and healing (not as contradictory as it might seem to people who mostly died in warfare or of associated injuries, or in childbirth). He became associated not only with the better-known Celtic gods Cernunnos and Nodens (see page 20), but with a variety of more local minor deities. These included Camulos who was worshipped in his martial guise in Gaul, in British Camulodunum (Colchester), in another centre with the same name at Almondbury, Yorkshire, and at a number of sites in southern Scotland, between the Roman Hadrian and Antonine Walls. Another Mars cognate was Braciaca, recorded in an inscription from Haddon Hall, Derbyshire, whose name may be derived from the Brythonic for malt (*brag/brac*) and the beer used to intoxicate warriors before battle.

The Gorgon's Head, the classical image reinterpreted as a Celtic warrior, second/third century AD. From the temple of Sulis Minerva, Bath.

Another important example of such cultural blending was the equation of the Celtic water-goddess Sulis with the Roman Minerva, at the impressive complex of religious buildings and healing thermal springs that formed the temple of Sulis Minerva at Bath (Aquae Sulis). This site seems to have attracted those in hope of a cure – or a partner – to its springs from at least Celtic prehistory until Jane Austen's era. It was also dedicated to a pair of Celtic deities widely worshipped in Gaul, namely Leucetius who was equated with Mars and Nemetona 'goddess of the sacred grove' (from *nemeton* for 'sacred grove', preserved in the Romano-British place-name Vernemeton, the 'especially sacred grove', in Nottinghamshire). Symbolic of this fusion of cultures, the mask that adorned its main pediment was a Medusa or Gorgon head, with some variations. The female, snake-haired physiognomy was transformed into a Celtic

Europe, acquired an astrological connotation. He was either depicted wrestling with a bull, whose shed blood ensured the fertility of creation, or as a winged, lion-headed deity, enclosed in a serpent's coils and covered with zodiacal symbols. He was sometimes equated with Aion, god of time, believed by many to be the Creator.

One of the many Pictish carvings of the Burghead bull, Moray.

Another Mithraeum was excavated at the Walbrook in the City of London (see page 36). The high quality of its sculptures indicated the wealthy status of its members; the cult often counted emperors among its initiates. The invincibility of the sun and the strict moral code demanded of the soldier of the faith ensured its appeal to the military, by whose agency it spread around the empire from the first century AD onwards. Aspects of this cult would have struck a chord with the native Celtic populace, for the bull had been considered sacred in prehistoric northern Europe and was often

moustached male, his face contorted into the warp-spasm – a frenzy through which the Celts prepared themselves for combat – and his hair arranged in the erect, lime-washed locks of the Celtic warrior. In his hair coiled the serpents that both traditions associated with healing. This also recalls the Celtic cult of the severed head and, like its classical architectural counterparts, would have served a protective apotropaic (evil-averting) function.

Celtic head, first century AD, from the Bon Marché site, Gloucester. For Celts, the head was the seat of the soul, reflected in the other-worldly gaze of the eyes.

The Celtic obsession with the head continued; the stylistic tendency towards symbolic representation and abstraction produced some striking artwork from the province, such as the youthful male head from Gloucester, with his almond-shaped eyes which strain from their sockets to stare blindly into the otherworld. An example of the female head comes from a funerary monument in Towcester, Northamptonshire. It sports the hairstyle of a fashionable Roman matron but the furrowed brow and ferocious stare of a Celtic druidess or warrior queen. The impact of Roman sculpture also added a further impetus to Romano-British depictions of both Celtic and Roman deities, or conflations of the two. Particularly interesting examples include: a little bronze figurine of Mars clutching the ram-headed serpents of Cernunnos, from Southbroom, Wiltshire; a stone relief of the three mother goddesses, the Deae Matres, from Cirencester (Corinium Museum); and a stela dedicated to Coventina who is portrayed on it as a reclining classical nymph (University of Newcastle-upon-Tyne Museum).

considered a suitable sacrificial offering. This, or the impact of Mithraism, may have stimulated the production of myriad bull depictions (see page 35) inscribed on stones at the Pictish promontory fort of Burghead during the first seven centuries AD (their dates are uncertain, but the site was obviously used over a lengthy period). At the heart of its rock lies a profoundly atmospheric cavern approached by a lengthy flight of rock-hewn steps, which recalls the labyrinthine dwelling of the minotaur or the Celtic cave of Cruachan, gateway to the otherworld.

The Mithraic secret societies originated in Persia and became especially popular within the Roman army during the third century AD, a time of particular political and economic upheaval within the empire, when insecurity was high and morale low. People looked to the afterlife to compensate for the shortcomings of the present and sought a superhero to secure their salvation. The essential basis of religious observance under Roman imperial rule was a confidence in the supreme importance of materialism and the need to ensure the physical and financial well-being of the individual during life. The activities of the gods mirrored these limited human concerns.

Mithraism was one of several mystical religions to have gained in popularity at

The Persian god Mithras slaying the bull, from the Walbrook Mithraeum, London.

this time, all of which were of eastern derivation and involved complex ritual practices and a belief in an afterlife. These have become collectively termed the 'mystery religions'. Another was the cult of Isis, mother of the god Horus, who together with her husband Osiris formed an influential trinity of deities from ancient Egypt. She is often depicted seated on a throne, suckling or holding Horus, in a pose later adopted by Christian artists when depicting Mary and Christ. When the Christian Copts occupied the ancient Egyptian temples they did not redecorate, but rather relabelled and reinterpreted some of the ancient iconography they found there. After Osiris was murdered by their brother, Set, Isis first embalmed him and then restored him to eternal life. Horus was miraculously conceived after Osiris's death. Isis also tricked the sun-god, Ra, into entrusting her with the knowledge of his true name, after she had fashioned a serpent that bit him – a wound that only her magic could cure. There are some intriguing parallels here with aspects of the Christian Eve and Mary. Eclipsing the other Egyptian goddesses, Isis became equated by the Greeks with Aphrodite, and was seen as the goddess of fertility and of the dead. The Romans termed her the 'star of the sea' (a forerunner of the Marian epithet *stella maris*) and patroness of travellers. Her cult was brought to northern Europe by seamen and slaves.

The third of the great mystery cults that swept across the empire during the third century was Christianity.

THE INTRODUCTION OF CHRISTIANITY AND THE GLASTONBURY GRAIL LEGEND

The Christian gospel (from the Old English *godspell*, 'good news') was probably first heard in Britain from those who had travelled elsewhere in the empire, notably merchants and military personnel and their families. Other incomers would have included those in service, and those who had been freed and were acting as secretaries, domestic staff, traders and the like. The egalitarianism of the Christian message and the hope it extended to the downtrodden and dispossessed was a significant factor in its popularity and early dissemination. This was despite the brutal persecution and heightened taxation applied by the authorities in an attempt to suppress it during the second and third centuries. Christianity has left overt signs of its presence in Britain from the third century onwards, and in Ireland from the early fifth; but that does not mean that it was not present in these islands beforehand, borne on the ocean waves that carried trade goods and other influences, and on the soundwaves of individual oral witness.

Following Nero's initial lead in the generation following Christ's death, systematic persecutions were implemented under the emperors Septimius Severus in the early third century, Decius and Valerian in the mid third century and Diocletian in the early fourth century. The remoteness of Britannia, or a perception that Christianity had not become too much of a problem to the authorities there, may have accounted for the lack of widespread persecution and martyrdoms compared to those that beset Italy, the eastern and southern Mediterranean provinces, and even Gallia and Germania.

The diaspora of the first followers of Christ spread throughout many regions of the empire, and even further afield with St Thomas's work in India, but there is no incontrovertible evidence of them reaching its farthest outpost, Britain. To fill this gap, a legend gradually evolved during the Middle Ages recounting a mission to Britain by Joseph of Arimathea. He was said to have brought with him the cup used by Christ at the Last Supper and into which Christ's blood flowed at the crucifixion – the holy grail. The New Testament recounts that Joseph was a Jewish councillor who followed Jesus in secret, played no part in his condemnation and, having beseeched Pilate for his body, laid it in a newly hewn tomb. To this core numerous myths were soon added, including a French legend connecting him with the grail, and the Sone de Nausay which had him driving Saracens out of Norway, wedding the pagan king's daughter and losing his power, causing him to retreat into the pastime of fishing as the 'Fisher King'.

The grail legend was taken up at Glastonbury Abbey, along with material concerning the monastery's alleged authorization by St Patrick, and the legend of King Arthur. Arthur's body, along with that of Guinevere, was 'discovered' there 'in the Isle of Avalon' in 1191 – as recorded in an 'ancient' inscription on a lead cross-shaped plaque within the coffin which is engraved in twelfth-century script and is blatantly a pious forgery. This was a time of crisis for the abbey, which was

The Virgin and Child, from the Book of Kells. This early Christian iconography was first derived by the Copts from ancient Egyptian images of Isis and Horus. Iona, possibly c.800.

Virgin and Child carved on the coffin of St Cuthbert, c.698.

fighting off rival claims to its authority and competing with Westminster Abbey and Christ Church Canterbury, which claimed the relics of its own favourite son, St Dunstan, its former abbot and a subsequent archbishop. The earliest Glastonbury record relating to Joseph is a thirteenth-century interpolation to William of Malmesbury's treatise on the antiquity of Glastonbury, written around 1125. This says that Joseph preached the gospel in Gaul with St Philip, who sent him to Britain with twelve followers. They failed to convert the local king but he gave them the inland island of Yniswitrin (Glastonbury), a mystical focal point in the surrounding marshland of the Somerset Levels, where they built a wattle church dedicated to the Virgin by Christ himself, so legend would have it. William of Malmesbury's original work makes no mention of Joseph, and the fuller tale recounted by John of Glastonbury around 1400 has him bringing not the grail, but two silver cruets containing the blood and sweat shed by Christ on the cross. This helped to foster a growing devotional interest in the physicality of Christ's Passion – a route to the appreciation of the immensity of the sacrifice made which is reminiscent of Mel Gibson's film, *The Passion of the Christ*.

In 1502 John's account was supplemented by a poem, 'The Lyfe of Joseph of Arimathia', containing stories of local cures, and from this stems the tale of a holy thorn that sprang from Joseph's staff and flowers at Christmas. A tradition also arose amongst local metalworkers that Joseph – presumably conflated with the Virgin's husband or, according to the apocryphal *Proto-evangelium of James*, her father Joachim – brought Mary and Christ to Cornwall. This became the source of William Blake's visionary hymn 'Jerusalem': 'And did those feet, in ancient times, walk upon England's pastures green?' Joseph's grave was sought, with royal permission, but even the monks of Glastonbury did not dare claim to have found it. Yet promoting the Joseph of Arimathea episode also allowed Glastonbury to claim seniority among the English Black Benedictine abbeys and the English clergy at large at the Councils of Constance (1414–18), on the grounds that England was the first western country to receive Christianity. Such myths are still perpetuated by recent works of fiction such as *The Holy Blood and the Holy Grail* and *The Da Vinci Code*, which flaunt conspiracies by the church authorities to subvert history. This may have been the case, but they would appear to have alighted on the wrong conspiracy theories: the medieval church promoted, rather than suppressed, the grail legend.

THE FIRST BRITISH MARTYRS

A credible candidate emerged as the British proto-martyr: St Alban. Gildas, writing around 540, and Bede, around 730, place his martyrdom c.305, in the reign of Diocletian, along with those of Julius and Aaron at Caerleon in South Wales. However, some scholars prefer a third-century date, with John Morris credibly proposing 209. Bede, following the account in the legendary 'Acts of Alban', relates that he was a Roman citizen who was converted and baptized by a priest named Amphibalus. He subsequently sheltered the priest and assumed his identity to cover his escape during persecution. Following arrest, Alban refused to offer sacrifice to pagan cults and was beheaded – but only after one of his executioners was converted and the other's eye had fallen out. The site of his *martyrium* was visited in 429 by Bishop Germanus of Auxerre and his companion, Lupus of Troyes, when they swapped other relics for dust from the shrine, famed for its healing propensity. This gave rise to his celebration in a number of French churches.

The shrine was still known in Bede's day and after the Norman Conquest it became the great medieval abbey of St Alban's – the wealthiest in England because of this association with the origins of Christianity in Britain – whose brethren, notably the mid-thirteenth-century chronicler, Matthew Paris, popularized the cult. Matthew Paris, one of the first desktop publishers, even authored and illustrated a work on the lives of two Anglo-Saxon kings named Offa who were both connected with the foundation of the early monastery, during which the original shrine is said to have been rediscovered. It can be no coincidence that Alban's grave was once more 'discovered' in 1257, whilst Matthew Paris was a monk there. Paris and the poet John Lydgate both wrote lives of St Alban, thus bolstering the abbey's reputation – especially in the face of rival claims to hold his relics, notably from Ely. At the time of World War I Alban began to be depicted as a Roman soldier, emphasizing the changing role of saints as superheroes and social role models in accordance with the needs and agendas of the day.

THE CONVERSION OF CONSTANTINE: CHRISTIANITY AS A STATE RELIGION

It was a soldier who finally made it possible for Christianity to 'come out of the closet' and be practised openly. In 306 Constantine, son of the general Constantius Chlorus who had made a successful bid for the imperial throne in 292, was declared emperor by his troops in York. His claim to succession was contested, and in the conflict that ensued Constantine is said to have had visions of Christ's cross, including one before the Battle of the Milvian Bridge in which it was delineated by stars. This is said to have ensured his decisive victory. His subsequent conversion marked the death-knell for emperor worship and was accompanied by the first grant of liberty of conscience to Christians. This was followed by Emperor Galerius's 'Edict of Toleration' towards those practising the Christian faith and, in March 313, by the famous 'Edict of Milan', which proclaimed complete religious toleration, freedom of worship and restoration of sequestered churches. An important Roman fort, Richborough, which formed part of the reinforced defences of the vulnerable British eastern seaboard during the fourth century, even acquired an elaborate hexagonal baptistery in which new converts, military and presumably civilian, were received into the faith. Nonetheless, there was a pagan backlash, with periods of apostatization by emperors and people alike at certain times during the fourth century.

Geoffrey of Monmouth (died 1154) claimed British birth for Constantine's mother, the empress St Helen/Helena/Ellen (c.250–330; feast, in the East 21 May, in the West 18 August). He described her as the daughter of the legendary King Coel of Colchester ('Old King Cole' of nursery rhyme fame), although in fact she was probably an innkeeper's daughter from Drepanum (Helenopolis) in Bythinia. She converted to Christianity in 312, in her sixties, and was renowned for her modest dress, her charitable works and her pilgrimage to the Holy Land, where she died. During her travels she is said to have conducted research on the ground into the location of the places associated with Christ and the biblical texts, and to have received a vision which led to the excavation of the true cross on the site in Jerusalem which was thought to be Calvary. Constantine subsequently erected the basilica of the Holy Sepulchre there. The finding, or 'invention', of the cross is usually dated to 335 and the association with Helen may be apocryphal. Her role was first ascribed to her by St Ambrose, but the earliest reference to the discovery is given by Cyril of Jerusalem, who wrote in 346 that the 'saving wood of the cross was found at Jerusalem in the time of Constantine and that it was disturbed fragment by fragment from this spot'. The recollection of Constantine's links with Britain may have played a part in the region's subsequent role, from the seventh century, in elevating the cross – initially eschewed as an instrument of death – to its place as the foremost symbol of Christianity and eternal life.

The periodic attempts by the Roman authorities to suppress the subversive Christian cult had meant that overt signs of faith had to be avoided. Affiliation therefore tended to be signalled by symbols: the fish, the Greek term for which, *ichthus*, was used as an anagram of Christ; the chi-rho – an X with a P superimposed upon it, based on the Greek letters *chi* (Latin 'X'), and *rho* (Latin 'P') – which is a contraction of the Greek *Christos*, 'the Anointed One'; its derivative the chrismon – a symbol resembling a cross with a hook to the right of its upper arm; the cross, which did not begin to assume prominence until the fourth century onwards; the marigold, symbolic of rebirth in the ancient world; the peacock, whose flesh was thought not to putrefy, making it a symbol of resurrection; and the eucharistic vine-scroll or Tree of Life. Iconographies (images imbued with meaning) adapted from those of Roman art, such as the Good Shepherd, were also adapted for Christian use. A number of artefacts from Roman Britain carry such motifs and may betoken Christian ownership; but these were, of necessity, discreet. Many of them are portable articles, such as strap ends, rings and pottery lamps, which were easily stolen or lost during travel, and their find-spots do not necessarily reflect a geographical spread of Christian belief. The distribution of more static Christian artefacts, along with such early churches as have so far been recognized, shows a concentration within south-east England and a northern military zone stretching from York to the area north of Hadrian's Wall in Northumbria, especially around its western end in the vicinity of Carlisle. The artefacts include mosaics, inscribed building components, funerary monuments, and a series of lead tanks bearing chi-rhos. The latter have been identified as possible baptismal tanks or containers for holy water. (Good examples have been found at Icklingham in Suffolk, Wiggonholt in Sussex, Ashton in Northamptonshire, and Walesby in Lincolnshire.)

This may simply reflect patterns of excavation over the past century, with an emphasis upon towns, forts and villas. But it does indicate that Christianity had achieved an overt presence in late Romano-British towns, amongst army families and those associated with them, and in a number of country estates which had become the focus of local life. Major structures of basilican plan, thought perhaps to be Christian churches, have been excavated inside the Roman town of Silchester, in the Roman 'Saxon Shore' fort of Richborough in Kent, and at Uley, on an ancient shrine site beside a hill fort. All of them are accompanied by stone baptisteries. In the case of the two former, the structures containing baptismal basins were detached in the usual continental fashion, whilst at Uley it was attached, a form also found in southern Europe. Further baptisteries have been identified at Icklingham and Witham. The baptismal pools could be hexagonal or octagonal to evoke biblical number symbolism. They were also shallow, as many of the baptisms that took place during conversion periods were of adults, and the usual rite was one of affusion (in which holy water was poured over the candidate's head as they stood within the pool or foot tank) rather than immersion.

Silver spoons inscribed with Christian motifs or inscriptions have been found in several late Roman hoards, such as the fourth-century Water Newton Hoard. This includes Christian inscriptions and metal leaves inscribed with crosses and

Early Christians in the orans attitude of prayer, a fourth-century fresco from a house-church at the Roman villa at Lullingstone, Kent.

may be an assemblage of Christian church altar-plate hidden during times of raids. Similar items have also been found in some early Anglo-Saxon graves, such as Sutton Hoo, and these may have been christening gifts or implements used during baptismal affusion and anointing. At Chedworth Villa in Gloucestershire (see page 29), the well of the nymphs was inscribed with chi-rhos during the fourth century and probably became a baptismal pool associated with a Christian house church. Likewise at Lullingstone Villa in Kent, the cellar nymphaeum was sealed up and replaced by two rooms above at ground level. It was cut off from the house itself with an external entrance to permit 'public' access. On the west wall of this house church was a large painted frieze of six figures in late-Roman eastern-style dress, their hands raised in the 'orans' position of prayer still observed in many eastern churches and as part of the Islamic sequence of prayer. They may depict the members of the Christian family that commissioned them, those who ministered there (some of the clothing perhaps representing early vestments), or favourite saints. On another wall was painted a large chi-rho symbol, flanked by the Greek characters alpha and omega ('I am Alpha and Omega... saith the Lord, which is and which was and which is to come' Revelation 1:8). The characters are set within a victor's laurel wreath with perching doves, flanked by a triumphal arch. These layers of meaning all reinforce belief in Christ's victory over death and in his role as the eternal *logos*, the Word – 'In the beginning was the Word, and the Word was with God and the Word was God' (John 1:1).

These precious fragments of painted plaster have been painstakingly reconstructed at the British Museum, where another of the most important examples of early Christian art is also to be seen: a fourth-century mosaic from the villa of Hinton St Mary in Dorset. This has a central roundel depicting a youthful, clean-shaven bust of Christ wearing Roman draped clothing, with a chi-rho behind his head serving as a nimbus, flanked by two pomegranates symbolizing eternal life. The mosaic was in the main reception room and is the first extant depiction of Christ from Britain and one of the earliest from the entire western part of the Roman empire. Other elements of the iconography of this mosaic accord with classical imagery but may have been given Christian interpretations, such as the four corner-heads, traditionally the winds, but here perhaps denoting the evangelists; and

Bellerophon spearing the Chimaera, which here may represent the triumph of good over evil, which was to be perpetuated in the Christian iconography of St Michael spearing the dragon. The mosaic at the villa of Frampton (Dorset) likewise combines Christian and pagan imagery, featuring a chi-rho, a *cantharus* (a wine chalice), dolphins, a rider spearing a lioness and Bacchic imagery perhaps adapted with reference to the eucharist. It adorned what was probably the dining room, a suitable venue not only for daily meals but also for the celebration of the Christian *agape* – the feast of love, in recollection of the Last Supper.

The *cantharus*, along with dolphins and other fish, recurs in a mosaic from Fifehead Neville (Dorset), and two silver rings inscribed with the chi-rho were found in a nearby hoard. The chi-rho flanked by alpha and omega is encountered again, cast into a lead tank from Icklingham that may have been used in baptisms. More controversial in their interpretation are the mosaics from the villa of Littlecote (Wiltshire), found in a religious building with three apses and a bath suite that stood apart from the house itself. They depict *Canthari*, marine life and panthers – which were to become symbols of Christ in the early Christian text of the *Physiologus* or 'Marvels of the East' (one of the sources of the medieval bestiary with its allegorical symbolism) – along with images of Orpheus in his guise as

The Head of Christ with chi-rho and pomegranates, in a fourth-century mosaic from the Roman villa at Hinton St Mary, Dorset.

Apollo. Both of the latter were considered to be saviour-gods, similar to Christ. This may be another case of Christian adaptation of pagan imagery, an extension of the process by which Celtic deities had become associated with those of Classical Antiquity. Conversely however, it might signal a fourth-century pagan householder's rebellion against what was becoming the Christian norm. Another intriguing find was a copper alloy sheet metal plaque decorated with high-quality repoussé images depicting biblical scenes of the sacrifice of Abraham (Genesis 22), Jonah reclining under the gourd (Jonah 4), Christ and the centurion (Matthew 8:5-14) and Christ healing the blind man (John 9). It was discovered folded and hidden in the fabric of the shrine at Uley, where it was remodelled in the late fourth century. It may have formed part of a box carrying Christian and classical pagan scenes, for which there are continental parallels.

PAGAN CONTINUITY

Apostasy was common during the early phases of a new faith's official reception within a society, and fourth-century Britain was no exception – especially when Emperor Julian himself apostatized in 361–63. After the pagan temple at Uley collapsed in the late fourth century it was rebuilt four times, in makeshift fashion. It went through phases of pagan reuse – allowing the cult of Mercury to continue functioning after the official adoption of Christianity – before its ultimate adaptation to Christianity. This culminated in the construction of a stone church in the late sixth or seventh century, complete with windows made of streaked red glass. Likewise, the temples at Bath and Lydney exhibit signs of rebuilding during the fifth century, and maybe even into the sixth in the case of Bath, where a series of pewter bowls inscribed with interlace crosses have also been found, indicating possible Christian use. During the first half of the fourth century, the shrine of Apollo at Nettleton was adapted by the construction of internal walls in the shape of a cruciform, as if it was being converted into a Christian church. However, finds dated by a coin to post-360 indicate that by this time it was pagan once more, perhaps indicating a period of apostasy. Brean Down and Lamyatt Beacon both had small

Holy Well, Sancreed, West Penwith, Cornwall. Wells such as this were used during the Celtic Iron Age and from early Christian times. Offerings such as ribbons and bandages tied to adjacent trees, nuts and berries, and sometimes little effigies and coins, were made as prayers for healing.

rectangular buildings, thought to be of Christian use, constructed next to their pagan temples; and the octagonal shrine at Pagan's Hill (Somerset) was adapted in the late fourth century and continued in use well into the Anglo-Saxon period. Its building was still being used during the Middle Ages and its name recalls its original function until the present day.

So who were the Christians of Roman Britain? At first they would have been few, and would most likely have been found amongst those who had contact with travellers who brought the news of what began as an eastern cult. Some may have been merchants themselves, or their servants, and were probably based in trading centres. By the third century the urban and military classes probably began to embrace Christianity in greater numbers as one of a number of exotic belief systems, as social and political instability promoted a quest for more spiritual, mystical meanings to life. Some of these people died for their faith, although persecutions were not implemented as thoroughly and ruthlessly in this remote province as elsewhere in the empire. Many would have lived for it, seeking to mould their lives to the image of Christ's teaching. When Christianity was adopted as the official state religion of the Roman empire during the fourth century, and the edicts of toleration were announced, most of the populace of Roman Britain would probably have given their religion as 'Christian' without perhaps actively practising its doctrines, as is often the case today. In remote rural areas however, pagan practices may have remained entrenched. As had been the case for millennia, the new religion probably merged, for many people, with pre-existing beliefs. Some prehistoric and Romano-Celtic shrines contined in use whilst others were abandoned, and in a few cases destroyed, and others were replaced by Christian churches, ensuring continuity of worship reinterpreted in the light of the revelation of the New Testament.

A proximity to nature developed into a distinctive appreciation of its value as a visible manifestation of God's bounty and beauty. Similarly, as elsewhere, the plethora of minor deities whose role was to intercede for the daily needs of humankind were gradually replaced by myriad local and international saints who assumed their functions (St Margaret of Antioch, patron of pregnant women; St Nicholas, patron of sailors, or St Clement with his symbol the anchor; St Cosmas and St Damian the healers, and so forth). Holy wells venerated for their healing propensities continued to receive offerings. Indeed, some still do today in the form of well-dressings (very popular in the Peak District of Derbyshire), and the ribbons, bandages, berries and nuts that can be seen around their sides or festooning surrounding trees and bushes in places such as Madron and Sancreed in West Penwith, Cornwall, and at numerous Irish wells. The existence of some of these ancient pools was sometimes ascribed to saints who settled beside them, using them as their water supplies and as baptismal and healing fonts, such as the well of St Winifred/Winefride/Gwenfrewi at Holywell, Flintshire (north-east Wales). The story goes that this was watered by the blood that fell from the marytr's head when it was severed by a rejected princely suitor in the seventh century. The well is now encompassed within an elaborate late medieval shrine, forming one of the best-preserved and most popular of British pilgrimage sites and a refuge for post-Reformation recusants. At Penmon Priory on Anglesey a well that was probably one of the druidic shrines destroyed by Paulinus in the first century AD was enclosed by a dry-stone beehive cell in the early Christian period. It later became associated with St Seiriol, sixth-century founder of Penmon church and the monastery on nearby Puffin Island (Ynis Seiriol or Priestholm). The pathway leading from the well heads for the cell at Caer Gybi (Holyhead, Anglesey), set within a Roman fort said to have been given to the saint by the local king, Maelgwyn Gwynedd and inhabited by his fellow hermit and friend, St Cybi. Cybi's well at Llangybi in North Wales was said to have burst forth when the saint struck his staff on a rock, but it may also have served as a sacred site during prehistory.

THE CHRISTIAN CHURCH IN THE LAST CENTURY OF ROMAN RULE

During the fourth century, British bishops attended Church Councils in Gaul, and a diocesan structure was put in place, with bishops exerting their pastoral authority from a seat (*cathedra*) within a town. The progressive decline of the urban economy and a migration of people and activity towards the countryside – and, in the cases of the wealthy, to villa estates – may have played a significant role in determining a regional distinction from the continent in the post-Roman period. In Italy, Gaul and Iberia the bishops stepped into the power vacuum left as the empire contracted and transformed under the pressure of external attack and the migration of the 'barbarian' peoples from beyond its frontiers. Many continental towns continued to function as cathedral cities, along with local markets and episcopal administration.

Wroxeter Forum, a late Roman town that stayed 'in business' into the fifth century, its walls remaining to remind the Anglo-Saxons of 'the work of giants'.

In Britain, however, the decay of many towns, a primarily agrarian economy and an inclination towards rural places of worship meant that many Roman settlements and structures fell to ruin. Their remains were later eulogized by their Anglo-Saxon successors as 'the work of giants' in the tenth-century Old English poem, 'The Ruin'. That said, archaeologists are beginning to question whether Christian churches from the late Roman period may have formed the basis, literally as well as ideologically, for a number of Anglo-Saxon and medieval churches which were constructed in former Roman towns near to the remains of principal buildings, such as the forum. Examples include: Holy Saviour church lying beneath Canterbury Cathedral; London (St Peter, Cornhill); Lincoln (St Paul-in-the-Bail); Colchester;

Chichester; Exeter; Gloucester and the church founded by King Edwin in York during the early seventh century, remains of which can still be seen in the archaeological excavations on display beneath York Minster. The memory of the Roman period, which had witnessed the beginnings of Christianity in Britain, lingered on.

The church in Roman Britain was therefore flourishing in late Antiquity, and it should be noted that it was in no way independent but formed a provincial component of the broader Christian church. Despite claims of a devolved Celtic – or as is currently being proposed – Greek Orthodox origin for British Christianity, the post-Roman Christian tradition which continued in Britain was thoroughly Roman in creed and origin. However, the empire had stretched from the Atlantic to the Middle East, making Britannia part of an international ecumen as yet unfragmented by the schisms and heresies that would contribute to the partition of East and West, both politically and in terms of religious tradition. This process culminated in the formal division of the two churches in 1054, but took shape during the fifth to ninth centuries.

CHAPTER 3

Warleaders, Settlers and Heretics: The Roman Withdrawal and the 'Age of Arthur'

THE ROMAN WITHDRAWAL

To Aëtius, thrice Consul, come the groans of the Britons... The barbarians drive us into the sea, and the sea drives us back to the barbarians. Between these, two deadly alternatives confront us, drowning or slaughter.

BEDE, *HISTORIA ECCLESIASTICA*, BOOK I

The dawn of the fifth century saw the gradual eclipse of the Roman empire. It was over-extended and beset by pressures on its frontiers from piratical raiders – in the case of Britannia from the Irish, Picts, Angles and Saxons – and migrants seeking entry to enjoy its economic benefits. Several British usurpers of imperial power arose during the early years of the century, the last of whom, Constantine III, withdrew the Roman troops to the continent in order to pursue his ambitions, leaving Britain poorly defended. Coins minted in his name at Lyon in 407–408 were the last to be circulated officially in Britannia, and the official gold coinage of 402–406 represented the last wage payment to the army. The province rejected the usurper, but by 410 the legitimate western emperor Honorius was forced to issue an order, the Honorian Rescript, instructing Britain to look to its own defences. The troops and civil servants were recalled and the monetary economy ruptured. In 446 an appeal from whichever authorities remained in the province to the Consul Aëtius, asking him to send relief, was declined.

A measure of trading contact remained, however, and some coins continued to be imported and to change hands. But it was not until after 600 and the conversion of the pagan Germanic settlers of Kent to Christianity that money was once more minted in Britain. Barter and bullion became the currencies of exchange as the province struggled to maintain existing lines of communication and trade with Gaul, Iberia and the Mediterranean and to preserve and establish new internal markets. Formal taxation ceased, but was doubtless replaced by the need to pay tribute, or protection money, to local leaders who emerged to fill the power vacuum. Any rejoicing at the absence of centralized authority would have quickly given way to anxiety over the alternatives and the prospect of far-reaching change. The world was being transformed, fast, and new relationships and ways of life had to be forged. That said, much of the late Roman military machine and the civil service had been manned by locals, federal auxiliaries and mercenaries recruited from outlying territories and frontier tribes. Retired soldiers were generally allotted a small-holding in the region in which they last served, and many of them married into the local community. There is ample evidence that members of the Romano-British establishment sought to maintain the status quo well after the province was jettisoned, and it has even been suggested that the Saxon Shore forts took their name from soldiers of Germanic origin manning their defence, as well as those attacking them. Bede's prose work *Life of St Cuthbert* relates an episode in which the saint predicted the fate of Carlisle (the Roman city of Luguvallium, known to the Anglo-Saxons by its British name, the fort, *caer*, of the god Lug) during a tour of the city led by its *praepositus* (a Roman official). Cuthbert's tour included the proud display of a working fountain, which has been taken as evidence of the continued maintenance of the city's Roman water supply system by its post-Romano-British inhabitants under Anglo-Saxon rule.

Despite the instability of the later fourth century, life in the province had been comfortable and relatively prosperous. The fear of raids is demonstrated by the large number of hoards of valued objects and coins that were buried by their owners, with the intention of retrieving them in safer times. They never did. Many of these buried treasures and life-savings were never reclaimed by the fleeing Roman citizenry, or discovered by their attackers; they lay hidden until they were discovered by modern workmen or archaeologists. Some were buried in the prosperous heartland of Britannia, such as the Mildenhall and Water Newton treasures and the recently discovered Hoxne hoard. The latter consisted of 15,244 coins and around 200 other

The Water Newton Treasure, thought to be a cache of church plates hidden during raids in the late fourth century. The silver 'leaves' carry chi-rho symbols.

COMES LITORIS SAXON PER BRITANIAM.

The *Notitia Dignitatum*, Renaissance copy of a Roman document dating from c.395. This page depicts the Saxon shore ports built to protect Britain against sea-borne raids.

gold and silver items. These included a pepper pot in the form of the bust of an empress (pepper was a valuable commodity and was one of the few possessions bequeathed by the priest-monk Bede on his deathbed in 735) and two ladles, possibly for liturgical use, which were decorated with the dolphins often associated with Christianity. The Water Newton treasure was even less ambiguously Christian in character and may be a cache of church plate (see page 49). Other hoards were found in hostile territory, where they were in turn hidden by those who had seized them – after some of the finely wrought metalwork *objets* had been broken up into hack-silver for its bullion value. These include the Traprain Law hoard, buried in a hillfort to the south-west of Edinburgh, and the Coleraine hoard from Northern Ireland, which consisted mostly of plundered military sword belt fittings and tableware, with coinage dating its deposit to after 410.

By the fourth century the church in Britain had been organized into territorial dioceses. At least four, and perhaps as many as six, bishoprics existed by the time of the Council of Arles in 314, which was attended by delegates from the civil diocese of Gaul. These included the provinces of Britain: Bishop Eborius of York, capital of Britannia Secunda; Bishop Restitutus of London, Maxima Caesariensis; and Bishop Adelphius, probably of Lincoln, Flavia Caesariensis. Others, less easily identified, were 'Sacer episcopus', 'Sacer presbyter' and 'Arminius diaconus', whom it has been suggested may have represented Britannia Prima, Wales and the West. The *Notitia Dignitatum*, a Roman document now preserved only in a copy made in 1436 from a ninth-century Carolingian copy of the original, contains a list with illustrations, maps and diagrams of the offices of the late Roman empire. It shows not only military installations but also centres of civil administration and the diocesan structure of the church. The terms 'diocese', 'bishop', 'priest', 'vicar' and 'rector' all stem from the Roman civil administration and its ecclesiastical derivatives which emerged at this time. This suggests the existence of significant Christian congregations. In the light of subsequent events however, the growth of this early British diocese/parish system would have to await the arrival of Archbishop Theodore of Tarsus in 667 to get underway properly, and would not be fully implemented until after the Norman Conquest in the eleventh century.

> *... The story of their banishment from Eden is in truth the story of how the human race gained its freedom: by eating fruit from the tree of knowledge, Adam and Eve became mature human beings, responsible to God for their actions.*
>
> PELAGIUS

PELAGIANISM AND THE MISSION OF GERMANUS OF AUXERRE

The church in Roman Britain had been a provincial and unremarkable one, and it was probably considered peripheral by the churchmen of the day. This was to change in the late fourth century with the rise of one of the most eloquent, rational philosophers and teachers of the day, the heretic Pelagius. Probably born and educated in Britain, which says something about the level of schooling available to British Christians, he left as a young man to pursue a career in Rome, probably in the 380s. It was probably Pelagius whom St Jerome had in mind when he wrote a letter in 393–94, attacking someone who had dared criticize his own aspersions against Jovinian and describing him as '…a certain gossipy monk, a wanderer around the streets, the cross-roads and the highways, a pettifogger, a sly detractor, who with a beam in his eye strives to remove the mote from another's'. As if his consorting with women were not evidence enough of his moral laxity, Jerome adds the final insult that Pelagius had only turned to religion when he failed to carve out a career in law. Jerome's pique may have had something to do with the fact that Pelagius had quickly filled the place he himself had formerly occupied in the intellectual Christian circles of Rome. As late as 411 St Augustine of Hippo described the Briton as 'a holy man, whom I am told has made no small progress in the Christian life'. But by 415 these two great minds, one from the Roman province of Carthage in North Africa and the other from Britannia, were locked in a vicious public conflict which could not be resolved. In the same year, by which time he and Pelagius were both based in Palestine, Jerome first coined the term 'Pelagiani', thus attributing Pelagius with a school of thought that he was called to defend at two diocesan synods (at Jerusalem and Diospolis). Pelagius's vindication on these occasions emboldened him to write his most controversial works: a lost treatise called 'In Defence of Free Will' and 'On Nature'.

Augustine mobilized the African bishops and influential contacts in Rome, pressurizing the Pope to excommunicate Pelagius and his key follower Celestius. They put up a spirited and articulate fight, but eventually Pope Zosimus was forced to expel them from the Christian communion. This was, however, only after the emperor, then based in Ravenna, had intervened through fear of civil unrest. Pelagius had passed out of the record by 431, when Celestius alone had his opinions condemned by the Council of Ephesus, and is thought to have retired to Egypt where his followers still had a safe base. There is evidence of the heresy lingering for centuries in Gaul, Italy, Dalmatia, Britain and Ireland, where its influence was still to be found as late as 807 in the 'Commentary of the Book of Armagh', made in support of its claims to primacy. Aspects of Pelagius's teaching, now referred to as Semi-Pelagianism, or Synergism, still find support in many Christian denominations today.

The crux of the debate lay in the nature of free will and of divine grace, which was later to become a key issue underlying the theological disagreements of the Reformation and Counter-Reformation during the sixteenth and seventeenth centuries. Augustine's hard line on the elect and predestination caused many to embrace Pelagius's cause, and no less than four Italian bishops were expelled from office for refusing to accept his condemnation. The Pelagian resistance, which espoused grace as a partnership between God and humankind, continued to dog Augustine's old age, and it found sympathetic, if not as extreme, support amongst respected churchmen such as John Cassian and Vincent of Lérins. Part of the problem was that, as a whole, the church had not formulated a universal position on original sin, but that the church in Africa had. Its view had been constructed in the face of the Decian persecutions and the associated fragmentation of whatever hard-won Christian unity had already been achieved. Building on the writings of Cyprian

A certain gossip monk, a wanderer around the streets… a pettifogger, a sly detractor.

St Jerome on Pelagius

A holy man, whom I am told has made no small progress in the Christian life.

St Augustine of Hippo on Pelagius

and Tertullian, Augustine had constructed a neat theological system linking the transmission of original sin, the need for infant baptism, divine grace and predestination. He was not going to allow this to be deconstructed.

Pelagianism was transmitted by teaching, face to face and through letters and tracts, and it sought to regain the innocence of the early church. Its core principle was that baptism bestowed a new life, potentially free from sin. For Augustine, on the other hand, only God's grace could prevail over the perpetual workings of inherited sin. The debate is often represented as one of an emphasis upon simplicity and individual freedom of choice versus the championing of ecclesiastical hierarchy and theological formalization. This is to overstate the case, but then so bitter was the contest that both sides did just that. Pelagius's British background was perhaps most clearly manifested in his belief that the beauty of nature was a reflection of God, which led him to urge his followers to care for animals and plants, as well as people, for their own sake. His espousal of a simpler, more austere Christian lifestyle

Pelagianism

A flavour of Pelagius's thinking may be gained from these passages from his *Letter to Demetrias* (as published by the Little Gidding Community in *The Letters of Pelagius, Celtic Soul Friend*, in which he is firmly claimed for the 'Celtic' spiritual tradition).

Within our minds there is a kind of natural sanctity, which we call conscience. This conscience presides over the mind as a judge presides over a court. It favours honourable and righteous actions, and it condemns hurtful and wrong actions. Just as a judge is guided by a book of law, so the conscience is guided by an inner law which has been written on the soul by God. But in one important respect the way in which conscience works is different from the way a court works. In a court lawyers on opposing sides try to win their case by brilliant argument; they are not trying to reveal the truth, but merely to win the judge to their side. Conscience, by contrast, rejects brilliant argument and instead wants only the truth of each and every situation; and only when it has discerned the truth will conscience make its judgement. When we read scriptures and remark that Moses or Abraham were good people, we are simply saying that in them conscience was a firm and strong judge.

When Adam and Eve ate from the tree of knowledge they were exercising their freedom of choice; and as a consequence of the choice they made, they were no longer able to live in the Garden of Eden. When we hear that story we are struck by their disobedience to God; and so we conclude that they were no longer fit to enjoy the perfect happiness of Eden. And we should also be struck by the nature of that tree and its fruit. Before eating the fruit they did not know the difference between good and evil; thus they did not possess the knowledge which enables human beings to exercise freedom of choice. By eating the fruit they acquired this knowledge, and from that moment onwards they were free. Thus the story of their banishment from Eden is in truth the story of how the human race gained its freedom: by eating fruit from the tree of knowledge, Adam and Eve became mature human beings, responsible to God for their actions.

won him followers from all walks of life, including formerly wealthy nominal Christians who responded to the challenge of actually trying to live out the gospel. Yet to claim him as the first British theologian would be a distortion, for his thought was also shaped by the intellectual ferment and the street life of Rome and the Middle East, where he spent most of his life.

Pelagius's arguments may appeal to a modern audience, but their implications for doctrines of sin and salvation were profound and extremely dangerous. His British origins, and his following there, turned the attention of the church authorities to the remote former province. In 429, at the request of the British, the bishops of Gaul dispatched Bishop Germanus of Auxerre and Bishop Lupus of Troyes (who had trained at the monastery of Lérins in the South of France) to refute the heresy at a conference held in Verulamium. There they affirmed the origins of Christianity in Britain by visiting the shrine of St Alban. For those citizens of late Roman Britain who were already alarmed at the prospect of being cut adrift from the political, economic and cultural framework within which they had operated for nearly four hundred years, the prospect of being cast off as an heretical or schismatic local church would have been terrifying.

In 447 Germanus paid a second visit, banishing those leaders of the Pelagians who were still operating in Britain. He is also said to have led the British in a bloodless battle against the Picts and Saxons, which they won by singing a chorus of Alleluias, thereby putting the enemy to flight by the element of surprise. Germanus may have been selected for his diplomatic experience: he had served as a legal advocate and as governor of Armorica (Brittany), which had strong traditional links with Britain, including their alliance against Caesar at the maritime Battle of the Gulf of Morbihan. His feast was widely celebrated in medieval Britain and St Germanus in Cornwall was named after him. Lupus must also have possessed considerable diplomatic skills, for he was later sent to treat with Attila the Hun when he was ravaging Gaul.

Pelagianism was not, perhaps, the only concern. Bede writes of a period of peace and stability in the Romano-British church until the time of Constantine, to whose reign he attributes the rise of heresy, rather than the championing of Christianity:

De Excidio Britanniae et Conquestu ('The Ruin and Conquest of Britain'). Tenth-century copy of a mid-sixth-century text by the British monk, Gildas.

This poisonous error [Arianism] after corrupting the whole world, at length crossed the sea and infected even this remote island: and, once the doorway had been opened, every sort of pestilential heresy at once poured into this island, whose people are ready to listen to anything novel, and never hold firmly to anything.

Bede, *Historia Ecclesiastica.*

Bede was undoubtedly referring pejoratively to the British – who in his own day still espoused an alternative dating for Easter to that favoured by Rome – rather than to his fellow Anglo-Saxons. Bede gives Pelagianism short shrift, but does add the details that the heresy was introduced to Britain by Agricola, the son of a Pelagian priest named Severianus, and that its representatives faced Germanus and Lupus at the Verulamium conference clad in rich ornaments and magnificent robes. This would have run counter to Pelagian teaching but, unless Bede is simply adding the detail to condemn the miscreants, the Pelagians may have felt that the dignity and pomp of the Gaulish bishops needed matching if they were to be taken seriously.

GILDAS AND THE EVIDENCE FOR CHRISTIANITY DURING THE FIFTH CENTURY

As we have seen, our main literary sources for the history of the fifth century are the accounts by the Anglo-Saxon monk Bede in his *Historia Ecclesiastica Gentis Anglorum* ('The Ecclesiastical History of the English People'), which was completed in 731. The authority upon whom Bede relied primarily for information concerning this mystery-shrouded period was Gildas, whose *De Excidio Britanniae et Conquestu* ('The Ruin and Conquest of Britain') was composed around 540. Gildas (c.500–570) was a British monk and abbot who is thought to have been born in the Clyde area and to have entered the monastery of Llaniltud in south Wales, perhaps after he was widowed. He later became a hermit on Flatholm Island in the Bristol Channel.

The details of Gildas's life and its chronology are debated, and it may be that the deeds of more than one man have become associated with this influential figure – as was the case with St Patrick. His influence as a monastic founder and teacher was disseminated by his travels in Britain, Ireland and Brittany, where he died in a monastery he had founded near Rhuis, Morbihan. He also attracted many Irish followers, visited Ireland in person and corresponded with members of monastic communities there, including St Finnian of Clonard who wrote to him about the problem of wandering monks. He received 'a most elegant reply', to quote St Columbanus, who in around 600 told Pope Gregory that he had read many of Gildas's writings. His literary style exhibits indebtedness to Scripture, to Virgil and to Church Fathers such as Ignatius of Antioch (who was thrown to the lions in the Colosseum around 107), indicating the kinds of sources available in Britain at this time. His influential form of polemic in the *De Excidio* castigated the moral inadequacy of the rulers of the day and sought the reason for the rising tide of Germanic incursions in the poor spiritual and educational health of the nation. Alcuin used something of the same tone in the letter of commiseration to the monastic community on Holy Island after it had become the victim of the cataclysmic first Viking raid in Europe in 793. Similarly, King Alfred's religious and educational reforms, launched in the late ninth century following the Viking partition of England, were based on the same assumptions as those adopted by Gildas. Archbishop Wulfstan of York's famous *Sermon of the Wolf to the English* also shows evidence of Gildas's influence. It was penned in the early eleventh century to rouse the English against the renewed Scandinavian threat during the reign of Aethelraed Unraed (the 'ill-advised'). The role of Christianity in rallying people to the defence of their nation, and in examining the moral, educational and spiritual health of that nation, was established early on in Britain.

'ARTHUR', VORTIGERN AND THE COMING OF THE GERMANIC SETTLERS

Gildas's account of the 130 years following the Honorian Rescript has formed the basis of the traditional scholarly version of events. He paints a picture of a Romano-British attempt to preserve the old order, led by the last man standing – one Ambrosius Aurelianus, whose parents had earned the right to wear purple, presumably by holding Roman office. This was undermined by the attempts of others to carve out power bases of their own, causing a reversion to Celtic tribalism. The foremost of these tribal leaders was Vortigern, the 'superb tyrant'. Like many others, Vortigern, following established Roman military practice, employed Germanic mercenaries to defend his territory against their fellows and against the Picts, the Irish ('Scotti') and, no doubt, some of his own British neighbours. The hounds of war he unleashed came to bite the hand that fed them, turning on their employers and enticing their kith and kin to join them in seizing the vulnerable former Roman province. Ambrosius led the resistance to the flood that followed. Gildas recounted that his battles culminated in the Battle of Mount Badon, usually dated to c.500, when Gildas was born. Badon has been variously located; suggestions include Bath and Badbury Rings. It marked a turning point and stemmed Germanic gains for some forty years, until the time when Gildas was writing – a time in which the complacency and divisiveness of the British leaders and people of the day were in danger of turning the clock back.

Sure enough, the Germanic settlements and raids resumed and by 600 a number of kingdoms had been carved out by groups of peoples drawn from around Germany, southern Denmark and the Netherlands, notably (as identified by Bede) the Jutes, Angles and Saxons. By the time that Bede wrote his history, some major players had emerged: the kingdoms of Kent, Sussex, Wessex, Essex, Mercia, East Anglia and Northumbria. Together these formed Anglo-Saxon England, or Bede's

Lamentable to behold, in the streets lay the tops of lofty towers, tumbled to earth, stones of high walls, holy altars, remains of human bodies, covered with livid clots of coagulated blood, as if crushed together in a press; and with no chance of burial, save in the ruins of their houses, or in the ravening bellies of wild beasts and birds.

GILDAS, *DE EXCIDIO BRITANNIAE ET CONQUESTU*

Gildas's Account of the Germanic Invasions

Chapter 23. Then all the council, with the superb [proud or supreme] tyrant Gurthrigern [Vortigern], the British king, were so blinded that, to protect their country, they sealed its doom by inviting in (like wolves to the sheep-fold), the fierce and impious Saxons, a race hateful both to God and to Man, to repel the invasions of the northern nations… A multitude of whelps issued forth from the lair of this barbaric lioness… in three warships… The barbarians being thus introduced to the island as soldiers, as they falsely maintained, any dangers in defence of their hospitable hosts, received provisions which, being for some time bounteously bestowed, stopped their doggish muzzles. Yet they complain that their monthly supplies are not adequately furnished, and industriously aggravate each chance for a quarrel, saying that unless more generosity is shown, they will break the treaty and plunder the island. Shortly, they follow up their threats with deeds…

Chapter 25. Some of the miserable remnant, therefore, having been taken to the mountains, were murdered in great numbers; other, forced by famine, came and yielded themselves in perpetual slavery to their foes… others passed over the seas with loud lament… Others, committing their safety, continually jeopardized, to the hills, precipices, densely wooded forests, and the rocks of the seas (and even if with trembling hearts), remained in their country. But meanwhile, an opportunity presenting itself, when these heartless robbers were returned home, the poor remnants of our nation… took arms under the conduct of Ambrosius Aurelianus, a modest man, who of all the Roman nation was then by chance, in the confusion of these troubled times, alone left alive. His parents who, for their merit were adorned with the purple, had been slain in these same traumas, and now his progeny in our own days, although shamefully degenerated from the worthiness of their ancestors, provoke to battle their cruel conquerors, and by the goodness of our Lord obtain victory.

Chapter 26. Afterwards, sometimes our countrymen, sometimes the foe, won the field, to the end that our Lord might in this land try after his accustomed manner these his Israelites, whether or not they loved him, until the year of the siege of Mount Badon, when occurred almost the last, if not the least, slaughter of our brutal enemies, which was (as I am sure) forty-four years and one month after the landing of the Saxons, and also the time of my own birth. And yet to this day neither are the cities of our land inhabited as before, but being forsaken and cast down, still lie desolate; our wars against the foreigners having ceased, but our civil troubles still remaining. For the recollection of such dire desolation of the island, as well as of the unexpected recovery of the same, remained in the minds of those who were eyewitnesses of the fantastic events of both, and in respect of this, kings, public magistrates and private persons, with priests and clergy, did each and every one live ordered lives according to their various vocations. But when these had departed from this world, and a new race succeeded who were ignorant of these troubled times and had only experienced present prosperity, all the laws of truth and justice were so shaken and subverted that not so much as a trace or remembrance of these virtues remained among the above-mentioned orders of men, except among a very few…

Gildas, *De Excidio Britanniae et Conquestu*

'Nation of the English'. This would assume a more consolidated identity following the unification of the country under a single West Saxon monarchy during the tenth century, after further Germanic migrants from Scandinavia – the Vikings – had partitioned the country and knocked out the other English contenders for power.

Gildas's account was, of course, written from a purely British perspective. Modern historians and archaeologists have increasingly challenged its description of mass genocide and immigration into the Highland Zone of western Britain and overseas to Brittany – the former Celtic territory of Armorica, which is thought to have taken its new name from these British migrations. Questions have been raised over the numbers of Germanic settlers, although genetic evidence supports the introduction of a significant Germanic component to the population, presumably stemming from this period and from subsequent Viking settlement. Intermarriage undoubtedly occurred, and an element of the Romano-British populace would probably have remained on the land occupied by their ancestors for countless generations, serving their new Germanic overlords. This may have been the case for the 'laets', a distinct semi-free class provided for within the early seventh-century law-code of the Anglo-Saxon King Ethelberht of Kent. There is growing archaeological and landscape evidence for continuity of land use, with the holdings of many late Roman villas being perpetuated and preserved within a medieval manorial and village context. In one such case, which is particularly informative, the DNA taken from a modern farmer living in the vicinity of Cheddar Gorge was compared with that taken from the remains of a Neolithic farmer found nearby. They were virtually identical, indicating continuous working of the land and enfranchisement by the same people across some five thousand years.

The Romano-British Christian resistance to the pagan Germanic incursions gradually crystallized around the figure of King Arthur – although Gildas, who was a boy at the time, names the hero of the day not as Arthur, but as Ambrosius Aurelianus. Arthur may have been another of his names, or that of a contemporary; or he may represent a heroic ideal rather than an historical figure. The works of the sixth-century British poets Taliesin and Aneirin contain a messianic vein. The poem *The Gododdin*, thought to have been composed by Aneirin in around 600, is an elegy for the British warriors who defended the territory around Edinburgh against Germanic encroachment and who launched an ill-fated expedition to Catraaeth (probably Catterick). It recounts their valour but notes that although they were great, they were not Arthur, suggesting the existence of a concept of a superhero who would save the day.

The poem *Preiddeu Annwfn* is narrated by Taliesin, one of Arthur's companions, who accompanied him on a raid of the otherworld to carry off its cauldron. Taliesin was one of the seven who returned. The poem has overtones of earlier Celtic belief and myth, and it is possible that Arthur represents an amalgam of earlier Celtic saviour figures, and that this name was in turn bestowed upon a military leader who led the British at the height of the Germanic influx. The beginnings of Arthurian legend can more clearly be traced, however, in a work copied by the scribe

Men went over to Catraeth [Catterick] with battle ranks and warcry, power of horses, blue armour and shields, shafts held on high, and spearheads, and shining coats of mail and swords.

THE GODODDIN, C.600

Nennius, a Welsh cleric who penned the *Historia Brittonum*, 'The History of the British', in around 830 (see page 61). Here the battles of Ambrosius are expanded upon and ascribed to Arthur, who is said to have once fought carrying the image of the Virgin on his shoulder (perhaps on a cloak, brooch or shield).

The *Historia Brittonum* also traced the derivation of Britain's name from that of Brutus, a Roman consul and a grandson of Aeneas of Troy. His genealogy stretched back to Japheth, son of Noah, and thence to Adam, thereby siting British history in relation to that of Greece, Rome and the Judaic Old Testament. The *Historia Brittonum*'s collection of texts and legends, some related by 'the old men around the fires', was composed in the face of two centuries of pressure upon the western British by the English. This had reached a peak during the second half of the eighth century under Kings Æthelbald and Offa of Mercia, the latter constructing a formidable earthwork, built in Roman fashion, called Offa's Dyke. It lay along the border of Wales and Anglo-Saxon Mercia (the Marches) and was presumably an official line of demarcation for trading and legal purposes. Raids in either direction

Tintagel Island – Arthurian icon, offshore emporium and early Christian community. Foundations of some of the fifth- to sixth-century post-Roman buildings on the cliff-shelf.

were commonplace. The Britons were known by the English as Wealas/Walas/Walh, 'strangers' or serfs/slaves in the seventh-century law-code of Wessex. Their continued presence within Germanic territory was signalled by the place-name element 'Wal-', as in Walton. The Welsh law-codes provide clear testimony to a mutual mistrust originating in the migration period of the fifth and sixth centuries. One of the severest of legal penalties, exile, was visited upon those Britons who committed treachery – specifically those who collaborated with the pagan invaders by giving them directions and acting as native guides. This prohibition on interaction with the newcomers is taken as one of the key reasons why the British church did not seek to convert their Germanic neighbours and aggressors. Bede's account of the period, from an Anglo-Saxon perspective, is indebted to that of Gildas, but adds:

> Among the other unspeakable crimes, recorded with sorrow by their own historian Gildas, they added this – that they never preached the Faith to the Angles or Saxons who dwelt with them in Britain. But God in his goodness did not utterly abandon the people whom he had chosen; for he remembered them and sent this nation more worthy preachers of truth to bring them to the Faith.
>
> Bede, *Historia Ecclesiastica*

This negation of any continuity of faith in England suited Bede's purpose in two ways. It enabled him to identify the Anglo-Saxons as God's chosen people, the new

Israelites, fresh from their wanderings in the wilderness in search of the promised land, and to attribute their conversion primarily to the Gregorian Mission with Augustine's arrival in Kent in 597. However, evidence for the continuity of the Christian tradition in British territory is considerable, and a measure of such continuity is also likely to have extended – if only in pockets – to the remaining Britons in England. It may also have embraced some of the Germanic peoples alongside whom they now lived.

The *Canu Aneirin, Canu Taliesin* and *Canu Llywarch Hen* (the Songs of Aneirin, Taliesin and Llywarch the Old) are, along with related material such as the *Canu Heledd*, preserved in some important Welsh manuscripts dating from the thirteenth century. These are the 'ancient books of Wales': the Book of Aneirin, the Book of Taliesin, the Red Book of Hergest and the Black Book of Carmathen. The spelling used in these texts shows that they were written down in Old Welsh as early as the ninth century, and they were probably recited orally prior to this. They relate the heroic exploits of a number of families, war-bands, and individual warriors such as Urien, who came from northern and north-western Britain but had relocated to Wales in the face of Germanic settlement. Such a migration is corroborated not only by the diffusion pattern of these poems and legends but also by the place-name evidence. For example, *cumbre* – the Brythonic term for a Briton, a fellow-countryman, or those sharing the same border – is recollected in the names Cumbria, Cumberland and other British and Welsh place-names, as well as in the name for Wales itself – Cymry. This would support Gildas's view that British territories consolidated within the western Highland Zone of Britain and that there was interaction between the regions, stretching in an arc from Edinburgh through south-western Scotland and north-western England, then across into Wales and down into the South West and Cornwall.

SITES OF THE ARTHURIAN AGE

There is growing archaeological evidence for the continued British occupation and renovation of Roman sites during the fifth and sixth centuries, such as the town of Wroxeter and the forts of Caerwent in South Wales and Birdoswald at the western end of Hadrian's Wall. At the latter a massive timber hall was erected on the foundations of the earlier Roman granaries by a post-Roman leader who continued to protect at least part of the Roman defences. Earlier Celtic hillforts and promontory forts were also reoccupied during this period, including the Iron-Age fort of South Cadbury, which was equipped in Roman military fashion with timber defences and parade ground. This site has become one of the foremost candidates as the location of Arthur's court of 'Camelot'.

Subsequent attempts by the British to withstand English rule, or to promote regionalism in the face of growing centralization, led to a number of other sites becoming associated with the fully developed Arthurian legends of the central Middle Ages. These included Tintagel (see page 59), the site of the castle built by

Then it was, that magnanimous Arthur, with all the kings and the military force of Britain, fought against the Saxons. And through there were many more noble than he, yet he was twelve times chosen as their commander, and was as often conqueror.

THE *HISTORIA BRITTONUM*,
NINTH CENTURY

The *Historia Brittonum's* Account of the Germanic Invasions

Chapter 28. Thus, according to the account given by the Britons, the Romans governed them four hundred and nine years. After this, the Britons despised the authority of the Romans and refused to pay them tribute or receive their kings; nor dared the Romans any longer attempt to govern a country, the natives of which massacred their deputies…

…Chapter 50. St Germanus, after his [Vortigern's] death, returned to his own country. At that time, the Saxons increased greatly in Britain, in strength and numbers… Then it was, that the magnanimous Arthur, with all the kings and military force of Britain, fought against the Saxons. And though there were many more noble than he, yet he was twelve times chosen as their commander, and was as often conqueror. The first battle in which he was engaged, was at the mouth of the river Gleni. The second, third, fourth and fifth, were on another river, by the Britons called Duglas, in the region of Linuis. The sixth, on the river Bassas. The seventh in the wood Celidon, which the Britons call Cat Coit Celidon. The eighth was near Gurnion castle, where Arthur bore the image of the Holy Virgin, mother of God, upon his shoulders, and through the power of our Lord Jesus Christ, and the holy Mary, put the Saxons to flight, and pursued them the whole day with great slaughter. The ninth was at the City of the Legion, called Cair Lion. The tenth was on the banks of the river Trat Treuriot. The eleventh was on the mountain Breguoin, which we call Cat Bregion. The twelfth was a harsher contest, when Arthur penetrated to the hill of Badon. In this engagement, nine hundred and forty fell by his hand alone, no one but the Lord affording him assistance. In all these engagements the Britons were successful. For no strength can avail against the will of the Almighty… The more the Saxons were vanquished, the more they sought for new recruits of Saxons from Germany; so that kings, commanders, and war bands were invited over from almost every province. And this practice they continued until the reign of Ida, who was the son of Eoppa, he, of the Saxon race, was the first king in Bernicia, and in Cair Ebrauc [York].

Historia Brittonum

Historia Brittonum. A copy made c.1100 of a text copied c.830 by the Welsh ecclesiastic scribe, Nennius. This passage recounts the battles of King Arthur, including Mount Badon.

St Michael's Mount, West Penwith, Cornwall: natural harbour, Iron Age shrine, Roman trading centre, early Christian hermitage, medieval priory and post-Dissolution castle. It is approached by a causeway at low tide.

Earl Reginald of Cornwall and Earl Richard during the twelfth and thirteenth centuries, as the focus of their bid for an independent kingdom. This dramatic promontory fort, now an island, was probably selected for its traditional identification as the birthplace of Arthur. Yet once again fact may have been stranger than fiction, for the underlying rock of this evocative island fortress has been found by archaeologists to have hosted an earlier Roman offshore trading centre. This centre was still occupied in the post-Roman period, trading with northern Africa and the eastern Mediterranean, as evidenced by the thousands of broken sherds of pottery in which wine and olive oil continued to be imported during the fifth to seventh centuries. At this period Tintagel may either have been a secular site or, less probably, an early monastery.

A similar scenario can reasonably be proposed for Gateholm Island, off the south Pembrokeshire coast in the heartland of St David's subsequent activities, where the foundations of Roman *insulae* – forerunners of urban 'blocks' of buildings – can still be traced beneath the greensward. Likewise at St Michael's Mount in Cornwall, which has yielded evidence of its prehistoric role as a cult focus. There is also evidence that it was used as a Roman offshore trading harbour and stronghold; an early monastic or eremitic settlement (with an early Christian stone cross still clinging to its rock-face) and subsequently a monastery that was given to the monks of Mont St Michel in Normandy because of their mutual association with the high places where the Archangel Michael combatted the dragon of evil; and an aristocratic castle. In the early tenth century the West-Saxon King Athelstan acknowledged the ancient importance of Marazion, the settlement on the mainland facing St Michael's Mount, by granting it one of the first privileges of holding a market. This was one of the acts by which he celebrated the absorption of Cornwall into the newly formed kingdom of 'England' – of which he was sole monarch – and his conquest of the Scilly Isles. Others included the founding of a college of canons at St Buryan's on the westernmost tip of Cornwall, the farthest end of Britain. The two crosses that still stand atop their stepped bases beside St Buryan's church probably helped to commemorate this event. The round churchyard (*rath*) surrounding the church proclaims its early Celtic origins – founded by an Irish nun, Buriana.

The post-Roman occupation of Tintagel island can still be seen in the traces of the huts and garden plots which still cling to the cliffs, although some scholars prefer to view them as part of the later medieval castle settlement. However, the recent find of a piece of stone bearing the inscription 'Artorius', in a style of script appropriate to around the sixth century, has been taken by many to corroborate of the presence of a post-Roman centre associated with Arthur. Inscribed stones known as the Drustan and

Stepped cross in St Buryan's churchyard, perhaps erected after King Athelstan of Wessex founded a college of canons here in celebration of his conquest of the Scilly Isles.

Cunomorus stones, found in the vicinity of the Iron-Age fort of Castle Dore near Fowey, also add a note of credibility to the legend of King Mark and the adulterous lovers Tristan and Iseult. The names inscribed upon them perhaps commemorate Tristan/Drustan and King Mark. On the mainland cliffs opposite Tintagel island sits the parish church, at some distance from the medieval village on the approach to the isle. Recent excavations in its graveyard have revealed a cemetery of the same period – its graves aligned west-east in Christian fashion – along with the remains of funerary feasts, the wakes of prehistoric and Roman tradition. Those buried in Tintagel churchyard were Christians who were continuing to enjoy at least some of the trappings of a romanized lifestyle: maintaining trading links with various parts of the Mediterranean world; using imported tableware; drinking wine and cooking with olive oil. Whether they themselves controlled the rocky citadel of the nearby island where these de luxe goods were imported, or whether it was occupied by a local king or a monastic community, Tintagel bears witness to the perpetuation of a late Roman Christian lifestyle and to sustained relationships with other parts of the Christian ecumen in the troubled generations that witnessed the fall-out of post-imperialism and the demise of a superpower.

CHAPTER 4

The British Church in the 'Age of the Saints' and the Missions to the Picts and the Irish

THE BRITISH AND THE POWER VACUUM

A number of British kingdoms emerged to fill the power vacuum left by the Roman administration. Gildas, writing perhaps in Chester, or Bangor in north Wales, names five British kings in his tirade against bad government. The correspondence of St Patrick highlights the misdeeds of another king, Coroticus. These admonitions are addressed to Christian rulers, however lax. Their kingdoms were Strathclyde in the vicinity of Glasgow; Rheged in south-west Scotland and north-west England; Elmet in Yorkshire around Catterick; Dumnonia in the South West (Dorset, Devon and Cornwall); Dyfed in south-west Wales; Venedotia or Gwynedd in north-west Wales;

Reconstruction of an Irish Iron-Age/early Christian ring-fort (*cashel*) at Cragganauen Archaeology Park near Limerick. Monastic *raths* may not have been dissimilar.

and Ercing/Ergyng in south Wales (named after the Roman town of Ariconium, later Archenfield, in the district of Herefordshire).

The most visible traces of the presence of Christian Britons within these territories are a remarkable series of stones carved with commemorative inscriptions, dating from the late fifth century onwards. These form part of a Christian epigraphic tradition that also embraced Gaul, Iberia and North Africa. Christian British presence can also be mapped through place-names, notably those retaining an 'eccles' element, from the Latin *ecclesia*. On the other hand, the English word 'church', from Old English *cirice* (kirk), derived from the Greek. Such places include Eccles and Exley, which come from the British for 'church' and the Old English *leah*, a clearing. The same Latin derivation applies for the Welsh place-name element *eglwys* and the Cornish *eglos*. However, the survival of Brythonic Celtic languages in Wales and Cornwall means that not all such names in these countries need date to as early as the Roman and post-Roman periods. The Brythonic Celtic equivalent was *Llan*, denoting a church enclosure, the equivalent of the Goidelic Celtic *rath* or the Latin *vallum*. When found in place-names this element can often be taken to imply the presence of an encircling earthwork. In an early Christian context this took the form of an earthen bank surrounding a church or monastic settlement, which demarcated its inner sacred space. Another early form of place-name is the Brythonic *Ty* (Goidelic *Tigh/Tech*), meaning 'house' in the sense of a monastic foundation. The Goidelic term for a monastic cell, *Cell-/Cill-* or *Kell-/Keill-* (as in Kells) can also denote a church.

Another defining feature of the areas that remained in British hands during the fifth to seventh centuries is the proliferation of church dedications to native saints. This predates the medieval papal process of canonization: sanctity was by popular acclaim and could be bestowed for a variety of contributions made in God's service during life (such as founding a church), or for miracles performed after death. Most of the men and women so commemorated do not appear in the fragmentary remains of the contemporary written record. Their names might appear on a roughly hewn stone, inscribed in the debased capitals or uncials of the late Roman world and now preserved in a chapel, graveyard or museum. Occasionally they are sited in isolation on some wild moor or coast where the saints themselves still lie, or where they performed some inspiring deed, for the age-old prehistoric practice of siting burial mounds and menhirs at meaningful points within the landscape continued into the Christian age. Indeed, on the Welsh border with England, near the medieval ruins of Valle Crucis Abbey, sits a cairn of stones – each one a prayer – marking the grave of Eliseg. It is surmounted by a monument, ironically of Anglo-Saxon Mercian form, known as the Pillar of Eliseg, which was erected by his great-grandson, Concenn (died 854). The monument commemorates Eliseg, proudly proclaiming his genealogy, and states that his fame was assured for saving Powys from the English. It also claims that Eliseg's descent stemmed from Vortigern, who was blessed by Germanus, and Severa, daughter of the usurper to the Roman imperial dignity, Maximus.

In the absence of such graphic early witness, the names of other early saints might simply be found stencilled upon the notice boards of a church, preserving the memory of its founder in its dedication. Some caution needs to be exercised here, for dedications can change. In the late eighth century, for example, King Offa of Mercia ordered all churches in his territory to be rededicated to St Peter. However, where an early Christian dedication survives, the likelihood remains that it is an authentic one. The details of the lives of such early saints tend only to be preserved in later medieval hagiography and in local legend, within which it is difficult to

✠ It is Eliseg who annexed the inheritance of Powys... from the power of the English, which he made into a sword-land by fire...
✠ Britu, moreover, [was] the son of Gworthigirn [Vortigern], whom Germanus blessed and whom Severa bore to him, the daughter of Maximus the king, who slew the king of the Romans.

GENEALOGY CARVED ON THE PILLAR OF ELISEG, WALES, MID-NINTH CENTURY distinguish fact from pious or superstitious fiction. What can nonetheless readily be deduced is that there was a considerable amount of interaction between many of these saints, and that they often operated beyond their local area, some ranging across several territories within north-western Britain, Scotland, Wales, Cornwall, Ireland, the Isle of Man and Brittany.

PALLADIUS AND PATRICK

According to the contemporary chronicle of Prosper of Aquitaine (who is thought to have been the secretary of Pope Leo the Great), in 431, Celestine, Bishop of Rome – then but one of many important patriarchs located around the Mediterranean – sent Palladius as bishop to those in Ireland who already believed in Christ. There must have been a significant community of the faithful who had come to the attention of the mainstream ecclesiastical authorities in the West and who required the ministrations of a bishop. The presence of a bishop would allow them to be received into the body of the church by the sacraments of baptism and confirmation, and to have priests ordained to serve them. It is noteworthy that Celestine did not deem it necessary to send bishops to Britain, other than Germanus of Auxerre, who was entrusted with a special mission to suppress heresy and who also made it his business to stiffen the resolve of those intent on resisting the pagan invaders. Prosper also mentions that a Palladius had been one of those who persuaded Celestine to dispatch Germanus to Britain in 429, and it has been suggested that the new 'apostle to the Irish' was a deacon of either Auxerre or Rome. He may even have accompanied Germanus to Britain and have reported the predicament of the Irish to Rome. Three churches in County Wicklow, south of the later Viking town of Dublin, claim to have been founded by Palladius – Donard, Tigroney and Cilleen Cormac near Dunlavin. It is also likely that this area, with its ancient trading links with Britain and Iberia, would have encountered the Christian faith through mercantile contacts with these and other parts of the Roman empire.

Palladius's mission does not seem to have made much of a tangible impact. He seems to have moved to Scotland, where he is still celebrated in the Aberdeen area and where he is thought to be buried at Forddun. However, scholars are increasingly inclined to view many of the deeds subsequently attributed to St Patrick as those of Palladius: the two figures appear to have become conflated in the later attempts by Armagh to bolster the reputation and territorial claims of its founder.

St Patrick/Patricius, 'apostle to the Irish', was a Briton. It is difficult to excavate the real person from the accretions of later legend and hagiography. His *Lives* commenced early with the ninth-century *Tripartite Life of St Patrick* by Tiréchan, and a *Life* by Muirchu, but there is much scholarly debate concerning when he lived and what he did. Fortunately there are two texts by the man himself that are taken as the core of the historical Patrick. One is his *Confession*, a partial autobiography possibly composed as an apologia in the face of attacks from the

I spread God's name everywhere, obediently and without fear, so that after death I may leave a legacy to so many thousands of people.

ST PATRICK, *CONFESSION*

British church on his intellectual competence, his probity (he is at pains to point out that his mission has cost him money and that he returned any gifts offered) and his authority, which he ascribed solely to God, rather than to the British church. The other is his *Letter to Coroticus*, in which he chastises a British ruler of that name for engaging in slave trading – an evil he had experienced at first hand when he was

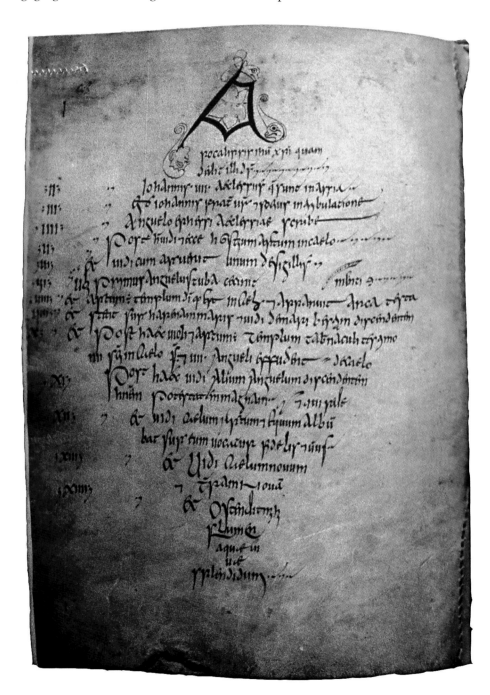

The Book of Armagh, compiled to help advance Armagh's claims of primacy, Armagh, c.807. It contains a collection of Patrician material along with a copy of the New Testament. This section was written by the master-scribe Ferdomnach.

captured in Britain by Irish raiders and which he subsequently strove to eradicate amongst his own people and those whom he evangelized in Ireland. Those seized by Coroticus's men were Christian converts, and no history of ethnic antagonism could justify such a breach of their shared fellowship in Christ.

WRITINGS ASSOCIATED WITH ST PATRICK

Patrick's writings are the earliest extant texts to have originated from the British church other than the teachings and correspondence of Pelagius and his followers, which were largely formulated on the continent. The faith, commitment and modesty of Patrick the man shine through the words of his *Confession*, in which he wrote:

St Patrick's Confession
I see this as a measure of my faith in the Trinity that, disregarding danger, I make known the gift of God and the eternal comfort He provides: that I spread God's name everywhere, obediently and without fear, so that after death I may leave a legacy to so many thousands of people – by brethren and my children whom I have baptized in the Lord... I entreat those God-fearing believers who agree to peruse or accept this document, which the unlettered sinner Patrick composed in Ireland, that none will attribute to an ignorant man like me any little thing I may have done, or any guidance I may have given according to God's will. Consider, and may it truly be believed, that it may have been rather the gift of God. And that is my testament before I die.

His Creed, if not actually written by him, was certainly composed before 600. It is a telling attempt to reconcile his native Celtic literary tradition and philosophical stance in relation to humanity, creation and the divine with those of the Mediterranean.

The prayer known as St Patrick's Breastplate, or 'Lorica' (quoted in extract here), was actually composed no earlier than the eighth century. However, it is typical of a traditional Celtic protective charm, similar to the encircling prayer known as a *caim*, which is characterized by its enumerative tendencies:

St Patrick's Breastplate
I gird myself today with
The Might of Heaven:
The rays of the sun,
The beams of the moon,
The glory of fire,
The speed of the wind,
The depth of the sea,
The stability of earth,
The hardness of rock.

He has a dwelling
in heaven and earth
and sea
And in all things
that are in them.

ST PATRICK'S CREED

Other popular literary devices included alliteration and grouping things in threes for mnemonic (memory-aiding) purposes – an ancient druidic practice which lent itself particularly well to the Christian doctrine of the Trinity. Here is another traditional prayer:

The Three Who are over me,
The Three Who are below me,
The Three Who are above me here,
The Three Who are above me yonder;
The Three Who are in the earth,
The Three Who are in the air,
The Three Who are in the heaven,
The Three Who are in the great pouring sea.

In his writings Patrick describes himself as 'a letter of Christ', sent to the farthest ends of the earth for their salvation. From his writings, too, we learn that Patrick's grandfather was a priest and his father was a deacon and *decurio*, a Roman town councillor. Patrick came from an unidentified town named Bannavem Taburniæ, somewhere in western Britain between the Severn and the Clyde. When he was sixteen he was captured, along with thousands of others, and enslaved in Ireland for six years where he served as a herdsman, probably in County Mayo, spending his time praying and repenting of his earlier life, when he was careless of Christian values. He escaped and travelled some 200 miles, probably to the south-east Irish coast, where he took ship. After adventures and destitution in a strange land he returned, like the prodigal, to the bosom of his family. He studied Scripture, but lamented that he did not receive a 'higher education', for which he seems to have endured criticism. That said, his literary style is clear and eloquent and shows knowledge of poetic metre. It was formerly considered that he received his clerical training at the important centre of Lérins, an island off the southern French coast (Côte d'Azur), but this is now questioned. There is also debate over whether the mission he subsequently undertook to Ireland, to save his captors and their people in the 'wood of Foclut', occurred from the 430s to 460s or the 460s to 490s. The weight of scholarly opinion currently favours the latter date range.

There are many stories associated with Patrick, including colourful episodes such as the casting out of snakes, explaining the Trinity with the aid of a shamrock, and lighting the Paschal Fire. Doubtless these have been embellished by a degree of artistic hagiographical licence, and have incorporated some deeds performed by other figures such as Palladius. Nonetheless, what shine through are his bravery, compassion and commitment to living out the gospel by forgiving his captors and placing the rest of his life at the service of their souls, trusting completely in the Lord. Over the course of time his popularity has increased, promoted by Armagh, one of his key centres, to establish its primacy. It has also been helped by the espousal of his cult by the Normans, and by the Irish diaspora that carried his cult around the world.

He has been credited with the conversion of most of Ireland, but his activities seem to have been concentrated upon the northern territories. Important places that have become associated with him – besides Armagh, which was situated close to the local royal centre of power – include Downpatrick, Saul and Croagh Patrick. Several English and Welsh churches are also dedicated to him, and medieval Glastonbury claimed to possess his relics, perhaps having equated him with a 'Patrick the Older' who was buried there. Old Kilpatrick near the British stronghold of Dumbarton may

St Patrick's Creed

Our God, God of all men,
God of heaven and earth, sea and rivers,
God of sun and moon, of all the stars,
God of high mountains and of lowly valleys,
God over heaven, and in heaven, and under heaven.

He has a dwelling
In heaven and earth and sea
And in all things that are in them.

He inspires all things,
He quickens all things,
He is over all things,
He supports all things.

He makes the light of the sun to shine,
He surrounds the moon and stars,
And He has made wells in the arid earth,
Placed dry islands in the sea
And stars for the service
Of the greater luminaries.

He has a son
Coeternal with Himself, like to Himself;
Not junior is Son to Father,
Nor Father senior to the Son.

And the Holy Spirit
Breathes in them;
Not separate are Father
And Son and Holy Spirit.

relate to him. During the eleventh century, Glastonbury claimed to have found the bodies of Patrick and his follower Benignus, but as their enterprising medieval brethren also claimed to have discovered the remains of King Arthur and Guinevere (complete with forged identification inscription), this was probably merely part of their attempts to boost their pilgrim trade. A significant aspect of Patrick's mission is that he was not a missionary monk, but a bishop. And it was to the episcopate that he looked to accomplish the conversion and pastoral organization of the Irish church, on the Romano-British and Gaulish models.

In addition to Palladius's mission to the Wicklow area in Leinster, others are thought to have evangelized in Ireland prior to Patrick, or at the same time as him. These include Ailbe who operated in north Munster; Declán who was active amongst the Déisi of Munster; and Ciarán who ministered to the Osraige and founded Seirkieran and Ibar. They are all named in an eighth-century 'Life' of Ailbe and are said to have operated in Leinster and Munster in the South East.

BELOW: St Benan's Chapel, seventh or eighth century, Inishmore, Aran Islands.

LEFT: The Monymusk reliquary, a Pictish house-shaped reliquary from the eighth century, perhaps resembling a church building.

One of Patrick's followers, Abbot Mochta, is said to have been of British birth and to have been educated and consecrated as bishop in Rome. Joining Patrick in Ireland, he operated in Meath and further north, founding an important monastery at Louth. His *Life* speaks of a mutual agreement with Patrick to ensure the continuation of each other's foundations after one or the other's death. Other men traditionally acknowledged to be Patrick's assistants, who may equally as well have operated independently further to the South, were Secundinus/Sechnaill who worked in Meath (where his foundation at Domnach Sechnaill/Dunshaughlin preserves his name) and Auxilius, who founded Cell Ausaile/Killashee near Naas, County Kildare. Missionary endeavours emanating from Armagh included that of St Benignus (Bennen), said to have been a disciple of Patrick's and his successor, who evangelized in Kerry and Clare. There is even a little seventh- or eighth-century stone chapel on Inishmore in the Aran Isles that may be dedicated to him and which resembles the portable metalwork Irish house-shaped shrines of the period. Iserninus, a fellow-bishop with Patrick, is said in Irish tradition to have served at Auxerre under bishops Amator and Germanus, and some Irish sources also assert that Patrick was himself a disciple of Germanus of Auxerre. A ninth-century appendix added to a metrical *Life of Germanus* by Heiric of Auxerre relates that Germanus also had another Irish disciple, Michomeri/Michomairle. Similarly, a Corodemus named by Germanus's contemporary biographer, Constantius, as a member of the church at Auxerre during the third century, is thought from his name to have been Irish. Such evidence is slight, but it does suggest that the traditional view of Ireland being isolated from the rest of Europe and from Christianity prior to the missionary activity of the fifth century should be questioned. Archaeological discoveries yet to be unearthed may further help to clarify this picture.

THE PICTS

Another mysterious but important culture present within the British Isles during this period was that of the Picts, who inhabited what later became known as Scotland. The Picts were first described by Caesar as 'Picti' because they painted or tattooed their bodies. They have left us little by way of written record, save a few inscriptions in Latin or ogham, rather than their own tongue, which is thought to have been a pre-Indo-European language. From archaeological evidence the Picts are considered to have been representative of an indigenous Bronze-Age population with a Celtic overlay. What can be reconstructed from later Scottish and Anglo-Saxon lists of their monarchy suggests that royal succession passed via the female line, and such matriarchal societies are anthropologically indicative of an early stage of social development, as maternity is more readily demonstrable than paternity. Ingenious attempts have been made to supply linguistic evidence to supplement the few references to the Picts by English authors, notably Bede. These include an interpretation of an inscription on a silver sword chape of eighth-century date which

The Picts

Sword scabbard chape
found in a Pictish hoard on
St Ninian's Isle, Shetland.
The inscription indicates
that the weapon was
dedicated to the Lord.
It was made during the
eighth century, possibly in
Anglo-Saxon Mercia.

Pictish stones, fifth–ninth century

Pictish Class I stone of the
fifth–seventh century with Pictish
symbols, Aberlemno roadside.

Pictish Class II stone of the eighth
century, Aberlemno churchyard:
cross, flanked by beasts, including
seahorses.

formed part of an important Pictish hoard found on St Ninian's Isle in the Orkneys (see feature on the Picts). Part of the inscription, which reads 'resadfilispuscio', was interpreted as the quaint Pictish names 'Resad son of Spuscio', but it is probably a corrupt piece of Latin reading 'res ad fili sp(irit)us s(an)c(t)io' ('things for the son of the Holy Spirit'). Indeed, it has even recently been suggested on stylistic grounds that the piece, with its distinctive muzzled beast-heads, is of Anglo-Saxon rather than Pictish manufacture.

Undoubtedly of Pictish manufacture, however, are the remarkably elegant and well-developed series of carvings incised upon stones, metalwork and cave walls throughout Scotland. They cluster especially around the focal points of Pictish kingship – initially around Craig Phadraig on the outskirts of Inverness, where St Columba is said to have converted the Pictish high-king Brude in the late sixth century – and then move southwards with the relocation of royal power to Fife.

The original functions of the Pictish stones were probably varied, some marking graves or territorial demarcations, others commemorating battles, alliances, marriages, shrines, synods and other important events or sites. They remain the most tangible manifestations of what was undoubtedly a vibrant Christian culture, with a well-developed sense of its own traditions and history that was effectively synthesized with a new Christianized world-view. One of the greatest masterpieces of Pictish carving, the St Andrew's sarcophagus (see feature on the Picts), was made around 800 and exhibits Mercian influence in its rounded figures, which depict scenes from the life of King David. It may have contained relics of St Andrew or of a Pictish king.

Only one book can be ascribed to Scotland with any degree of certainty during the early Christian period. It is the Book of Deer, created c.900 (see feature on the Picts), and its images are no match for the carvings of the sarcophagus. There is, however, a possibility that the Book of Durrow and the Book of Kells (see feature on St Columba between pages 152 and 153) were made on Irish Iona. Recent excavations at Tarbat (Porthmahomack) in north-east Scotland are yielding signs of manuscript production as well as high-class sculptures.

NINIAN AND THE CONVERSION OF SCOTLAND

'The apostle to the Picts' was probably a contemporary of Patrick's, traditionally named Ninian/Nynia. He was a fifth-century British bishop, perhaps from the vicinity of Carlisle and the Hadrian's Wall frontier zone. An eighth-century poem concerning him survives, and a *Life* of the same era is known to have existed but is now lost. The main *Life* was composed by Ailred of Rievaulx in the twelfth century, when he was attached to the court of King David I of Scotland. Bede's *Historia Ecclesiastica* remains our principal written source for Ninian's mission, however. This uncharacteristic interest in a British ecclesiastic seems to be largely attributable to the fact that Ninian's major foundation – the see of Whithorn in Galloway (south-west Scotland) – was refounded under Bishop Pechthelm as part

Pictish Carvings

Pictish sculptures are usually classified in three groups, although there is some overlap between them. Class I consists of Pictish symbols incised upon undressed or roughly dressed stones, featuring a range of stylized symbols reminiscent of the hieroglyphs of the ancient Egyptians and Mayans. These include animal forms, such as the eagle, bull, otter, dog, horse, bear, and 'swimming elephant' or 'Pictish beast' that was probably derived from classical depictions of the dolphin. These stones may represent clan badges. Different 'tribes' were known at one time to have taken their names from animals, such as 'the otter people' of Orkney where there are also Bronze- and Iron-Age communal burials distinguished by the accompanying remains of particular animals, such as the 'Tomb of the Eagles'. At Burghead the imposing symbol of a bull, its outline articulated by a characteristic Pictish double line that spirals at the limb joints, was repeated on over fifty small slabs of stone, presumably as part of a cult site. This probably focused upon an atmospheric cavern in the area that may have symbolically represented the entrance to the otherworld; or it may have formed part of a cult such as that of Mithras, perhaps transmitted by traders or by contact with Roman troops.

Other early Pictish symbols, which may have originated as early as the time of Christ, include: the crescent; a notched rectangle perhaps representing the characteristic Pictish stone towers known as brochs; a double disc with linking rod perhaps representing a stylized horse bit or brooch pair; and a circle with two shields perhaps meant to be a cauldron with handles, seen from above. These were sometimes combined with a superimposed 'v' or 'z'-shaped rod, resembling a broken lance or ceremonial sceptre. Other symbols include the mirror, comb and shears, motifs that continued to be used on Scottish grave-markers into the sixteenth century to denote status, gender or profession, which they may also have helped to signify at this earlier date. Such symbols were also sometimes engraved with great precision and finesse upon silver plaques used as earrings and other personal adornments, or as horse-trappings, on which the symbols were picked out in niello, a sulpherous carbon black rubbed into the engraved lines.

No 'Rosetta Stone' equivalent, with parallel bilingual inscriptions, has yet emerged to aid in the deciphering of the enigmatic Pictish symbols. Various hypotheses have been advanced concerning their meaning, including an ideographic and/or syllabic substitution, in Egyptian fashion. For example, the crescent might stand for the word for 'bright', which might in turn be part of a personal name. Another favoured interpretation includes the heraldic identification of individuals, families or tribes, along with accompanying symbols indicating status, gender, role – priest, king, queen, warrior, landowner, smith and so forth. Human figures also occasionally appear, depicted in profile, the men with hooked noses and pointed beards, sometimes wearing knee-length tunics and leggings or hunting capes and carrying small rectangular shields, short stabbing swords and spears. During the time that the Class I symbols were carved, the Picts received the Christian faith through the agency of British missionaries such as Ninian and Mungo.

Class II stones are thought to date from the early eighth century onwards when, as Bede recounts, King Nechtan invited the English church to reform that of the Picts. The earlier Pictish symbols continued in use, suggesting that they were probably not primarily associated with pagan symbolism. They were now used along with more deeply carved representations of the cross, or with figural scenes probably depicting

Old Testament themes. Some may also depict scenes from Pictish life or history, such as the regal image of a beautiful woman, well-dressed and sporting a fine penannular brooch, who rides side-saddle amidst her entourage, heralded by trumpeters and escorted by her hounds. She dominates one side of a great cross-slab found adjacent to a chapel site at Hilton of Cadboll (Rosshire). Is she a Pictish queen, or the Queen of Sheba in contemporary Pictish garb?

Other images refer to Christian texts such as the *Physiologus*, or 'Marvels of the East', an early Christian work discussing the mythical inhabitants and fauna of Africa and Asia and imbuing them with a Christian moral symbolism. Thus a Pictish house-shaped gravemarker at Meigle, probably of eighth-century date, carries a carving of a little man looking back over his shoulder as he flees in terror from a lion with a human head – the *Physiologus*'s manticore, harbinger of death. Restenneth Priory contains extensive early masonry which may also date to this phase of Northumbrian influence, its architectural construction *more romanum* ('in Roman fashion') recalling that of Monkwearmouth / Jarrow.

The influence of the Columban Church and the coming of an Irish Dalriadan king, Kenneth McAlpine, to the Pictish throne in the mid ninth century led to an injection of Irish influence which can be seen in the Class III stones (see feature on the Picts between pages 72 and 73). These develop Christian themes – such as the cross, King David's life, Daniel in the lion's den, Paul and Anthony in the desert – alongside contemporary scenes, and usually relinquish the ancient Pictish symbols. The carving technique favours a higher relief, with more rounded rather than incised forms, and features bosses to the crosses. At Abernethy an Irish round tower also made an appearance in late Pictish Scotland – which took its new name as a kingdom from the Irish settlers of Dalriada, the 'Scotti'.

Fine collections of Pictish stones can be seen at the little museums of Meigle and St Vigeans, whilst many others remain in situ, some under post-modernist glass shelters to combat erosion, or in adjacent churches, or within the National Museums of Scotland. At Aberlemno three fine stones remain in place: a superb Class II cross-slab, flanked by classical sea-horses, with a battle scene from the Old Testament and/or from Pictish history, sited in the churchyard; an imposing Class I stone with symbols; and a monumental Class III cross-slab by the roadside (see feature on the Picts).

of the Anglo-Saxon church of Northumbria during the early eighth century. Bede names Ninian's church as 'Candida Casa', the 'white house', its name preserved in the Old English 'Whit hearn'. Excavations on the site over the last couple of decades have revealed a substantial early monastic settlement. Here, there is a church that was painted white on the outside, recalling the white plaster used, as a cheap alternative to marble, to clad some late Roman shrines/churches in Britain. This may, however, be a later structure than Ninian's original church. A number of other communal buildings, burials and inscribed and decorated stones have also been found on the site. If Bede is correct in his assertion that Ninian dedicated his church to St Martin of Tours, the founding father of western monasticism, Gaulish influence may have helped to inspire him. An inscribed stone at the mouth of the nearby harbour carries a dedication to St Peter, indicating another strand of influence from Rome. St Ninian's cave, which opens onto a nearby beach, is said to be the site of Ninian's own hermitage. It contains a number of early medieval symbols and graffiti scratched onto its walls, some in Pictish style.

It is difficult to tell how widespread Ninian's mission was. He may have worked beyond south-west Scotland in the vicinity of Stirling (where a place-name commemorates him), Forfar, Perth and Fife. Outlying dedications can be found in northern England, and one of the smaller Orkney islands is named after him and was the find-spot of a remarkable hoard of Pictish and Anglo-Saxon metalwork of eighth-century date. Amongst those trained at Whithorn was St Enda, an Irish princely soldier-turned-monk who is thought to have pioneered the introduction of monasticism to Ireland. St Enda worked initially in the Boyne Valley and then, until his death in around 530, from a base on Inishmore in the Aran Islands in Galway Bay which became an important monastic training ground. Other Irish pupils of Whithorn's are said to have included Tigernach of Clones, Eógan of Ardstraw, Finnian of Moville and Cairpre of Coleraine.

A remarkable collection of early medieval sculptures, dating largely from the ninth century, is all that remains of another major Scottish centre – St Govan's on the outskirts of Glasgow, which was founded in the ninth century by the Scottish king, Constantine. The Glasgow church itself had been founded by St Kentigern/Mungo (died 612), whom later *Lives* say was British and who may have been the illegitimate son of Prince Urien. He was trained in the Irish monastic tradition at Culross by St Serf, the apostle of western Fife who is also commemorated in the Orkneys. St Kentigern was active as a bishop and monastic founder in Strathclyde, and perhaps also in Cumbria, north Wales and Hoddam near Dumfries, where he lived for a while and which has yielded important eighth-century sculptures of Northumbrian style. The type of monasticism exported to Ireland by the followers of Ninian of Whithorn had evidently returned home to assist in the conversion of the rest of Scotland. This was accomplished over a period of time by numerous individuals and communities, although much of the work was claimed on behalf of the Irish missionary St Columba (died 597), who left Ireland on *peregrinatio* (voluntary exile) in 563. He founded the monastery of Iona off the coast of Mull, initially to minister to the northern-Irish expatriate kingdom of Dalriada in west Argyll.

Figures other than Columba and his followers who have been associated with the conversion of Scotland include: Ronan (a seventh-century hermit); Kessog; Kentigerna and her son Fillan; Canice (an Irish hermit-scribe active in the Hebrides); Modan; and Mirin, a seventh-century Irish abbot and follower of Comgall, who trained at Bangor, County Down, and founded a monastery at Paisley. During the early eighth century King Nechtan of the Picts invited representatives of the Northumbrian Church to reform that of Pictland. This phase, and that of the earlier Columban mission, are discussed further in chapter seven.

THE EARLY WELSH CHURCH AND ITS SAINTS

Moving on from Scotland to Wales, another probable contemporary of Palladius and an influential follower of Germanus was St Illtud/Illtyd/Eltut/Hildutus, founder and abbot of Llanilltud Fawr (Llantwit Major) on the coast of south Wales. An early 'Life' of St Samson of Dol claims that Illtud was a disciple of Germanus, and served as abbot of a monastery he founded in South Glamorgan. It also praises him as the foremost British scholar of Scripture and philosophy, uniting Judaeo-Christian mysticism with the philosophical thought of Greece and Rome.

The medieval church of Llantwit Major, with its early Christian inscribed stones, lies close to the site of a Roman villa in which burials were found, recalling Gildas's lament that the British were buried in the ruins of their dwellings. (Another important collection of Welsh stones can be found at Margam, west of Cardiff.) However, it appears that a thriving Roman rural estate continued to form the focus for the succeeding Christian monastic community – one

St Govan's Chapel, Pembrokeshire, an early hermitage in Wales enshrined in a later medieval chapel set into the cliff face. A holy well springs onto the beach below.

which recalled its villa roots by continuing its agricultural traditions and which was famed for the fertility of its land and the quality of its produce. The *Life* of St Samson tells of the herbs that were cultivated there and brewed into medicines, perhaps perpetuating the learning stored in the Graeco-Roman herbals compiled by authors such as Apuleius Platonicus. The twelfth-century author of Illtud's *Life* praised the site for its abundant harvests, describing it as a land blessed with flowers and honey. Supporting a community, even a monastic one, required land and careful stewardship. The early Penitentials, which contain recommendations for the penances to be imposed upon miscreants, indicate that even a reduced diet was a reasonably varied and

The St Chad Gospels
(or Lichfield Gospels/Llandeilo
Gospels).
Luke miniature, with marginal
inscriptions added in Wales during
the ninth century. It was swapped
by Gelhi, son of Arihtiud, for his
best horse and presented to the
altar of St Teilo at Llandeilo Fawr,
made at Lindisfarne or one of its
daughter houses. Second quarter of
the eighth century.

balanced one. The *Preface on Penance* ascribed to Gildas prescribes bread, butter (on Sundays), relish, cheese, milk, buttermilk, eggs and vegetables, with those who were not performing penance also being allowed meat and beer.

Early monasteries were not the only places to preserve aspects of a Roman lifestyle. Excavations at Llangorse Crannóg, an artificial manmade island settlement of Celtic Iron-Age derivation, and the fort of Dinas Powys, some four miles from Cardiff, have revealed that each was the *llys* (court) of wealthy native chieftains who aspired to a civilized lifestyle. The Iron-Age hill-fort of Dinas Powys was refortified during the fifth century and occupied into the seventh. Pottery imported during this reoccupation phase included: amphorae and fine red slipware from North Africa; eastern Mediterranean tableware probably from the Bordeaux region (grey bowls known as 'D' ware); beige kitchen jars ('E' ware) from northern France; and Anglo-Saxon and other Germanic glassware and jewellery. Manufacturing debris indicates that high quality metalworking took place on the site. The same is true of Llangorse Crannóg, which also imported exotic pottery and trade goods. Set in the largest freshwater lake in Wales, renowned in the twelfth century by Giraldus Cambrensis for its prophetic qualities which were doubtless of Iron-Age origin, Llangorse sits at the western foot of the Brecon Beacons in the kingdom of Brycheiniog. The *crannóg* form of defensive settlement and ogham stones from the area indicate probable Irish influence in this kingdom. Both sites are likely to have been periodic courts of local rulers, who had luxury metalwork made there because of the secure nature of the defences, and accumulated imports that were probably for further distribution. According to the Book of Llandaff/Liber Landavensis – one of the most important sources for the early history of Wales – Llangorse and its territory were given in the eighth century to Bishop Euddogwy by King Awst, who also bequeathed to the church his body and those of his sons, presumably as royal saints. Llangorse was occupied as late as 916, when the Anglo-Saxon Chronicle records that the queen and 33 others were captured at Brecenanmere by the English forces of Aethelflaed, Lady of the Mercians.

According to later tradition – as preserved in the Book of Llandaff and a 'Life' by Benedict of Gloucester – another of Germanus's followers was St Dyfrig/Dubricius/Devereux (died c.550). He was a bishop-abbot who worked in the Hereford-Gwent region, focusing upon the Roman town of Ariconium (Archenfield) and perhaps Caerleon, another important Roman military centre. His background is firmly sited within the Romano-British Christian tradition. One of his foundations, Whitchurch, recalls in its English name the Latin *Candida Casa* which Bede said was founded by Ninian at Whithorn in Galloway. The *Life* of St Samson says that Dyfrig ordained Samson and appointed him abbot of Caldey Island (Ynys Byr), an important early monastery near Tenby, south-west Wales. Dedications to Dyfrig as far afield as Porlock in Somerset and Gwenddwr in Powys may reflect the extent of his and his followers' mission. These included numerous offspring of the Welsh king St Brychan, who became saints themselves: Morwenna, Ninnoc/Gwengustle, Nectan, Endellion and Clether, who are said to have travelled from Brecon to work in Devon and Cornwall. However, the extensive properties claimed for Dyfrig in the Book of Llandaff probably reflect the territorial ambitions of the twelfth-century bishops of Llandaff itself, where Dyfrig's relics had been taken in 1120. His prominence at this period may also have accounted for Geoffrey of Monmouth naming him as the bishop who crowned King Arthur. Dyfrig is thought to have died in retirement on Bardsey Island, north-west Wales, which was founded by St Cadfan – one of the few to have migrated in reverse direction, from his native Brittany to Wales. Towyn (Gwynedd), another of his churches, possesses a holy well that retained its renown as a healing centre even after the Reformation.

St Paternus/Padarn was active in Cardiganshire and Radnorshire during the fifth-sixth century, serving as abbot and bishop at his principal monastery of Llanbadarn Fawr (Dyfed). The proximity of his foundations to Roman roads testifies to the continuing importance of the pre-existing communications infrastructure.

Another prominent Welsh saint was Cadoc/Cattwg/Sophias (died c.560), founder of Llancarfen, a contemporary of Gildas and St David. Fifteen dedications to him are known to exist in south Wales (such as Raglan), with one outlier in Cornwall. St Finnian of Clonard is said to have studied the monastic discipline with Cadoc, Gildas and David, contributing to their fame in Ireland. Cadoc's reputation for vigorously and effectively cursing his adversaries perhaps owed much to eleventh-century hagiographers, who wished to emphasize the saint's power to protect his territory and his people on behalf of the contemporary community of Llancarfen.

Other important early Welsh ecclesiastics included St Beuno, sixth-century abbot of Clynnog Fawr, who was principally active in Anglesey and the Lleyn peninsula; and his niece, Winefride/Gwenfrewi, who was decapitated by a rejected suitor, Caradoc. A famous well is said to have sprung from the spot at Holywell (Clwyd), which

ABOVE: Eighth-century cross slab, now in the south transept of St David's Cathedral, Pembrokeshire.

RIGHT: The Calf of Man Crucifixion slab, eighth century, from a little island at the southernmost tip of the Isle of Man.

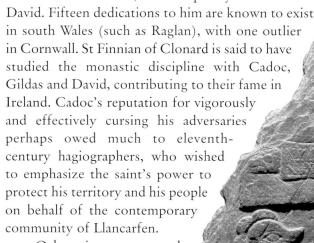

became a major medieval shrine. Shrewsbury was another of her cult centres. Beuno is said to have restored her to life, enabling her to enjoy a lengthy career as abbess of Holywell. The impressive late-medieval well chapel was commissioned by Margaret Beaufort, mother of King Henry VII, after the Battle of Bosworth in 1485 to celebrate the coming of the Welsh Tudor dynasty to the English throne.

There are many more early Welsh saints of note, including: Sts Seiriol and Cybi of Anglesey; Gwenfaen; Kew; Kyned/Cenydd/Kenneth; Kinemark/Cynfarch; Briavel; Tathai, a fifth to sixth-century Irish hermit-monk, renowned for his hospitality and his defence of ancient woodlands, who founded Llantathan (St Athan) and a monastic school at the Roman *civitas* capital of Caerwent; and Govan, said to be a follower of the Irish St Ailbe during the sixth century. His remarkable chapel and cell, preserved within a later medieval structure are still to be found clinging to a cleft in the cliff above a wild boulder-beach in south Pembrokeshire – a real Atlantic desert where the saint might encounter his God alone, through solitude, meditation and the physical rigours of survival in a challenging environment.

St David (died c.589–601) was the only Welsh saint to be canonized and has been the patron saint of Wales since the twelfth century. His cult was based at St David's Cathedral, on the site of his early foundation, Rosina Vallis. He is said by his eleventh-century hagiographer, Bishop Rhygyfarch of St David's, to have been the son of St Non. She was a nun at Ty Gwyn near Whitesand Bay (Dyfed) – where her holy well survives – who was either seduced by or married to Sant, a Pembrokeshire chieftain. She subsequently settled at Altarnon in Cornwall and died in Brittany where she lies entombed at Dirinon. The Irish 'Catalogue of the Saints' of c.730 says that the Irish received the Mass from Bishop David and from the Britons Gillas (Gildas) and Teilo, implying that Welsh missions to Ireland preceded those from Ireland to Wales and Cornwall. Several Irish ecclesiastics are said to have studied with David in Wales, including Máedóc of Ferns, Scuithín of Slieve Margy near Carlow and Modomnóc of Tibragny/Tibernachy in County Kilkenny, a prince of the Ui Neill who is said to have taken the art of bee-keeping back to Ireland with him. Other Irish prelates who visited David for guidance were Finnian of Clonard, Senán of Slattery Island, Brendan of Clonfert and Findbarr of Cork. Finnian is also thought to have corresponded with Cadoc and Gildas concerning the monastic discipline to be followed at his foundation. Britons from Wales and southern Scotland evidently played an important part in helping to shape early Irish monasticism. David is also commemorated, in turn, in the earliest Irish martyrologies which were composed around 800. His principal foundation was Menevia, St David's, in the vicinity of which there are numerous early remains. These include part of a particularly fine eighth-century cross-slab, which resembles a similarly fine slab of Irish inspiration from the Isle of Man, known as the 'Calf of Man Crucifixion slab'. Other dedications indicate his activity throughout south Wales and Herefordshire. There is also some suggestion that David, or his followers, may also have operated in Cornwall and Brittany.

Bishop Asser, who was recruited from St David's to Sherborne by King Alfred the Great in the late ninth century, ensured his popularity in England too.

By the ninth century the church at Llandeilo Fawr, Carmathenshire, was assuming a growing significance, along with the cult of its founder, St Teilo. At its core was a mid-eighth century Gospelbook, the St Chad Gospels (see page 78). These were strongly influenced by the Lindisfarne Gospels and were probably made in a centre associated with Holy Island. In the mid ninth century they were obtained by a Welshman, Gelhi, in return for his horse and presented to the altar of St Teilo. The Gospelbook remained there for a century, during which time legal transactions, oaths and dedications enacted at the shrine were inscribed in its margins along with the record of Gelhi's gift. This makes it one of the earliest witnesses to the written Welsh language and to Welsh handwriting – with the possible exception of the Hereford Gospels, now in Hereford Cathedral, which although in Latin is the foremost candidate as an early Welsh book and which dates to around 800. The St Chad Gospelbook is now in Lichfield Cathedral from where it had moved by the 960s–970s and where, it has been suggested, it may originally have served as the cult focus of Lichfield's founder, St Chad of Holy Island. It may have been redeemed during the turbulent ninth century from raiders – analogies for redemptions from Vikings are known – and restored to the Christian Church through donation to an important local centre in Wales.

According to his twelfth-century *Life* by Geoffrey of Llandaff, St Teilo/Elidius/Eliud was a pupil of Dyfrig and Paul Aurelian during the sixth century. He worked in Dyfed (south-west Wales) until plague led him to join Samson at Dol in Brittany. He subsequently returned to Llandeilo Fawr where he died. Llandaff and Penally, his alleged birthplace (graced by a fine early Christian cross), were also important centres of his cult.

THE SAINTS OF CORNWALL AND BRITTANY

The early conversion of south-western Britain was essentially a pretty gradual and peaceful affair. We cannot tell to what extent, if at all, Christianity impinged upon the consciousness of the communities that occupied villages such as Chysauster and Carn Euny from the Iron Age to the early Christian period. In these places there are well-preserved custom-built houses – hybrids of the Iron-Age round house and the Roman villa, resulting in the distinctive Cornish courtyard houses with their array of rooms of different functions arranged around a well-drained central court. Some of these settlements, like their Irish, Scottish and Welsh counterparts, feature underground passages and chambers known as souterrains or fogous, which may have served a purely pragmatic storage function such as keeping foodstuffs cool; but some are more complex and suggest ritual use. By the sixth century, however, such rural communities can have been in no doubt of the impact of the energized and committed men and women who arrived at the ports of Padstow and the Hayle

Estuary and established hermitages, churches and monasteries throughout the region – some of which can still be seen, such as St Helen's Oratory at Cape Cornwall, the hermitage at Roche and the chapel at Madron (see pages 84 and 85). These were local saints for local people, but they were tied into a collaborative network of evangelization that embraced much of the northern-Atlantic seaboard.

Many Cornish churches still sit within their early circular *raths* or *llans*, often identified by the name of the founder or patron saint. A number contain Roman milestones or early Christian inscribed stones, some of which remain standing in situ in the field, such as the Men Scryfa, West Penwith. Carved crosses dating from the eighth- to eleventh-century mark the perimeters or other key spots in churchyards, as at St Levan's, Sancreed, Phillack, Paul and Cardinham. Wayside crosses nestle into hedgerows marking stations in the journeys along pilgrimage routes. This practice spread to Brittany, leading in the central Middle Ages to the construction of elaborate sculptured shrines on columns – a regional variant on the theme of the Celtic high-cross. Holy wells are still visited for healing and baptism and used as a focus of faith by both Christians and 'new age' pagans. Some have probably been used continuously since prehistory and have received both pagan Iron-Age and early Christian votive offerings. Good examples can be found at Sancreed, Madron, Morvah and St Levan's (see page 85). St Levan's is set within a cliff-top baptistery with the foundations of the saint's cell nearby, overlooking a windswept rock-strewn cove into which cascades a stream choked with watercress and wild herbs.

TOP: Iron-Age and early Christian courtyard houses. Carn Euny, West Penwith, Cornwall.

BOTTOM: The Carn Euny souterrain or fogou, an underground ritual and storage chamber.

The early Christian histories of Cornwall and Brittany are closely intertwined. St Paul Aurelian is probably to be identified with the Welsh Paulinus, who was a hermit near Llandovery. He is commemorated in a sixth-century inscription at Cynwyl Caeo and is thought to have been a disciple of St Illtud. He is said to have left Wales on *peregrinatio*, visiting his sister in Cornwall where he founded Paul in West Penwith before travelling to Brittany where he founded Paul-de-Léon (St Pol). His *Life* was composed in the tenth century by Wrmonoc, a monk at the important Breton house of Landevennec.

The most influential British missionary to Brittany during the sixth century was St Samson of Dol (died 565). His *Life* is earlier than most, dating linguistically to the seventh or ninth centuries. Born in Wales, he entered Illtud's monastery at Llantwit Major as a child and was priested there. To escape the jealousy of Illtud's nephews he retreated to Caldey Island, where he became cellarer and abbot. He is said to have been active in Ireland and the Severn Estuary in Cornwall (Padstow, Golant, St Kew and Southill being associated with him), and in the Scilly Isles where an island is named after him. He then moved on to Brittany, where he founded Dol and Pental in Normandy, from which he evangelized the Channel Isles. It was probably he who subscribed to the acts of the Council of Paris in 557. He signed himself 'Samson peccator episcopus' ('Samson, sinner and bishop'), indicating, in

St Helen's Chapel, Cape Cornwall, West Penwith,; an early oratory chapel on the site of an Iron-Age promontory fort, later converted to a medieval priest's house.

Celtic fashion, that he was a bishop as well as an abbot. The monastery formed a focused spiritual powerhouse for pastoral work in the world.

This phenomenon of the bishop-abbot, which became a distinctive feature of many Celtic monastic federations (*parochiae*), may have arisen through the influence of the early church in Gaul, where the practice subsequently disappeared. St Martin of Tours (c.316-397), a Pannonian soldier in the late Roman army, founded the first monastery in the Western empire

St Levan's, West Penwith, Cornwall. Early Christian well within a medieval baptistery.

around 360 and was popularly acclaimed as bishop in 372. He continued to live as a monk, initially in a cell near Tours cathedral and then at the monastery of Marmoutier. He seems to have viewed his monasteries as valuable tools in the conversion of rural areas, as Christianity was still focused upon towns in Roman fashion, with *pagani* still denoting country-dwellers. The rural basis of the Celtic tribal social structure meant that Martin's solution to outreach was particularly suited to the British and Irish situation. The popularity of his *Life*, written by his friend Sulpicius Severus, ensured the diffusion of his influence. This may be detected in Bede's report that Ninian dedicated Whithorn to Martin and likewise in St Augustine's dedication of his first base in Canterbury to the Gaulish saint.

The role of *peregrinus pro Christi* (voluntary exile for Christ) is one usually

Roche Chapel, near St Austell, Cornwall. Early Cornish hermitage enshrined in a later medieval chapel.

associated with Irish monks such as Sts Columba and Columbanus. But the concept of placing oneself outside of the protection of the law and ties to family and earthly rulers in order to follow the will and work of the Lord certainly seems to be well attested earlier in the sixth century, and perhaps even as early as the fifth. The need to move on in the face of the plagues and famines which swept through Britain and Ireland in the sixth and seventh centuries may also have had something to do with the phenomenon of wandering Celtic and British monks and nuns, as well as other members of the populace.

A procession of saints is said to have migrated from Ireland and/or Wales to Devon and Cornwall, evangelizing there before, in some cases, moving on to Brittany. Some have only left a name in a church dedication or in an inscription, such as that of Selus/Selinus/Selnius, whose funerary memorial is carved upon a fifth- or sixth-century stone pillar, along with a chrismon symbol, now in the church of St Just, West Penwith. St Piran/Perran, patron saint of Cornwall, was a monk from Ireland or Wales who founded Perranporth and is thought to have died around 480. His hermit's cell, cross and oratory chapel (where three skeletons with severed heads were found) are still resurrected from the engulfing sands each year on his feast day, when local folk ceremonially dig them out of the dunes.

The Selus (or Selinus) stone, with chrismon and inscription commemorating the resting place of St Selus, fifth century, St Just's Church, West Penwith, Cornwall.

Many other early saints are only really known by name. A little more is known from local legend or later *Lives* of the aforementioned children of King Brychan of Wales, who included Austell and Endellion, Brannoc, Branwalader (alleged son of a Cornish king, Kenen), Carantoc, Enoder, Enodoc, Germoe, Goran, Gwinear, Gwythian, Helen, Justus, Kerrian, Keverne, Meriasek, Merryn, Meubred, Mewan, Rumon, Selevan/Levan, Wethinoc, Winnoc, and Probus. Sherborne Abbey in Dorset was originally named after the last, perhaps reflecting its post-Romano-British origins. The saint's Latin name presumably reflected his reputation for probity. Of particular note was St Petroc, founder of Padstow, whose cult became focused at Bodmin where his relics and the Bodmin Gospels were held. These consist of an early ninth-century Breton Gospelbook which came to Bodmin later that century where it served as its 'book of the high altar', upon which the oaths accompanying any important legal transactions were sworn. Its margins contain the earliest surviving examples of written Cornish in the form of records of property transfers and manumission (freeing) of slaves. The ninth century, during which the *Historia Brittonum* was written, was a defining period in the evolution of the cults of British saints, with an upsurge in awareness of British/Welsh identity in the face of Anglo-Saxon and Viking incursions.

The litany of Cornish saints also includes many women, such as Sennen, Juliot/Juliana, Stithian, Teath, the Irish nuns Breage and Buryan/Buriana, Minver, Newlyn, Gwen/Wenn (sister of Non, St David's mother) and the rather gullible Juthwara of Lanteglos, near Camelford – another possible candidate for Camelot — who was persuaded by her wicked stepmother to place cream cheeses upon her breasts to cure a chest ailment. Her stepmother then informed Juthwara's stepbrother that she was pregnant, the moisture on her garments convincing him that she was lactating, upon which he promptly decapitated her. A spring welled up and Juthwara carried her head to the local church where she was duly restored to life. A graphic representation of Juthwara's little-known story is included in the extensive programme of exquisite illumination in the Sherborne Missal (now in the British Library), made at Sherborne Abbey around 1400–1407. The Missal acted as one of a number of allusions to Sherborne's importance within the post-Roman and early Anglo-Saxon churches, by which it sought to remind Salisbury that it was a Norman parvenue whose authority rested upon that already established by Sherborne in the age of the saints. The emphasis in Juthwara's legend upon holy wells and the severed head, a common feature of many early Celtic saints' lives, perpetuated the pagan Celtic preoccupation with both of these features. Legends concerning such murdered saints helped to compensate for the almost embarrassing dearth of Celtic martyrs as victims of the persecutions of imperial Rome – even if

The Bodmin Gospels. Canon tables with marginal inscriptions, recording legal transactions conducted at the altar of St Petroc at Bodmin, added second half of the ninth century to a Gospelbook made in Brittany earlier that century.

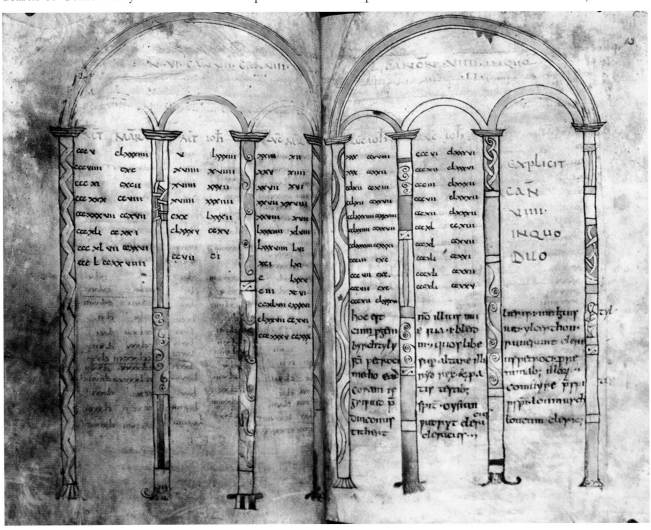

their misfortunes owed more to family and feuds than to self-sacrifice for religious beliefs.

The wild and romantic landscape of the western seaboard of Britain and its hinterland is punctuated not only by imposing prehistoric monuments, but by dry-stone structures, carvings, holy groves, caves and wells. Many of these are still inextricably bound in local memory to the communities and individuals who devoted themselves to living God-focused daily lives in the centuries following Rome's withdrawal. During this time, western and northern Britain evolved its own distinctive Christian identity and established an uneasy *modus vivendi* with its voracious pagan neighbour – the patchwork of kingdoms that formed early Anglo-Saxon England.

CHAPTER 5

Early Christian Ireland and the Growth of Monasticism

EARLY IRISH SOCIETY

The work of Sts Palladius and Patrick shows that the conversion of Ireland was a multi-faceted endeavour in which the churches of Rome, Britain and Gaul all played a part (see feature on Early Christian Irish Artefacts between pages 104 and 105). Their authority was episcopal, a prerequisite of the process of conversion in which the pastoral and sacramental role of the bishop was essential. However, unlike Britain and continental Europe which had witnessed the growth of towns under Roman influence, Iron-Age Celtic Ireland had no such urban centres or networks in which to site the *cathedra*, the bishop's seat. Nor was there an administrative bureaucracy in place for the episcopate to inherit. Alongside the fundamental work of baptizing and saving souls, and of transforming the spiritual and moral outlook of a people, one of the roles of these early Christian prelates was to integrate the church, and themselves, into the fabric of society, which in the case of Ireland was rural, tribal and hierarchical.

At the top of the pyramid were the *ri*, the 'kings' who were in fact individual chieftains of a *tuath* (tribe). The most powerful amongst them at any time assumed the title of *ard ri* (high-king). This, however, did not become in any sense a centralized, established monarchy until the time of Brian Boru and his stand against the Vikings at the Battle of Clontarf in 1014 (which acted rather as resistance to the Danes strengthened the West Saxon monarchy in late ninth to tenth-century England). Next came those of free status, headed by a warrior; then cattle-owning aristocracy, the *bó aire*; and then the slaves. There was a degree of social mobility achievable within Irish law: men and women could be equal, depending upon who brought the most wealth into a household. Lesser freemen could work their way up the social ladder by combining free birth with growing material assets, of which the most important were cattle, and clients whose allegiance was obtained by renting them cattle on a hire–purchase basis. Slaves could earn enough during their time off to buy their way to freedom. Everyone,

Do not sink upon a bed of sloth, do not let your bewilderment overwhelm you; Begin a voyage across the clear sea, to find if you may reach the Land of Women.

'BRAN AND THE EARTHLY PARADISE', IRISH, SEVENTH-EIGHTH CENTURY

Caryatid figures including a Bishop-Abbot with crozier and bell. Ninth century, White Island, County Fermanagh.

however, was constrained by the law and by the bonds and obligations owed to kindred and kings.

Irish law was well-developed and orally transmitted. It was later committed to writing during the early Christian period in corpuses such as the *Crith Gablach* and the *Senchas Már*. The jurists and judges who preserved and dispensed the law were part of an important high social class termed the *Aes Dana* (people of the deity Danu). These were the intelligentsia, preservers and transmitters of culture (the legal specialists and the bards), the professional priesthood (the druids), and the craftspeople responsible for making the wealth of stunning de luxe material goods that signified social status, ritual and belief. This group enjoyed special privileges consistent with those appropriate to the aristocracy and it was at this level that the new Christian priesthood, with its own internal hierarchy, was absorbed and equated. There are some indications in the hagiographical and other early written sources to suggest that, despite some spirited resistance, some druids quickly converted to Christianity and carried on fulfilling much of their earlier function. Some Christian schools continued to flourish in the raths where for centuries the druids had passed on their sophisticated bodies of oral learning.

There was much in Christian teaching and ritual that would have struck a cord with the Celtic folk memory and that could be integrated with existing beliefs and ceremonies. For example, *agape*, the eucharistic feast, would have been welcomed into the culture of hospitality and social communion at meals, and the waters of life and rebirth would already have offered a welcome to the baptismal candidate. Similarly, a long list of heroes, willing to sacrifice themselves for their fellows and for their ideals, had prepared the way for Christ's ultimate sacrifice and victory over the common enemy – death. Trinities of deities would also have made the concept of the Trinity of Father, Son and Holy Spirit a familiar and approachable one. *Tír na nÓg* and the otherworld made way for heaven and hell, as indicated by this Christianized seventh- or eighth-century account of the invitation issued to the ancient Celtic hero-figure, Bran, to the 'Islands of the Earthly Paradise':

There is an island far away, around which the sea-horses glisten;
Flowing on their white course against its shining shore; four pillars support it.

Pillars of white bronze are under it, shining through aeons of beauty,
A lovely land through the ages of the world, on which many flowers rain down.

There is a huge tree there with blossom, on which the birds call at the hours;
It is their custom that they all call together in concert every hour.

Weeping and treachery are unknown in the pleasant familiar land;
There is no fierce harsh sound there, but sweet music striking the ear.

Riches, treasures of every colour are in Cíuin, have they not been found?
Listening to sweet music, drinking choicest wine.

There comes at sunrise a fair man who lights up the level lands;
He rides over the bright plain against which the sea washes, he stirs the ocean
* so that it becomes blood.*

The host rides across Magh Mon, a lovely sport which is not weakly;
In the many-coloured land with great splendour they do not expect decay nor death.

Do not sink upon a bed of sloth, do not let your bewilderment overwhelm you;
Begin a voyage across the clear sea, to find if you may reach the Land of Women.

By the time of Patrick's arrival, the tribal conflicts and alignments of Irish prehistory had crystallized into a series of recognizable provinces called the Five Fifths: Connacht, Ulster, Meath, Leinster and Munster. Tribal chieftainships had given rise to dynastic septs, such as the powerful Ui Neill (later the O'Neills). They were the descendants of the semi-legendary Niall of the Nine Hostages, whose expansion eastwards from their traditional Connacht territory contributed to the Ulster emigrations of the Dal Riata to western Scotland, where they founded the kingdom of Dalriada. The focal point of kingship there was the

The Rock of Cashel, ancient ceremonial seat of king and church in the Irish kingdom of Munster, now capped by medieval buildings.

ceremonial rock-fortress of Dunadd, where de luxe metalwork was also made. In Ireland each king had an ancestral seat, often in the form of a stone built ring-fort (a *cashel* or *rath*) or an ancient hill or promontory fort. Most significant of these – both as symbolic places of royal inauguration and assembly and as de facto power bases – were the rock of Cashel in Munster, the hill of Tara in Meath and Emhain Macha in Ulster. It was by the site of the latter that Patrick located his *cathedra* of Armagh.

St Brigid of Kildare and the Role of Women in the Irish Church

Women played a significant part in Celtic society. They could be queens in their own right, they could lead households, they could go into battle as well as into childbirth and they could be druids and teachers. It is therefore not surprising to find that they achieved prominence within the Christian church.

A leading early saint of Ireland was St Brigid/Bridget/Brigit/Bride of Ireland, abbess of Kildare (died c.525). There are several *Lives* of Brigid, the first (*Vita I*) perhaps composed by Aileran the Wise of Clonard (died 665) and the second (*Vita II*) by Cogitosus around 650. These ascribe to her a humble birth and a period as a nun–cowherd following her baptism by St Patrick, and she is sometimes reported by legend to be the daughter of a druid, Dubhtach. In the late twelfth century Giraldus Cambrensis, in his *Topographia Hibernica* ('The Topography of Ireland'), described her shrine at Kildare, where a perpetual fire was tended by twenty nuns and surrounded by a hedge. If any man set foot inside this enclave he was struck dead by the taboo (a feature of pagan religion, along with the anathema or curse) and died. A Celtic goddess of valour, Brig, was honoured by the fire feast of Imbolc and attempts have been made to identify her with Brigid, whose feast also falls on that day. The saint's historical authenticity has accordingly been questioned. It is likely that, as with Patrick, one historical figure has attracted a number of earlier and subsequent legends along with the deeds of other near-contemporaries. In Brigid's case these probably included the attributes and wonders of an earlier Celtic goddess. It is not unthinkable that those who won sanctity by popular acclaim during the early centuries of Christianity in Britain should have been equated with various minor deities who for centuries had been the popular recourse for ensuring safety, fertility, peace and plenty. Brigid, who is the patroness of poets, blacksmiths and healers, was renowned for generosity and nurturing – even turning her bath water into beer for her clerical guests. One tradition relates a vision of Bishop Ibor in which he saw the Virgin ('Mary of the Gael') of whom Brigid was the likeness. He is subsequently said to have consecrated Brigid as a bishop – often cited as a precedent, if a unique and highly uncertain one, for the ordination of women.

If this event ever actually occurred it may have had something to do with the tendency to invest the leader of a monastic community with episcopal authority – the same person being simultaneously abbot and bishop, or in this case, allegedly, abbess and bishop. This effectively allowed both the monastery to function as the cathedral and its diocese to embrace the territory of the *tuath*, facilitating the travels of its priests/monks to convert, to minister and to preach. Networks of houses and hermitages founded by its members grew to form *parochiae*, monastic federations united under the name and traditions of the original founder – for example, the Columban *parochia*. It was these, rather than the Roman model of dioceses and parishes, that underpinned the church structure. Such federations often found themselves competing for resources and position in subsequent centuries, having become victims of their own worldly success, attracting pilgrimage, donation and property ownership. The greatest competition was that between the cults of Sts Brigid and Patrick. Cogitosus's biography of Brigid even goes so far as to omit any reference to Patrick. Kildare's rival, Armagh, retaliated by compiling the Book of Armagh, around 807, which brings together the New Testament, *Lives* of Patrick and other Patrician material in support of its claims to primacy. In its counter-claim it was necessary for Kildare to claim episcopal authority for its founding abbess, whose cult spread to Britain (with dedications in Fleet Street, London, and at several churches named Llansantaffraid in Wales) and the continent. Her popularity nonetheless remained secondary to that of Patrick.

Kildare, like some other early monasteries in Gaul and England (such as Chelles and Whitby), was a double house in which monks and nuns lived alongside one another, always under the motherly care of an abbess. Details from the early lives summon up an image of the church at Kildare, by the mid-seventh century if not necessarily during the time of Brigid herself, which resembles that of a Coptic church. It had an iconostasis screen, covered with painted icons, separating the chancel from the nave. The latter was divided by a wooden partition into male and female prayer halls where men and women could worship side by side without the distraction of sexual temptation.

Among the many other Irishwomen who devoted their lives to the service of God was St Bega, foundress of St Bee's in Cumbria. The bracelet relic that was the focal point of her hermitage shrine there was called 'beag' in Old English, and perhaps lent its name to this woman, whose life is shrouded in the mists of time. Another was the holy virgin Samthann (died 739) who came from a good enough family to have been fostered by a king and to have a promising match arranged for her, which she declined in favour of studying with St Cognat at Ernaide (County Donegal). She went on to found a convent at Clonbroney (County Longford). She won renown for her wisdom and some of her sayings are preserved in her later *Life*. These include her response to someone who asserted that he was going to give up his studies for more prayer time. She told him that he would not be able to set his mind properly upon prayer if he neglected study, for in prayer, as in other forms of conversation, it is difficult to have something valuable to say if you take nothing in. She discouraged gifts to her foundation, preferring poverty, and maintaining a herd of just six cows to support her community.

Samthann is commemorated in the litany of the early ninth-century Stowe Missal (an important source, along with the Antiphonary of Bangor, for early Irish liturgical practices). Her cult was introduced to Salzburg by her pupil, the Irish monk Virgil, who also founded it. He was criticized by the Anglo-Saxon missionary to Germany, Boniface, on account of his dating of Easter and his teaching that there was another world underneath this one, with other inhabitants and another sun and moon. Could he have been referring to the ancient Celtic concept of the underworld and the 'little people', or *Sidhe*? Did he have cognizance of early voyages to the new world, or was he perhaps an early advocate of quantum physics and parallel dimensions?

There were many other notable Irish foundations on the Continent including St Kilian's Wurzburg, Trier, Mainz, Cologne, Vienna, Reichenau, Berne, Milan, Verona, Fiesole, Lucca and Taranto.

THE GROWTH OF IRISH MONASTICISM

During the sixth century, the new trend of monasticism swept throughout Ireland. An important factor in this was the eremitic, ascetic model of the eastern desert fathers, such as Paul of Thebes (died c.345) and Antony of Egypt (died 356), whose lives were related by St Jerome. Another ascetic of the desert was

---

St Pachomius (died 346), a soldier-turned-hermit-turned-monastic-founder, who combined an austere regime of regulated sleep and food and drink consumption with meditation, work and obedience. His organizational aptitude brought the discipline of the army to the flocks of people who were retreating to the wilderness places in the face of punitive taxes and the persecution of Christians. His Rule was preserved by Jerome and influenced those of Sts Basil and Benedict. Another significant figure was John Cassian (died 433), who interpreted Egyptian monasticism for a Gaulish audience at his foundations in Marseilles and through his *Institutes* and *Conferences*.

The influence of the hermits and early eastern monastic founders helped to mould a distinctive response to monasticism that was akin to that of the Syro-Palestinian *lavras*, in which individuals could live a semi-eremitic lifestyle but come together communally for worship. This contrasted with the more consistently communal way of life advocated by western monastic founders such as St Martin of Tours, Cassiodorus and St Benedict of Nursia, whose influences were also felt. The lives of monks and nuns were governed by the shadows moving across the sun-dial and the tolling of the hand-bells which announced the 'Hours' – the eight services of the Divine Office conducted at periodic intervals during the monastic day and night.

The Irish, never ones to do things half-heartedly, responded to the challenges of a life of asceticism with alacrity. The monastic model also mapped well onto the rural tribal model by which Irish society was organized, focusing upon a figure of authority at its centre. The *ri* equalled the bishop/abbot/abbess and was based within a *rath*. The *cashel* became the *monasterium*, which was inhabited by the *tuath* – the monastic brethren and the lay people, who were also attracted to live a God-focused life attached to the monastery. The legal ties of mutual responsibility and accountability were also important in the monastic context, and the emphasis upon obedience and authority allowed royalty to continue in many of their old roles if they became monastic leaders. St Columba, for example, was a prince of the mighty Ui Neill.

When St Patrick arrived in Ireland the prehistoric practice of local king-priests was ongoing. The most important of these was chosen or fought his way to the symbolic seat of Tara, assuming the status of high king. This was where Patrick converted King Laoghaire. Such a tradition of combined royal and religious authority would have led to many of the converted royals – and their druidic advisors, no doubt – trading their secular positions for ones within the church. Swapping royal for abbatial authority was not a completely self-fulfilling prophecy, however. The Christian ethos meant that the church could also offer an alternative social model in which the poorest, in background and in spirit, could rise to the highest position by virtue of their vocation. One such example was St Finbar (died 610), who is said to have been the son of an illegitimate metalworker who married a slave-girl. Finbar founded the monastery at Cork, around which a town developed, and was renowned for his teaching and the school that he founded at Etargabail. His cult also spread to Scotland, where he became patron of Barra in the Outer Hebrides. Sanctity was not bestowed by a central authority or inherited as a status. It could be won by popular acclaim by living out the Christian life as a valued role model, or by performing heroic feats of ascetic endurance or constructive scholarship.

This was the case with St Kevin of Glendalough (died c.618). His *Lives* date from at least 400 years later and were written to help the monastery and diocese of Glendalough to extend its claims. There is therefore little early written evidence concerning him or his foundation, save the references in the Annals. A number of early archaeological remains at Glendalough relate to his time, however. There is an exposed section of excavated wooden trackway at the top of Wicklow Gap which is part of the original St Kevin's Way, the route by which pilgrims subsequently journeyed to the site of his foundation, which nestles in a cleft in the Wicklows beside two loughs. The Upper Lake was the site adopted by Kevin. He

is said to have been the scion of a dispossessed noble Leinster family, and was educated by monks after he had been ordained and chose to embrace the life of a hermit. St Kevin's Bed is a Bronze-Age rock-cut tomb in the mountainside on the edge of the lough accessible only by boat. This he adopted as his refuge, along with Teampall na Skellig (the 'rock church') – a rectangular church accompanied by wattle huts on a ledge nearby – and a dry-stone beehive hut perched on an outcrop above the beach. Below this is a cluster of early dry-stone raths and rough-hewn stone crosses, where those who flocked to follow the solitary man of God established a monastery. It

ABOVE: St Kevin's Kitchen and the round tower, part of the monastic city that subsequently grew up around the lower lake. Glendalough, County Wicklow.

RIGHT: the upper lake, site of St Kevin's original early eremitic retreat and monastery.

subsequently became the burial place of kings (at the Reefert church), and by the tenth century more formal masonry churches had been built here and the monastery had spread to the Lower Lake. Its sophisticated tenth- to thirteenth-century structures include the little Romanesque church now known as St Kevin's Kitchen (on account of its tiny tower resembling a chimney), and an imposing round tower which served as a bell-tower. Round towers first appeared in Ireland from the late ninth century, perhaps in response to Viking attacks. They might also have functioned as scriptoria and as a safe and a stronghold in which the monks would seek safety during times of attack from Viking and other secular forces – and also, on occasion, from rival monks. Glendalough later produced another renowned saint – the only officially canonized Irish saint – Laurence O'Toole, who was successively abbot of Glendalough and archbishop of Dublin (died 1180).

The monastic city of Glendalough, which would have housed several thousand in its heyday, was a far cry from the desert wilderness that had first attracted Kevin with its solitude, its awe-inspiring feral beauty, its natural amenities and its physical challenges. Legend records him feeding his followers on salmon caught for him in the lake by an otter. This could also be a metaphor for learning and is depicted as an artistic motif. An appreciation of humanity's place within the natural order and the need to survive within and alongside it is a distinctive feature of Celtic religious experience and of its Christian literature, poetry and prayer. Its origins lay deep within prehistoric tradition and Celtic paganism, enabling the Celts to make a unique contribution to Christian thought. One of Kevin's miracles, reported to a Norman audience in the late twelfth century by Giraldus Cambrensis in order to demonstrate this devotional trend, concerned his sensitivity to the needs of a fellow-creature. A blackbird nested in his hand whilst he stretched it out of his oratory window in prayer and, to keep from disturbing it, he did not move until its young had hatched. However far-fetched, this image of a social contract with the rest of creation is a powerful one.

St Columbanus also wrote of how nature was a second revelation, to be 'read' alongside Scripture to deepen our knowledge of God. This resulted in what might be considered today to be a more creative Christian environmentalism than the conventional theology of stewardship and the assumption that we have been set above the rest of creation to do with it as we will:

Seek no further concerning God; for those who wish to know the great deep must first review the natural world. For knowledge of the Trinity is properly likened to the depths of the sea, according to that saying of the Sage, 'and the great deep, who shall find it out?' If then a man wishes to know the deepest ocean of divine understanding, let him first if he is able scan that visible sea, and the less he finds himself to understand of those creatures which lurk beneath the waves, the more let him realize that he can know less of the depths of its Creator.

The Blackbird

Blackbird, it is well for you Wherever in the thicket be your nest, Hermit that sounds no bell, Sweet, soft, fairylike is your note.

Irish, eleventh century

In the Old Irish poem 'Pangur Bán', probably written in Austria where the poem was found written in the margins of a book now in St Paul in Carinthia, a ninth-century monk and scribe celebrates his bond with his cat.

Irish Nature Poetry

Irish monastic authors used their own language to convey, to great effect, their love of creation, blending an ancient Celtic affinity for nature with their Christian theology. Some are short, like Japanese haiku; others are long and epic. Here is a selection.

Writing out of doors

A wall of forest looms above
And sweetly the blackbird sings;
All the birds make melody
Over me and my books and things.

There sings to me the cuckoo
From bush-citadels in grey hood.
God's doom, may the Lord protect me
Writing well, under the great wood.

Admiration and joy was laced with a due respect for the awesome power of nature.

Forever Cold

Forever cold!
Weather grim and grimmer still,
Glittering brook a river
And ford a brimming lake.

The lake a great sea
(Each meagre band a company)
Rain-drop like shield-boss
And snow-flake like wether skin.

The dirty puddle is a great pit,
Level land is risen, the moor a wood,
No shelter for the flocks of birds
And white snow reaches up to haunch.

Sudden frost has closed the roads
Encircling with cunning the standing stone at Colt;
Grim weather lies entrenched on every side
And no one utters anything but: 'Cold'.

Pangur Bán

Myself and White Pangur are each at his own trade; he has his mind on hunting,
My mind is on my own task.
Better than any fame I prefer peace with my book, pursuing knowledge;
White Pangur does not envy me, he loves his own childish trade.
A tale without boredom when we are at home alone, we have –
Interminable fun – something on which to exercise our skill.
Sometimes, after desperate battles, a mouse is caught in his net;
As for me there falls in my net some difficult law hard to comprehend.
He points his clear bright eye against a wall; I point my own clear one,
Feeble as it is, against the power of knowledge.
He is happy and darts around when a mouse sticks in his sharp claw,
And I am happy in understanding some dear, difficult problem.
However long we are like that, neither disturbs the other;
Each of us loves his trade and enjoys it all alone.
The job he does every day is the one for which he is fit;
I am competent at my own job, bringing darkness to light.

The influence of secular love poetry can also sometimes be detected:

The Dawn

Come into my dark oratory,
Be welcome the bright morn,
And blessed He who sent you,
Victorious, self-renewing dawn.

Maiden of good family.
Sun's sister, daughter of proud Night,
Ever-welcome the fair morn
That brings my mass-book light.

Touching the face of each house
Illumining every kin,
White-necked and gold-bedecked –
Welcome, imperious one. Come in.

THE HERMIT'S LIFE

No one lived a more closely integrated life with nature than the hermit. Caves, clefts in mountainsides, ancient tombs, a pile of stones arranged into a beehive hut, some wattles lashed together and plugged with mud to form a hut, rocky isles off the coast or set within lakes, or boglands – these all meant home to the hermit or anchorite, both male and female alike. The discipline of the eremitic life, its hardships, attractions and aspirations, are summed up in the words of this eighth- or ninth-century Irish ascete.

The Hermit

Alone in my little hut without a human being in my company,
Dear has been the pilgrimage before going to meet death.

A remote hidden little cabin, for forgiveness of my sins;
A conscience upright and spotless before holy Heaven.

Making holy the body with good habits, treading it boldly down;
Weak tearful eyes for forgiveness of my desires.

Desires feeble and withered, renunciation of this poor world, clean live thoughts;
This is how I would seek God's forgiveness.

Eagerly wailing to cloudy Heaven, sincere and truly devout confession,
Fervent showers of tears. A cold anxious bed, like the lying-down of the doomed,
Brief apprehensive sleep, invocations frequent and early.

My food, my staple diet – it is a dear bondage – my meal
Would not make me full-blooded, without doubt.

Dry bread weighed out, well we bow the head; water of
The fair-coloured hillside, that is the draught you should drink.

A bitter meagre meal, diligently feeding the sick, suppression of quarrelling
And visiting, a calm serene conscience.

It would be desirable, a pure, holy blemish, cheeks dry and
Sunken, skin leathery and lean.

Treading the paths of the Gospel, singing psalms every Hour;
An end of talking and long stories; constant bending of the knees.

My Creator to visit me, my Lord, my King, my spirit to
Seek him in the eternal kingdom where He is.

THE WIND

It has broken us, it has crushed us, it has drowned us, O King of the star-bright kingdom; the wind has consumed us As twigs are consumed by crimson fire from Heaven.

IRISH, EIGHTH CENTURY

Let this be the end of vice in the precincts of churches,
A lovely little cell among many graves, and I alone there.

Alone in my little hut, all alone so, alone I came
Into the world, alone I shall go from it.

If being alone I have done wrong at all, through the pride
Of this world, hear my wail as I lament all alone, O God!

A telling response to the call to Christian life and morality is preserved in the Suibne (Sweeney) poems, composed by an anonymous Irish author during the twelfth century but based on the life of a famous hermit, Suibne. He had been a king in north-east Ulster, but became so traumatized and appalled by the carnage of the battlefield in 637 that he lost his mind and fled to take refuge in the wild. The contrast between manmade atrocity and the balance of the natural order is poignantly conveyed in the poem 'Suibne the Wild Man in the Forest'.

A Celestial Feast

Not every call to serve the Lord was austere. The congenial aspects of secular life could also play a role in shaping thought on the service to be rendered to God in the world, as this Irish poem of tenth- or eleventh-century date demonstrates:

I Should Like to Have a Great Ale Feast

I should like to have a great ale feast for the King of Kings;
I should like the heavenly host to be drinking it for all eternity.

I should like to have the fruits of Faith, of pure devotion;
I should like to have the seats of Repentance in my house.

I should like to have the men of Heaven in my own dwelling;
I should like the tubs of Long-Suffering to be at their service.

I should like to have the vessels of Charity to dispense;
I should like to have the pitchers of Mercy for their company.

I should like there to be Hospitality for their sake;
I should like Jesus to be here always.

I should like to have the Three Marys of glorious renown;
I should like to have the Heavenly Host from every side.

I should like to be rent-payer to the Lord; he to whom He
Gives a good blessing has done well in suffering distress.

Suibne the Wild Man in the Forest

Little antlered one, little belling one, melodious little
Bleater, sweet I think the lowing that you make in the glen.

Home-sickness for my little dwelling has come upon my
Mind, the calves on the plain, the deer on the moor

Blackthorn, little thorny one, black little sloe-bush; water-cress,
Little green-topped one, on the brink of the blackbird's well

Bramble, little humped one, you do not grant fair terms;
You do not cease tearing me till you are sated with blood

Holly, little shelterer, door against the wind; ash-tree,
Baneful, weapon in the hand of a warrior…

Aspen as it trembles, from time to time I hear its leaves
Rustling, and think it is the foray…

If on my lonely journey I were to search the mountains of
The dark earth, I would rather have the room for a single hut
In great Glenn mBolcáin…

TOP: The Gallarus Oratory, an early chapel surrounded by sixth- to seventh-century burials, Dingle Peninsula, County Kerry.

BELOW: Upturned boatsheds, Lindisfarne, Holy Island. Such structures may have inspired the builders of the Gallarus Oratory.

Close to the original eremitic impulse is the Gallarus Oratory on the Dingle Peninsula in County Kerry. Here a simple stone rath protects a little burial ground with simple small upright stones inscribed with crosses and invocations of the name of the Lord in early half-uncial script. Amidst these early graves, which commemorate believers of sixth- and seventh-century-date, is the little oratory chapel in which they worshipped. It has one small window and door, piercing a corbelled stone skin which looks like the upturned keel of a boat. Real upturned boats are still used for storage buildings on modern Lindisfarne and demonstrate how this age-old practice could have inspired a new form of stone building. The chapel is often dated to the same period as the grave-markers but its stones are set in place with mortar, indicating that it either post-dates 900 or was at some point rebuilt.

Certainly of early date, however, is the cluster of tiny dry-stone beehive huts that cling like nesting gulls to the craggy ledges of Skellig Michael (see page 105), a rocky island off of the Kerry coast – next stop *Tír na nÓg*. During the sixth or seventh centuries a band of hardy monks, possibly led by St Finan, first leapt onto its slippery rock and carved from it a lengthy flight of steps leading to terraces along a rock saddle some 550 feet above sea level. There they built two rectangular oratories, six beehive huts, rough cross slabs and a little 'garden' in which to grow a herb or two. In the twelfth century they added a church, dedicated to St Michael – as are so many high places – where heaven and earth meet and good battles with evil. The little beehive cells are the Atlantic seaboard's equivalent of the sketes of the eastern deserts: places where there was nowhere to hide from the elements, from God or yourself. In them one monk, perhaps accompanied by a pupil or amanuensis, would live, study and pray. They must have struggled to claw a living from this inhospitable place, nurturing vulnerable vegetation, gathering gulls' eggs, fishing by line whilst perched on the rock-face. This last practice was movingly depicted in the early twentieth-century film 'Man of Aran', when Aran Islanders would regularly get swept away whilst fishing with the line fed through their naked toes. Skellig Michael was also prey to any passing piratical raid, should anyone believe it harboured anything worth seizing. Sometimes even the monks were seized by Viking raiders and enslaved or starved.

By the thirteenth century life on Skellig Michael had proven too hard. The few remaining stalwart monks who had kept its community alive retreated to the mainland and their new home, Ballinskelligs, sited almost within view of the Skelligs – but resolutely turning its back upon them.

St Ciarán of Clonmacnoise and his Contemporaries

Such extreme eremitic establishments were, however, the exception rather than the rule. Most monasteries and nunneries were situated on the best lines of communication and the most fertile land. One such is Clonmacnoise (County Offaly), set on the broad banks of the River Shannon, which was founded by St Ciarán/Kieran (died 545), the son of an itinerant carpenter from Connaught who studied under St Finnian of Clonard. With ten companions and assisted by the local Prince Dermot, he built the monastery at Clonmacnoise. This became a leading centre of learning (the Annals of Tighernach were compiled there in the eleventh century and the Book of the Dun Cow in the twelfth) and the focus of the cult of St Ciarán. The cult was established despite the saint's injunction to his disciples that when he died they should leave his bones on a hilltop 'like the stag's', and preserve his spirit rather than his relics. One such relic may be preserved within the Clonmacnoise crosier in the National Museum of Ireland. Legend relates that the other 'saints' of Ireland were so jealous of him that, with the exception of Columba, they prayed and fasted so that he would die young. This he did, at the age of 33 (perhaps a hagiographical convention paralleling him with Christ, who was crucified at that age). Church politics could evidently be as cut and thrust then as now.

At the monastery there is an impressive array of recumbent grave-slabs with incised crosses and inscriptions in the vernacular (many favouring the characteristic formula 'Or do...', 'a prayer for...'). These date from the eighth and ninth centuries, and would have marked the graves of the monks who continued to follow the saint and those wealthy lay people who sought burial close to him in order that their souls might be saved by association. Two high-crosses also date from the ninth century, whilst the most complex and beautiful, with its didactic figural scenes from the lives of Christ, King David and Ciarán, is the 'Cross of the Scriptures' or 'Flann's Cross' which, like the round tower, dates from the tenth century. Subsequent Romanesque churches also adorn the site. This important monastery survived until 1552, despite frequently being plundered and burned (26 times between 841 and 1204). It faced a particularly focused raid in 845 when Viking longships sailed up the Shannon and their leader, Turgesius, an avowed enemy of the Christian faith, set his wife up as an oracle upon the high altar. This offers a rare insight into the motives that may, on occasion, have underlay the Viking raids upon Christian Europe. Their attacks on Ireland commenced in 795 and by the 840s they had established settlements, including the towns of Dublin, Wicklow, Arklow, Wexford, Waterford and perhaps Cork and Limerick. Until the Battle of Clontarf in 1014 they were a power in the land, tying Ireland into a new international trade network as part of the Viking empire. Rape and pillage were by no means the only incentives for such emigration: overcrowding in their Scandinavian homelands and the need to seek new territories, new opportunities and new trade outlets were important factors. So too might be a proselytizing pagan zeal on the part of some war-leaders, such as Turgesius and his 'Valkyrie' wife.

An influential early figure in the Irish Church was St Finnian of Clonard (died 549), who had studied the models of Sts David, Cadoc and Gildas in Wales and spent time at Kildare upon his return to Ireland. His tenth-century 'Life' records that he was born in Leinster and that he died of the 'yellow pest', one of the waves of plague that swept across the land during the sixth century. His monastic foundations included Clonard (County Meath), in a well-placed central location, where he promoted an eastern form of ascetic monasticism coupled with a stong focus upon study, especially of Scripture. This is said to have attracted a staggering 3000 or more followers to join Clonard during Finnian's lifetime, earning him the title of 'Teacher of the saints of Ireland'. Each missionary monk who left Clonard was equipped with a Gospelbook, a crozier and a reliquary to furnish their own church. Finnian also stressed a penitential strand, and composed the first of the Irish Penitentials, drawing upon the thought of Jerome and Cassian and upon Welsh and Irish sources. This in turn influenced the Penitential of St Columbanus, who carried the practices of monastic discipline and study to post-Roman Europe.

Another famous teacher was St Finnian of Moville (died 579), an abbot of royal descent from the Dal Fiatach sept. He studied at Ninian's Whithorn and returned to Ireland to found Moville (County Down) and Dromin (County Louth). His deeds have sometimes been conflated with those of his namesake, Finnian of Clonard, and

The Athlone Crucifixion Plaque

The Athlone Crucifixion Plaque (NMI R554). Christ is flanked by angels and by the spear and sponge bearers, Stephaton and Longinus, perhaps from a book cover or shrine; Irish, eighth century.

The Ardagh Chalice

The Tara Brooch

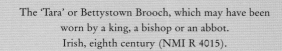

The 'Tara' or Bettystown Brooch, which may have been
worn by a king, a bishop or an abbot.
Irish, eighth century (NMI R 4015).

BELOW: front of pin head
RIGHT: equally decorative back – an object to be
displayed as well as worn.

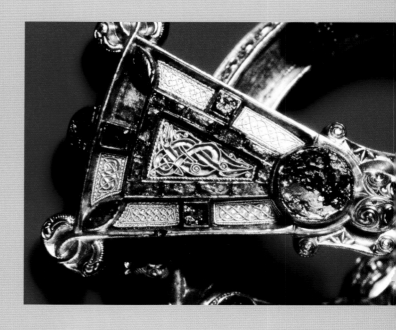

The Ardagh Chalice (NMI 1874:99).
Irish eighth century communion chalice,
with inscription defined by a punched
ground naming the apostles.

of Frigidian of Lucca. The *Penitential of Vinnian* has been ascribed to him, but may in fact relate to one of these other figures.

St Columba

Finnian of Moville's pupils included one of the most famous Irish missionary saints – Columba /Colum Cille ('dove of the church', died 597), who also studied with Finnian of Clonard. Born at Gartan (County Donegal) in 521 (see feature on St Columba between pages 152 and 153). He was a prince-abbot par excellence, a leading member of the Ui Neill, one of the most powerful and territorially ambitious of the royal dynasties of Ireland. Such ambitions may have been the true motivation for one of the greatest blood baths in Irish history – the Battle of Cúl Dremne in 561. This battle was blamed upon Columba, who was accused of copying and claiming as his own a Roman Psalter owned by his teacher, Finnian of Moville, which may have been brought back with him from Whithorn. The judgement in the case went against Columba, the jurists concluding 'to each cow its calf' and thereby

Early monastic settlement with beehive huts, sixth or seventh century. Skellig Michael, County Kerry.

convicting Columba of plagiarism and assigning legal copyright to Finnian. In penance Columba chose to embrace *peregrinatio*, the monastic equivalent of one of the harshest of secular punishments: exile. This meant relinquishing the mutual ties of support of kith and kin and effectively made the person concerned an 'outlaw'.

Columba's feelings as an exile are evoked in the following terms in an eleventh-century poem:

Colum Cille's Exile

This were pleasant, O Son of God,
With wondrous coursing
To sail across the swelling torrent
Back to Ireland.

To Eórlarg's plain, past Benevanagh,
Across Loch Feval,
And there to hear the swans in chorus
Chanting music.

And when my boat, the Derg Drúchtach,
At last made harbour
In Port na Ferg the joyful Foyle-folk
Would sound a welcome.

I ever long for the land of Ireland
Where I had power,
An exile now in midst of strangers,
Sad and tearful.

Woe that journey forced upon me,
O King of Secrets;
Would to God I'd never gone there, to Cooldrevne...

I have loved the land of Ireland
– I cry for parting;
To sleep at Comgall's, visit Canice,
This were pleasant.

Columba had already founded monasteries at Derry, Durrow and perhaps Kells, but in 563 he set sail in 'the boat with no oars', trusting in the Lord to take him wherever he wished him to serve. He set off from the northern coast of Ireland, and a number of sculptures in the area are

Cross slab with projections to carry extensions to the arms of the cross. Fahan, County Donegal, seventh or early eighth century.

witness to vibrant religious activity here during the sixth to ninth centuries. These include: the pillars and crosses of Carndonagh and the Fahan cross (County Donegal); the enigmatic little figures of apostles from Boa Island; the stooping bishop carved on a rough standing stone at Killadeas; and the ninth-century caryatid figures of kings, queens and abbots from White Island (all of these latter from County Fermanagh). With his twelve disciples, Columba voyaged just far enough to ensure that their beloved homeland was no longer in sight. This took them, in 563, to the little island of Iona near the Isle of Mull in the Inner Hebrides. It can have been no coincidence that this formed a bridgehead between Ireland and the 'expat' Irish kingdom of Dalriada in Argyll on the adjacent Scottish mainland, with its ceremonial fortress of Dunadd. Here much metalwork manufacturing debris has been found, along with a little pebble inscribed with a prayer.

Dalriada was founded by the Dal Riata, a tribe that had been pushed out of Ulster during the third and fourth centuries, as more powerful clans such as the Ui Neill expanded. From here Columba launched a mission to the Picts, continuing the work begun by Ninian, Kentigern (Mungo) and their followers, targeting King Brude at his lowering hill-fort of Craig Phadraig near Inverness. In 574 he consecrated the Dalriadan King Aidan, thereby conferring legitimacy on this royal house. This produced a partnership between church and state which helped both to extend their power within Pictland (which accordingly came to be known as Scotland – the 'Scotti' meaning the Irish). The extent of Columba's own apostolic mission is now thought to have been somewhat exaggerated: of the multitude of Scottish churches dedicated to him only a handful in Dalriada and the Hebrides are likely to have been his personal foundations. However, many further monasteries were established by his followers and his influence was considerable. The prime source concerning him is the *Life* by Adomnan (627–704), a later abbot of Iona who was himself an important figure in the history of the Insular Church. The picture he penned of his saintly predecessor has a ring of authenticity, portraying a vigorous, imposing, somewhat impetuous and driven man, a ruler, scholar, scribe and poet who could be both wise and harsh, but who mellowed with age. Bede was evidently much impressed by his work, and that of subsequent members of his *parochia*, which included the monastic houses of Melrose and Lindisfarne. Bede's approval comes in spite of their vigorous defence of their traditions and rights which led in 664 to the Synod of Whitby and its aftermath, in which the primacy of authority between the Columban and Roman Churches was contested.

Columba retained influence in Ireland, attending the important Convention of Druim-Cetta around 580 at which he mediated between the high king and Dalriada. The subject of the mediation was the dues owed by the latter, and Columba also

Pebble inscribed 'in nomine' ('in the name of') in half-uncial script. From the Irish ceremonial site of Dunadd, Dalriada, Argyll, eighth century. Perhaps a devotional object or a scribal motif-piece, it may recall a miraculous healing stone blessed by St Columba.

successfully negotiated naval service but exemption from military service. He championed the cause of the poet bards – of whom he was one – whose privileged status was threatened, thus ensuring their perpetuation as a legal class and the continuing role of a lay intelligentsia in Irish society. They were an articulate group, well capable of self-advocacy, as the sarcasm of this ninth-century poem aimed at a less than generous patron illustrates:

The Boorish Patron

I have heard that he does not give horses for songs of praise;
He gives what is natural to him – a cow.

They could also ensure good reputation and perpetuatual fame, as this twelfth-century poem shows:

Finn's Generosity

If the brown leaves were gold that the wood lets fall, if the white wave were silver,
Finn would have given it all away.

SCHOLARSHIP IN IRELAND

There has not drunk bravely of death, there has not reached the fellowship of the dead,
the cultivated earth has not closed over a sage more wonderful than he.

In addition to the ecclesiastical Latin literature of early Christian Ireland, much early Irish poetry is in the vernacular, including most of the examples given here. Learning Latin as a foreign language inspired Irish scholars to think about grammar and the graphic manifestation of language as writing. They rapidly applied these lessons to their own language, making Old Irish (along with Old English) one of the earliest written western vernaculars. They also introduced several new and valuable features into the history of writing, including systematic punctuation and the separation of words. This had much to do with new patterns of reading.

In Classical Antiquity texts were for reading out loud. Schoolchildren would be taught the art of oration, sometimes with the aid of an actor who would come into the schoolroom to perform readings. Pronunciation and style of delivery were crucial. Yet early Christian authors such as Isidore of Seville and Bede advocated the practice of silent reading, to foster meditation and understanding of the text. Anything that helped to make writing easier to read was useful and the *scriptura continua* of classical scripts, in which all the words were joined together, soon gave way at the tips of Irish quills to the sorts of layout with which we are familiar today. The work of the scribe was a gruelling physical and intellectual task. Writing out

Let me, while in Colum's care, be guarded by the heavenly throng; When I tread the path of fear I have a leader, I am strong.

Hymn to St Columba, by a seventh-century monk of Iona

entire books by hand in less than optimum conditions was tough, but it had its rewards, the greatest of which was the possibility of achieving a glimpse of revelation. By the processes of *meditatio* and *ruminatio* (chewing over the meaning of the text), the scribe-teacher-preacher sought *revelatio* – that moment of incisive clarity and sublime joy in which the reality of the divine order was glimpsed. Even the physical labour had its pleasures, as revealed by this ninth-century note written into the margins of a book by an Irish scribe on the Continent:

Sunshine Through the Window

*Pleasant to me is the glittering of the sun today upon these margins,
because it flickers so.*

Another ninth-century Insular scribe working on the continent would complain, however, that he could not write because his fingers were too frozen!

Of the three poems attributed to Columba, one, the *Altus Prosator*, may actually have been composed by him and is a powerful vision of the afterlife and the Last Judgement. He is also said to have been a scholar-scribe, who spent much of the final illness-ridden years of his life copying manuscripts. The relics that came to be associated with his widespread cult included over a hundred books, the earliest of which is the Cathach of Columcille (see feature on St Columba between pages 152 and 153). This Psalter was long thought to be the one that he plagiarized from Finnian of Moville but is now usually dated to the early seventh century, after his death. It contains calligraphic initials which are adorned with Christian symbols such as the fish and the cross, resembling those in manuscripts copied in Rome during the time of Gregory the Great, and also with traditional Celtic abstract motifs such as trumpet spirals and *peltae*. They are enlarged, and the letters following them decline in size until reaching that of the main text script, a feature termed 'diminuendo'. These initials were an important step in the development of the Insular 'illuminated manuscript', which became one of the highpoints of early medieval artistic endeavour and an eloquent vehicle of the Word. The script of the Cathach begins to assume the settled appearance that came to distinguish Insular half-uncial script, and exhibits both influence from Rome and independent local input. The ways in which the authoritative new medium of the book was made in the Irish context are consistent with the multi-faceted nature of the conversion of Ireland. Some of the greatest Insular Gospelbooks are associated with Columban foundations, notably the Book of Durrow, the Lindisfarne Gospels and the Book of Kells (see feature on St Columba).

THE BOOK OF DURROW AND THE BOOK OF KELLS

The Book of Durrow combines the following features: Celtic La Tène decoration with animal interlace of Germanic origin; an early half-uncial script; a Latin text

ON MAEL MHURU THE POET

The choice earth has not covered, there will not come to the towers of Tara, Ireland of the many fields has not enfolded a man like the pure gentle Mael Mhuru.

OLD IRISH EPITAPH, 887

exhibiting the influence of Jerome's Vulgate; 'carpet-pages' with crosses embedded within them introducing each Gospel (a feature of Coptic derivation); and evangelist miniatures in which a number of stylistic traits are combined. The symbol used to represent 'man' looks like an Anglo-Saxon or Frankish belt-buckle on legs, and its eagle symbol resembles a Germanic cloisonné brooch, whilst its lion and calf symbols feature the hip-spirals of Pictish carvings. The Book of Durrow has been variously dated to the seventh to ninth centuries and its making has been ascribed to Ireland, Pictland and Northumbria, indicating just how hotly debated the origins of the art of this period have been, particularly in view of nationalistic considerations. If there is any consensus of opinion it is that it was made in a Columban house, possibly Iona, during the later seventh century, following the Synod of Whitby. Its prefaces to the Gospels are very closely related to those in another great book associated with the cult of Columba, the Book of Kells, suggesting that they may have been made in the same place.

The Book of Kells is as contentious as that of Durrow, if not more so, with any consensus favouring production on Iona around 800. This stunningly inventive book is a veritable encylopaedia of Insular art, and also displays the influence of contemporary southern English art and that of the Carolingian empire. Its images are complex and multi-layered in their meanings. The Insular mind was such that it would have been considered naïve to 'read' only one literal meaning into images and texts when a dozen or more symbolic meanings could also be peeled away, like the layers of an onion, to reveal a kernel of wisdom at the core. So, for example, the miniature depicting Christ atop the temple in Jerusalem, being tempted by a spindly Byzantine-style devil, simultaneously forms a sacred *figura* (diagram) of the Communion of Saints. In this reading Christ literally forms the head of the body of the church (depicted as an Irish house-shaped metalwork shrine). Above him hover angels, representing the Church Triumphant – those who already dwelt in heaven. Beside him are watching crowds, representing the Church Militant – those working for the kingdom of God on earth in the present. Beneath is a figure resembling Osiris, Egyptian god of the dead, who presides over a group of people representing the Church Expectant – those dead but not yet resurrected to eternal life.

The Book of Kells contains a riot of amusing little figures and beasties: sea serpents (recalling the Loch Ness monster, which Columba is said to have bested), hens, otters, horses and hounds, beard-pulling wrestlers and priests riding off to preach. One detail was thought to offer a coded clue as to where the book was made. In the genealogy of Christ a merman grasps the name 'Iona' (Jonah). Unfortunately the island was not known by this name until the sixteenth century, being formerly called Hy/Hii ('the island'). However, 'Iona' is Hebrew for dove, which in Latin is *columba* – Columcille, 'the dove of the church' – thereby affirming the link between this remarkable book and the cult of St Columba.

Several stylistic features of the Book of Kells are paralleled on the high-crosses that still stand on Iona, including the snake bosses of Pictish art. They are also reflected on a cross erected in the churchyard at Kells later in the ninth century, after the community of Iona had moved there at the beginning of that century in the face of escalating Viking raids on the vulnerable island. When they moved, they took with them many of the relics of Columba, probably including the then unfinished Book of Kells, which was subsequently carried around the nearby territory claimed by the monastery at Kells on a ceremonial 'visitation' or 'circuit' in which legal ownership was demonstrated. It was stolen from the altar at Kells later in the Middle Ages and found abandoned in a ditch with its metalwork binding torn off. Evidently not everyone respected the authority of the Word or the power of the saint. Several other high-crosses marked the different zones of the monastic rath at Kells and an oratory on the site, known as St Columba's House, resembles the temple in the Book of Kells, with its steep, sloping stone roof. This is thought by some to be the chapel known to have been erected when the Iona community moved there in 804, but it was probably built during the eleventh century, along with the mighty round tower.

The Book of Durrow may have taken a similar route to another of Columba's original foundations. It may be the book seen in use at a Mass depicted on the shaft of the high-cross that was erected there in the tenth century, and which now stands waiting in the dappled light of an abandoned churchyard (see feature on St Columba). Columba's actual remains, however, were taken to Dunkeld in Scotland in 849 when Iona was finally relinquished, where his reputation as the 'apostle of Scotland' continued to grow alongside the aspirations of the Scottish Crown.

THE SPREAD OF IRISH INFLUENCE – ST COLUMBANUS AND HIS MISSION TO THE CONTINENT

A friend of Columba's, who had also studied with Finnian of Clonard, was St Canice or Kenneth (died 600). He was the son of a bard, and became a renowned hermit and preacher who left the monastery of Glasnevin when it was devastated by plague. Having spent some time at Llancarfen in Wales he returned to Ireland to found a number of houses, including Aghaboe, the most important church in Ossory. He then went on to evangelize in the Hebrides and mainland Scotland. His close relationship with nature was celebrated and he was famous for writing a Gospelbook single-handed (perhaps influencing the later creator of the Lindisfarne Gospels). Another energetic Irishman who subsequently worked in Pictland was St Maelrubba (died 722), a monk from Bangor in northern Ireland who founded the remote and beautiful monastery of Applecross (with its assembly of eighth- and ninth-century sculptures) in the dramatic landscape of Ross and Cromarty, opposite Skye which he also converted.

One of Finnian's other pupils, Sinell, taught another influential Irish saint – Columbanus/Columban (died 615). He came from a wealthy family and faced maternal opposition to his vocation, which he took up in the face of carnal temptation following the advice of a woman hermit. He also studied with Comgall

Let us concern ourselves with things divine, and as pilgrims ever sigh for and desire our homeland; for the end of the road is ever the object of travellers' hopes and desires, and thus, since we are travellers and pilgrims in the world, let us ever ponder on the end of the road, that is of our life, for the end of our roadway is our home.

ST COLUMBANUS

at the important monastery of Bangor (County Down) where he remained for many years before departing on *peregrinatio* around 590. He was then almost fifty, but with twelve companions in tow he set off for Gaul.

Upon arrival Columbanus attracted the patronage of the Merovingian King Childebert II, who gave him an abandoned Roman fort in which to found the monastery of Annegray. He went on to found Luxeuil in the Vosges, which became one of the most influential centres of learning in post-Roman Gaul/Frankia. Its scriptorium produced many books and devised its own distinctive form of script, which combined features from older Roman scripts and those of Ireland, as well as initials formed from animal, fish and bird forms, in Frankish fashion. Upon Childebert's death the Frankish church turned upon Columbanus, criticizing him for his adherence to idiosyncratic Irish practices, including the calculations used in determining the timing of the moveable feast of Easter. In response he wrote to

Columbanus's Journey

Some of the writings of Columbanus survive, including his monastic 'Rule of Life', his Penitential, and some letters and poems, including a Latin rowing-song that vividly evokes his voyages. In this song you can feel the muscles of the monkish oarsmen straining as they join in the chorus refrain.

Columbanus to his monks

See, cut in woods, through flood of twin-horned Rhine
Passes the keel, and greased slips over seas –
   Heave, men! And let resounding echo sound out 'heave'.

The winds raise blasts, wild rain-storms wreak their spite
But ready strength of men subdues it all –
   Heave, men! And let resounding echo sound out 'heave'.

Clouds melt away and the harsh tempest stills,
Effort tames all, great toil is conqueror –
   Heave, men! And let resounding echo sound out 'heave'.

Endure and keep yourselves for happy things
You suffered worse, and these too God shall end -
   Heave, men! And let resounding echo sound out 'heave'…

Stand firm in soul and spurn the foul fiend's tricks
And seek defence in virtue's armoury –
   You men remember Christ with mind still sounding 'heave'…

Supreme, of virtues king, and fount of things,
He promises in strife, gives prize in victory –
   You men remember Christ with mind still sounding 'heave'.

Pope Gregory the Great, assuring him of his allegiance to the See of St Peter but defending the ancient rites of the Irish church, which he presented as purer than those of other nations. Such representations may have helped to alert the pope to the dangers of allowing such divergent practices to disrupt unity in the fragile network of Christianized successor states and individual centres that he was nurturing within what had been the western part of the Roman empire. The primacy of the papacy in Rome was far from assured at this time. The competing claims to supremacy by the eastern patriarchates and the territorial ambitions of the Byzantine emperors, with their Italian bridgehead of Ravenna, may have posed a potential threat to Gregory's vision of reviving the western empire – in Christian form, with the papacy at its head. Such considerations may have contributed to his decision to send Augustine and his mission to convert the pagan Anglo-Saxons rather than leaving their salvation (and allegiances) to potentially schismatic Irish missionaries such as Columba and Columbanus, or to the equally dangerous post-Romano-British church.

Lack of papal support led Columbanus to seek toleration from the Synod of Chalon, allowing him and his communities to follow their Irish traditions. His refusal to bless the illegitimate son of Theuderic II alienated the Frankish royalty and led to his deportation, which was however prevented by a storm. Columbanus sought the support of another Frankish ruler and rejoined some of his Luxeuil brethren. Together they rowed up the Rhine, intending to settle on Lake Constance where they again encountered the opposition of Theuderic. They continued across the Swiss Alps, pausing to found the dramatically situated monastery of St Gall. They then proceeded to Bobbio in the Italian Apennines where the local Lombardic ruler, Duke Agilof, was an Arian heretic whose Catholic family was in dispute with Rome. Columbanus tried to mediate, but his correspondence displays both integrity and a lack of political astuteness and seems to have irritated the papacy. It also drew attention to the irregularities in Irish and British practice that helped to stimulate Augustine's mission to the English. Under their patronage, in the site of a ruined church at Bobbio, he founded the monastery where he later died. Both St Gall and Bobbio also became important places of learning and book production, and together with Luxeuil served as valuable conduits of two-way influence between Ireland, Frankia and Italy, exchanging artefacts and personnel.

Columbanus was one of the most influential of the many Insular missionaries to the continent, who sought to revive and reform what they perceived to be flagging Christian commitment there. His Rule, with its emphasis upon corporal punishment and self-mortification, was too harsh to recommend itself widely, and was rapidly overtaken by St Benedict's gentler 'Little Rule for beginners'. In this period individual monastic houses followed the rule of life advocated by their abbot/abbess or founding saint, rather than adhering to that of a specific 'Order'. Anyone who is seduced by the idea of a 'cuddly Celtic Christianity' characterized by a lack of observance of authority, an otherworldly spirituality and a New-Age environmentalism, should perhaps temper their desire to revive early Celtic practices by reading the Rule and Penitential of Columbanus, as well as critically analyzing other Insular sources. Standing up to the neck in fast-flowing freezing water is as good an introduction as any to Celtic ascetic spirituality.

PENANCE, *PEREGRINATIO* AND PILGRIMAGE

The Irish Penitentials, which were initially inspired by those of the early British church, prescribed physical penances for every sin imaginable, from bestiality to over-indulgence, and were essentially handbooks to assist confessors in guiding the penitent. Such injunctions seem strange to us today. More accessible, however, is the sense of remorse and repentance encapsulated so succinctly and movingly in the verse, 'Tears'.

The regime of St Maedoc/Aedh/Aidan (died 626) is also salutary. He founded Ferns in County Wexford upon returning from studying at St David's in Wales, and is said to have subsisted on barley bread and water for seven years and to have recited 500 Psalms each day. Priests had to be *psalteratus* – able to recite the Psalms by heart. One of the earliest examples of Irish handwriting consists of psalm verses scratched with a metal stylus onto the wax covering a set of wooden tablets, found preserved in the peat of Springmount Bog and dating from around 600. Perhaps the travelling priest who owned them became so absorbed in learning the Psalms on his journey, as many monastic rules of life advocated, that he took a tumble into the bog and lost his precious tablets. The ascetic tendencies of the Irish religious led to feats of physical endurance and deprivation worthy of St Symeon Stylites (who spent over 30 years sitting on top of a pole) and the spiritual athletes of the early Christian Middle East. They culminated in a religious reform movement of the ninth century, the Culdees (or *Celí dei*, 'servants of God'), hard-liners who expected much of their flocks and too much of themselves.

Irish society was well structured and well regulated. Its populace had for centuries been accustomed to formal religion led by a professional priesthood of druids and druidesses. Gaining the allegiance of the *rí* brought with it that of the *tuath*, and once any initial resistance to change was overcome and the aristocracy and intelligentsia had converted, the rest of society would have been quick to follow. The monastic explosion meant that everyone, in however remote a location, would have fallen under the pastoral care of a church or its travelling priests. Just looking at the mighty tome compiled by Kenney, *The Sources for the Early History of Ireland. Ecclesiastical. An Introduction and Guide* (1979), which lists and discusses (but does not reproduce) the written sources of the period, shows how active the church in Ireland was, and demonstrates its impact upon lives, laws and culture. A special language – hisperic – was even invented by a small group of clerical elite, who may actually have come to study in Ireland from the continent. It allowed them to communicate in a secret scholarly tongue which included loan words from Hebrew, Greek, Latin and Old Irish.

TEARS

God give me a well of tears
My sins to hide,
Or I am left like
arid earth
Unsanctified.

IRISH, NINTH CENTURY

The saints that the Irish church produced are too numerous to recite their litany and deeds here. Many are recorded in the annals (yearly notes of events, initially added to tables used in the calculation of Easter, but gathered together by the eleventh and twelfth centuries into chronicles such as the Annals of Tighernach, the Annals of Ulster, the Annals of the Four Masters and the Book of the Dun Cow) and in the Irish Martyrologies of the ninth century. Their names are preserved in church dedications and their relics – skeletal remains, the fabrics or vestments they were wrapped in, or objects owned by them or later associated with their shrines – are enshrined in metalwork. The superlative craftsmanship of Celtic Iron-Age metalworkers was skilfully perpetuated by their Christian heirs, who perfected the techniques of engraving, chasing, gold filigree, enamelling and millefiori glass studs (in which rods of glass were fused together and cut into slices, the pattern running all the way through, like Brighton rock). Amongst the masterpieces of early Christian Irish artefacts are the Tara Brooch, the Ardagh Chalice, the Moylough belt-shrine, the Athlone Crucifixion Plaque (with its heroic figure of Christ triumphant upon the Cross) and the Derrynaflan Hoard (see feature on Early Christian Irish Artefacts between pages 104 and 105). The latter was a stunning collection of altar-plate, inspired by that of Byzantium, buried beneath a bronze cauldron in the face of Viking raids during the ninth century. It lay hidden in the earth until discovered by modern metal detectors. What other treasures lie buried in Irish soil? Many fragments survive in Viking graves, with plates from bookcovers converted into jewellery for wives and sweethearts back home.

In his *Topographia Hibernica*, Giraldus Cambrensis would later write of an alleged encounter with two Aran islanders who were found sailing their *curragh* off the western coast of Ireland. Giraldus in fact never got further west than Waterford, but he used the tale to demonstrate that the Irish were noble savages in need of the evangelization and good government of the Angevin rulers of England. The men were said to be vegetarians of gentle disposition, naturally good but ignorant of the gospel. Giraldus was evidently unaware that since at least 500 AD, Arann na niamh (the isles of the saints) had been the equivalent of a high-

The Springmount Bog Tablets, Dublin. Extracts from the Psalms, inscribed on wax tablets. Ireland, early seventh century. One of the earliest examples of Insular handwriting.

PILGRIMAGE TO ROME

Pilgrim, take care your journey's not in vain,
A hazard without profit, without gain;
The king you seek you'll find in Rome, it's true,
But only if he travels on the way with you.

IRISH, NINTH CENTURY

powered theological seminary. In 490 St Enda had founded Killeany on Inishmore, the largest island, and here he trained many of the next generation of scholar-monks, including St Ciarán and St Finnian of Moville. The patchwork of stone-walls which divide its rock into a myriad of tiny fields merge with an astounding array of prehistoric, early Christian and medieval stone structures: ring forts, promontory forts, beehive huts, monastic raths, oratories, crosses and burial grounds. One of these, Templebrecan, includes the early gravemarkers of the 'VII Romani', seven unknown Roman saints. Could it be that even the inhabitants of Rome had once acknowledged, and sought out, the value of the learning and spirituality to be found in this religious training-ground, a desert on the very edge of the world?

The wander-lust of the Irish saints, the impulse towards *peregrinatio* and, no doubt, the ravages of famine and plague at home, carried them far afield. Their influence upon Scotland, Wales, Cornwall and Brittany was widespread, as we have seen, and often reciprocal. Many won renown far afield in Europe, being particularly valued for their learning (the scholars at the Carolingian court including Irishmen such as John Scottus Eriugena and Sedulius Scottus). Their writings fuse Celtic learning with that of the Graeco-Roman past, forming a new early medieval rhetoric in which they became the heirs of leading early Christian poets such as Sedulius, Prudentius and Venantius Fortunatus, as demonstrated in this Latin poem composed by Sedulius Scottus in the mid ninth century:

I read and write and teach, philosophy peruse.
I eat and freely drink, with rhymes invoke the muse,
I call on heaven's throne both night and day,
Snoring I sleep, or stay awake and pray.
And sin and fault inform each act I plan:
Ah! Christ and Mary, pity this miserable man.

Pilgrimage also became increasingly popular during the period. A note of caution in pursuing it for its own sake was sounded by the nun Samthann who issued the following challenge to a teacher named Dairchellach:

'I wish to go across the sea in pilgrimage', he said. She replied: 'If God could not be found on this side of the sea we would indeed journey across. Since, however, God is nigh unto all who call upon Him, we are under no obligation to cross the sea. The kingdom of Heaven can be reached from every land'.

For such free spirits could indeed pose a problem and some commentators were disparaging in their treatment of the *gyrovagues* – Irish itinerant hermits who could not settle anywhere and who were almost viewed as tramps, 'slaves to their own wills and gross appetites'. The exploits of the Irish missionaries caught the popular imagination, however, and one of the most widely copied and translated texts from early Christian Ireland was the *Navigation of St Brendan*. A romance, it was composed in the eighth or ninth century and loosely based upon the life of St Brendan the Navigator (died 575). In this his motivation is summed up as follows:

We went on our pilgrimage
At the blast of the whistling wind
To obtain forgiveness of our sins
There is the cause of asking.

He was educated by Erc, bishop of Kerry, and went on to found many houses, including Clonfert and Ardfert. His voyages took him around the western coast of Ireland and, perhaps, to Scotland (where Adomnan relates that he visited Columba on Hinba), Wales, Brittany and even across the Atlantic. This epic voyage from the *Navigation* was memorably reconstructed by Tim Severin as 'The Brendan Voyage'; the *curragh* he sailed can still be seen at the Cragganauen archaeology park near Limerick, along with a *crannóg* and a *rath* from the early Christian period.

In the *Navigation*, Brendan and his followers set sail into the unknown, searching for a blissful otherworld synonymous with the Christian heaven, the antique Elysium and the pagan Celtic *Tír na nÓg*. The ancient Celtic bards often grouped their tales into genres, one of which was 'voyages'. In the Christianized Navigation the pagan voyager-chieftain Bran gives way to the monastic father Brendan, in a seamless cultural transition that is representative of the process of conversion in Ireland.

CHAPTER 6

The Conversion of the English to Christianity

ST AUGUSTINE AND THE ROMAN MISSION TO ENGLAND

*Non Angli,
sed angeli
(not Angles,
but angels)*

POPE GREGORY THE GREAT

In 597 Columba departed Iona on that final journey which is common to us all. That same year the pagan Germanic king of Kent, Ethelberht, journeyed from his hall in Canterbury to Ebbsfleet in the Isle of Thanet on the Kentish coast. There he had agreed to meet Augustine, the ambassador of a new religion and of a potential new web of relationships and trading contacts. He was not taking any chances, however, for this was a shaman whose powers were as yet unknown, and so he would only encounter him in the open, lest he should be ensnared by some spell. The elderly patrician he encountered, St Augustine (died c.604), would have been equally wary, concerned that he and his little band of followers would be cut down by the king's bodyguard before their interpreters had had a chance to convey the purpose of their visit. They had doubtless been regaled with tales of the uncivilized Anglo-Saxons over the dinner tables of Gaul and had tried to turn back several times, but were held to their purpose by the mastermind behind their mission – Pope Gregory the Great.

The well-educated Augustine had been one of Gregory's monastic brethren, and was latterly prior of St Andrew's on the Celian Hill in Rome before becoming the reluctant recipient of his spiritual overlord's charge to travel to Britain. By the time he arrived, Augustine was accompanied by forty monks, some of them from Gaul. They would have been an imposing sight, as they knew that the initial visual impression could make the difference between life and death. They therefore no doubt displayed the painted icons, vestments, metalwork reliquaries and books in bejewelled treasure bindings that they had brought with them, and which they subsequently carried before them as they entered the old Roman city of Canterbury, where king and court now squatted amidst the 'work of giants'. Ethelberht accorded them permission to remain in his territory, to give him and his people a chance to assess the 'Good News' that they purported to bring. In so doing he bought himself time to make the transition from pagan warleader to Christian monarch without alienating his people by appearing to reject their age-old values and traditions.

One cannot resist speculating that the initial superstitious posturing on the part of this astute ruler was more for the benefit of his thegns and pagan priestly advisors than out of fear for his personal safety. For Ethelberht had successfully petitioned one of the Merovingian kings of neighbouring Gaul for the hand of his daughter, Bertha. One condition of the marriage contract was that she should be accorded tolerance to follow her Christian faith; and her entourage included her confessor, Liudhard. It is unlikely that she did not impart any knowledge of Christianity to her husband, or that it was not still practised (even if surreptitiously) by some of the native post-Roman inhabitants of Kent (who may be the unusual semi-free class of 'laets' referred to in Ethelberht's law code). Women played an important role in the conversion process, often embracing the faith ahead of their menfolk, and – especially when of royal or aristocratic status themselves – they could serve as guarantors of an entrée into court and society, as was the case with Bertha.

A chapel, now St Martin's Church, was granted to the queen for the performance of her rites and devotions. It was a little Roman structure of brick and stone set atop the rising ground that carried the road eastwards out of Canterbury. This road passed through the ancient Roman cemeteries in which stood the ruinous walls of ancient mausolea and chapels, such as the brick-built St Pancras, which still stands amidst the ruins of the medieval abbey to this day. The stone foot basins with their decoration of carved arcades which have been assembled to form the chapel's font may be those used by the Augustinian mission for baptisms. The early rite consisted of the pouring of water over the head of the baptismal candidate – who during the conversion period was more often an adult than a babe in arms – whilst they stood in a pool or basin. The spoons used to pour the water gave rise to the custom of bestowing a silver spoon upon the person being baptized, and of the phrase 'born with a silver spoon in the mouth'. A small gold pendant depicting Liudhard was found, many centuries later, in the churchyard of this chapel, part of which can still be discerned today in the surrounding chancel fabric of St Martin's church. The church itself was significantly extended by Augustine and his disciples as the base for their mission (see page 32). It was built *more romanum*, of reused Roman masonry and brick coursing, in basilican fashion.

Another Romano-British chapel was enshrined by the missionaries within a slightly larger church at Stone-by-Faversham in Kent, its ruined walls now a precious obstacle to the ploughed furrows of a field. A larger, imposing church was built during the early seventh century at Reculver. It survived intact until the nineteenth century when the misguided mother of the incumbent led the villagers there to torch it, intending her son to receive a more fitting modern church. Its lengthy, lofty nave was flanked by rows of porticus chapels and contained a column carved in the fashion of Trajan's Column and other Roman triumphal monuments, which depicted scenes from the life of Christ, including the turning of water into wine at Cana, and the Ascension. This important sculpture may even date from Augustine's time, as may a Gospelbook penned in a script favoured in the scriptoria of Gregory's Rome, which contained a page of images again depicting the life of Christ. The images are arranged in registers like a comic strip, perhaps resembling an altarpiece of the day, and there is a miniature portraying St Luke as an author–scribe, accompanied by his half-length calf symbol – modelled upon the mosaics of early Christian Rome, such as that at Santa Pudenziana and that in the basilica of Sts Cosmas and Damian in the Forum. This book, known as the St Augustine Gospels, was certainly in England by the eighth century, when notes were written in its margins in an English script, and it is thought to have been brought to Canterbury by Augustine. Now at Corpus Christi College, Cambridge, it is still used at the enthronement of the Archbishop of Canterbury in the cathedral that stands on the site of that established by Augustine, near to the royal palace. Outside the city walls, closer to St Martin's, Augustine founded an abbey, initially dedicated to Sts Peter and Paul and later named St Augustine's. Here he lies interred, alongside Ethelberht and Bertha. He also established a bishopric at Rochester in 604, occupied initially by one of a band of assistants sent to help him in 601, St Justus (died 627).

The St Augustine Gospels, Cambridge, Corpus Christi College. St Luke miniature from a Gospelbook traditionally associated with St Augustine's mission.

Pope Gregory, having conducted research in the archives of Rome, had drawn up a blueprint for the conversion of the Anglo-Saxons. Their pagan status made them virgin territory, ripe for evangelization and organization, and a potentially more straightforward prospect than the conversion of those 'barbarian' kingdoms that had already converted to the Arian heresy, such as Ostrogothic Italy and Visigothic Spain. The latter successfully made the transition to Catholic orthodoxy, whilst the promising Ostrogothic state remained resolutely Arian and perished, largely due to lack of collaboration from the indigenous Italian intelligentsia, both clerical and lay.

Gregory's advice and instructions to Augustine can be traced through their correspondence. Augustine was made archbishop, and was to have independence of the bishops of Gaul, without exercising authority over them. This alienated his nearest neighbours and source of support, and Gregory hinted that he might wish to adopt Gallican customs in his new See. Intending to revive the administrative structure of the late Roman Church in Britain, Gregory envisaged London as the seat of the archbishopric of the southern province, and York as that of the northern, each with twelve suffragan bishops. This ambitious scheme was never fully realized, but was a landmark in ecclesiastical planning and organization in the West. But London lay in East-Saxon territory, and although Ethelberht held sway as the overlord (or 'bretwalda' as Bede later termed it) of many of the other Anglo-Saxon rulers, he was evidently unable to guarantee the same level of safety and success there that he could in Canterbury. Political expediency therefore led Augustine to site the centre of his archdiocese in Canterbury.

Augustine is also thought to have founded the church of Old St Pancras in

Sutton Hoo

The helmet from the great Sutton Hoo ship burial, early seventh century. A family heirloom from Denmark, perhaps worn by King Redwald of East Anglia.

Burial ground of the early Germanic kings of East Anglia

And then they laid their dear lord,
The giver of rings, deep within the ship
By the mast in majesty; many treasures
And adornments from far and wide were gathered there.

(Beowulf)

The skeleton of the ship in which the main royal burial lay, during excavation in 1939.

The ceremonial burial ground of the Wuffing kings has been partially excavated. It is sited close to their woodland palace of Rendlesham, and to what became the important Anglo-Saxon town of Ipswich, on a spur of land that commands a sweeping view of the strategic inlet of the River Deben and which could be clearly seen by all who approached it. This is called Sutton Hoo.

In the 1930s one of the largest mounds in this pagan cemetery was first excavated and revealed a royal burial that has fired the imagination of those interested in the period ever since. The shadowy skeleton of the hull of an Anglo-Saxon ship emerged against the sandy soil, its iron rivets still intact and the ribs of its planks still visible as darker soil, although acidity had long since eaten the wood away. Amidships was a timber room covering the burial, fully equipped with the trappings of worldly status, in readiness to ensure the continued comfort and authority of the deceased in the afterlife. These opulent grave-goods were designed to emphasize the international links of diplomacy and trade

Sutton Hoo burial mounds, Suffolk
This mound was restored to its original height in 1993, following th
excavation of a prince's burial.

Shoulder clasps, made in Anglo-Saxon England in the early seventh century, and modelled on Roman parade armour. The intersecting boars on their sides, the animal interlace and the carpet-like panels resemble later manuscripts, such as the Book of Durrow.

Hanging bowl of Celtic
manufacture, its decoration
including crosses and a fish,
perhaps indicating Christian use
as an ablution bowl.

London, where a dedication stone in the altar is dated to his period. Its location outside of the ancient city of London might suggest that it marked the site of a Roman mausoleum or martyrium in an extramural cemetery. One of his followers, St Mellitus (died 624), did however found a cathedral in London in 604, dedicated to St Paul, apostle to the Gentiles. This was built at the command of King Ethelberht on the site of what is now Sir Christopher Wren's baroque masterpiece, St Paul's – the first newly and specifically built cathedral of Anglicanism. St Mellitus's cathedral crowned the dominant hill within the Roman city of Londinium and may earlier have been the seat of Restitutus, who was documented as bishop of London in 314. Prior to this, it may have acted as a focal point, and may have witnessed pagan Celtic and Roman religious activity. Ludgate hill, which forms the ceremonial approach to St Paul's imposing western portico, preserves the recollection of the Celtic deity Lugh (King Lud) after whom the city may have been named.

Mellitus, a Roman nobleman turned priest, headed a group of missionaries dispatched by Pope Gregory in 601 to reinforce Augustine. Correspondence between Mellitus and Gregory preserves a new set of instructions concerning the stance to be adopted towards paganism, and represents a papal rethinking of his original instructions to Augustine. Part of this dialogue involved Mellitus pointing out that the people had religion(s) already, and seeking guidance on how to proceed. Gregory's wisdom and growing sensitivity to the processes of integration and transformation is illumined by his response. In essence, this was to suggest that if there was an appropriate religious-festival-cum-party taking place, the Christian missionaries should join in, adopting the timing of a traditional pagan festival as a Christian one. Hence the close correspondence in timing between many of the ancient Celtic festivals and landmarks in the Christian year. Gregory also advised that if a place had been the focus of faith for generations it should not necessarily be destroyed (although any idols it contained might be), but should be embraced as a Christian place of worship. Thus the siting of Christianity within the continuum of world history, and its assimilation therein, could be presented as part of the ongoing revelation of God's masterplan. This meant that the practices and beliefs of a society's ancestors need not be condemned out of hand and their prospects of salvation need not be denied when Christianity was accepted by their descendants.

The conversion of Kent progressed rapidly after King Ethelberht's baptism, along with many of his courtiers, in 601. His overlordship was vital in making inroads into certain areas of the patchwork of petty kingdoms which had been carved out by the Germanic migrants since they began arriving in Britain in greater numbers, and which had assumed ascendancy over the native Romano-British populace from around 550 onwards. The Tribal Hidage, a ninth-century tax/tribute assessment document which may originally have been compiled for the rulers of Mercia, still records the existence of a multitude of peoples who have long since been forgotten, such as the Gywre, the Maegonsaetan and the Hwicce. For this was a world in which big fish ate little fish, and the identities of individual groups were lost as they were subsumed into larger territories. The most important Anglo-Saxon

> *... There in the harbour stood the ring-prowed ship, The prince's vessel, icy, eager to sail; And then they laid their dear lord, The Giver of rings, deep within the ship...*
>
> BEOWULF

kingdoms to emerge were Kent, Wessex, Sussex, Essex, East Anglia, Mercia and Northumbria – composed of its northern kingdom of Bernicia focusing on the royal citadels of Yeavering and Bamburgh, and its southern kingdom, Deira, centred upon York. Bede claims that the Kentish settlers were Jutish; those of East Anglia, Northumbria and Mercia ('people of the Marches') were Angles; and the rest were Saxons. Grave goods excavated from Migration period burials indicate that the pattern of ethnicity was in fact more complex, and it is likely that many different Germanic peoples from southern Scandinavia, Germany and the Netherlands coalesced in the transit camps of Frisia into what were sometimes mixed groups, which derived any group identity from the ethnicity of their leaders.

Essex and East Anglia

Ethelberht encouraged other client kings to follow his example, standing as Godfather to King Saeberht of Essex and to Redwald, the up-and-coming ruler of East Anglia whose power would soon eclipse that of Kent (see feature on Sutton Hoo). In the *Historia Ecclesiastica* – our main source of detailed (if highly structured and carefully selected) information concerning the conversion of the English – Bede laments the superficial nature of Redwald's conversion in the following terms (when discussing subsequent events of 627):

Redwald had in fact long before this received Christian baptism in Kent, but to no good purpose; for on his return home his wife and certain perverse advisers persuaded him to apostatize from the true Faith. So his last state was worse than the first: for, like the ancient Samaritans, he tried to serve both Christ and the ancient gods, and he had in the same shrine an altar for the holy Sacrifice of Christ side by side with a small altar on which victims were offered to devils. Aldwulf, king of that province, who lived into our own times, testifies that this shrine was still standing in his day and that he had seen it when a boy. This King Redwald was a man of noble descent but ignoble in his actions: he was son of Tytila, and grandson of Wuffa, after whom all kings of the East Angles are called Wuffings.

Many other pagan burials have been excavated in England, although none as breathtaking as Sutton Hoo, with its parallels to the famous ship burial and the treasure-mounds of the epic poem Beowulf:

Beowulf

…There in the harbour stood the ring-prowed ship,
The prince's vessel, icy, eager to sail;
And then they laid their dear lord,
The giver of rings, deep within the ship

By the mast in majesty; many treasures
And adornments from far and wide were gathered there.
I have never heard of a ship equipped
More handsomely with weapons and war-gear,
Swords and corslets; on his breast
Lay countless treasures that were to travel far
With him into the waves' domain.
They gave him great ornaments, gifts
No less magnificent than those men had given him
Who long ago had sent him alone,
Child as he was, across the stretch of the seas.
Then high above his head they placed
A golden banner and let the waves bear him,
Bequeathed him to the sea; their hearts were grieving,
Their minds mourning. Mighty men
Beneath the heavens, rulers in the hall,
Cannot say who received that cargo…
…A newly built barrow
Stood ready on a headland which overlooked
The sea, protected by the hazards of access.
To this barrow the protector of rings brought the heirlooms…
…Then the hoard was raided
And plundered, and that unhappy man
Was granted his prayer. His lord examined
The ancient work of smiths for the first time…
…The warden of the hoard
Prowled up and down, anxious to find
The man who had pillaged it while he slept.
Breathing fire and filled with fury,
He circled the outside of the earth mound
Again and again; but there was no one
In that barren place…
…Much against his will,
He conducted them to the entrance of the cave,
An earth-hall full of filigree work
And fine adornments, close by the sea…

Amongst the most prestigious burials were the mound at Taplow (Buckinghamshire) and that recently discovered on the outskirts of Southend at Prittlewell (Essex). The latter included beautiful blue glassware made in southern England, Coptic vessels carrying depictions of mounted saints (such as St Menas), weapons, jewellery, a reliquary buckle and continental coins. On the eyes of the corpse had been laid crosses of gold foil – a Christian burial practice from northern

Italian Lombardy. The Christian orientation of this important burial, probably that of an East-Saxon royal, is less ambiguous than that at Sutton Hoo. Many of the early Anglo-Saxon cemeteries of the seventh century that have so far been excavated have contained grave-goods: swords, knives, jewellery, and in the case of women, small workboxes attached to the belt and containing needlework or cosmetic implements and chatalains for suspending keys from belts. It is interesting and telling to note that it was only recently demonstrated by a woman historian that while references in the early Anglo-Saxon law codes show that penalties for a woman who was *lokborra* (lock-bearing) were harsher than those for other women, this was due not, as male historians had thought, to the fact that they were virginal maidens with long flowing locks of hair, but rather to the fact that they were the bearers of the keys to the household and functioned as estate managers from whom probity was especially expected. For Anglo-Saxon women could have equal legal status to their male counterparts and enjoyed the best legal rights of any women in the world until the 1930s.

ABOVE: Gold crosses placed upon the eyelids of the deceased, in Christian Lombardic fashion. From the recently discovered burial at Prittlewell, Essex.

Burials accompanied by artefacts have generally been assumed to be pagan, although many of them have contained objects with a Christian association, notably a series of cross-shaped pendants and brooches (such as the magnificent Kingston Down brooch, see page 126). This begs the question of when a cross is a pleasing geometric design and when it is a symbol of faith. If the latter, did its wearing betoken genuine commitment to Christian life or could it merely denote nominal allegiance or an exotic fashion statement, as is often the case with jewellery featuring crosses today? One of the most resplendent of these pendants, the Wilton cross, consists of a gold cross with garnet inlay (a traditional technique of Germanic metalwork) with a Byzantine coin set at its centre, displaying a cross on a stepped base which has been set upside down within the pendant's mount. This was either because the coin was purely decorative and its imagery not meant to be read, or so that the stepped cross could be more easily contemplated as an object of devotion by the wearer when he or she looked down. The assumption that such accompanied burials could not be Christian may need to be qualified, however. One has only to consider the rich deposits of relics and gifts deposited over the centuries in the coffin that was made to contain the incorrupt remains of St Cuthbert in 698 – including his gold and garnet pectoral cross – to realize that important Christian leaders could also be buried with material objects without entailing the belief that they literally needed such things in the afterlife.

BELOW: The Wilton Cross, from the second quarter of the seventh century. Anglo-Saxon gold and garnet cross, with a Byzantine coin (solidus) of Heraclius (613–32) depicting a stepped cross set upside down, perhaps so that the wearer could view it.

Redwald's son, Earpwald, remained staunchly pagan until persuaded (or commanded) to convert by his overlord, King Edwin of Northumbria – the next of Bede's bretwaldas – in 627. Perhaps as a result he was soon killed by a pagan challenger for power, Ricbert, and East

Anglia apostatized for three years until Earpwald's brother, Sigebert, succeeded in 630. During his brother's reign he had gone into exile in Gaul, where he became a devout and learned Christian. In order to assist him in converting his recalcitrant realm, Sigebert recruited a Frankish bishop, the Burgundian St Felix (died 647), who was eager for the task and was appointed by Archbishop Honorius of Canterbury. Felix, whose own Burgundian people were Germanic settlers and to whom Anglo-Saxon society may not have seemed as alien as it did to the Roman missionaries, established his See at Dunwich on the coast (which is rapidly eroding into the sea, its burials sadly exposed in the cliff face). He also founded a monastery at Soham, where he was buried until his relics were later translated to Ramsey Abbey. This collaboration between ruler, archbishop and bishop was a fruitful one and Felix 'reaped a rich harvest of believers', ruling the East Anglian province for seventeen years and passing away peacefully there. He was assisted in his mission by a band of Irish *peregrini* led by St Fursey (died 650), who arrived in East Anglia around 630 and were welcomed by King Sigebert. The king gave them the old fortress of Cnobheresburg, thought convincingly to have been the Roman Saxon shore-fort of Burgh Castle outside Great Yarmouth, as well as adjacent land on which to found a monastery. This was the first recorded Irish mission to the English. The trajectory of their exile for Christ suggests that their intention may always have been to head for the continent, and this was soon precipitated by Sigebert's death at the hands of an invading Mercian army. Once in Gaul, Fursey was given land by the Merovingian mayor of Neustria, Erchinoald, on which to found the monastery of Lagny-sur-Marne. He was buried at Péronne (Peronna Scottorum) in Picardy, which became the centre of his cult and was popularized by Bede's graphic account of a vision in which he was shown heaven and hell. This genre was reflected in the visions of St Brendan the Navigator and of the Mercian Fenland hermit St Guthlac, and was to mould Dante's *Divina Commedia*.

St Cuthbert's pectoral cross, made of gold, garnets and shell, discovered in his coffin. It had seen plenty of use and had been repaired. Anglo-Saxon, second half of the seventh century.

CHRISTIAN KINGS AND THE PAGAN BACKLASH

Sigebert wished to share with his people the benefits he had enjoyed in Gaul, and founded 'a school for the education of boys in the study of letters', for which Felix provided him with 'teachers and masters according to the practice of Canterbury'. (He thereby pre-empted the schools founded for the sons of the laity by King Alfred the Great during the late ninth century – the origins of the grammar school.) As Sigebert's devotions grew ever deeper, he relinquished more of the affairs of state to his kinsman Egric, before finally becoming a monk in one of the monasteries he had founded, 'devoting his energies to winning an everlasting kingdom'. This phenomenon of kings in holy orders (*in clericatu*) subsequently achieved a level of popularity in both England

and Ireland, sometimes at the ruler's own behest and sometimes representing a de facto deposition and enforced retirement. At this early stage in the process of social transformation it posed a threat to the very fabric of society and to traditional expectations of leadership. Herein lay the crux of the potential confrontation between pagan and Christian morality, before church and state together refined the concept of 'righteous warfare' and rulers could present themselves as literal as well as spiritual *miles Christi* (soldiers of Christ). When the pagan Mercians attacked in 635 the East Anglians asked Sigebert to lead them into battle to bolster morale:

When he refused, they dragged him out of the monastery regardless of his protests, and took him into battle with them in the hope that their men would be less likely to panic or think of flight if they were under the eye of one who had once been a gallant and distinguished commander. But, mindful of his monastic vows, Sigebert, surrounded by a well-armed host, refused to carry anything more than a stick, and when the heathen charged, both he and King Egric were killed and the army scattered.

The Kingston Down brooch. Anglo-Saxon, early seventh century. Its design features a cross, although Christian meaning cannot be proven.

Whatever the opinion of his secular contemporaries, King Sigebert certainly displayed an absolute commitment to his newly acquired Christian principles.

These could of course be variously interpreted. For example, bishops Mellitus and Justus had viewed discretion as the better part of valour when, following King Ethelberht's death and the temporary apostatization of Kent and Essex in 616, they fled to Gaul, deciding 'that it would be better for all of them to return to their own country and serve God in freedom, rather that to remain impotently among heathen who had rejected the faith' (Bede, *Historia Ecclesiastica*, Book II). They had fallen from favour, having opposed the marriage of Ethelberht's son and successor, Eadbald, to his stepmother. They had also refused to administer communion to the pagan sons of the late King Sabert of Essex, who had demanded to receive the same 'white bread' as their father, but without sharing his faith. Augustine's successor as archbishop, Laurence, had planned to follow them abroad, but having delayed to await the outcome of the volatile political situation in southern England (in response to a good telling off and scourging by St Peter in his dreams), he was able to convert the new king of Kent, Eadbald. Mellitus and Justus were recalled. Justus returned to Rochester, but London refused to relinquish its reinstated pagan priests, leaving Mellitus to become the third archbishop on Laurence's death in 619. Towards the end of his life his courage was certainly not lacking when, despite suffering from painful gout, he had his litter laid in front of the flames of a fire which was engulfing Canterbury, deterring it with his prayers and encouraging others to fight it too.

GREGORY THE GREAT, THE MISSIONARY POPE

From the preceding episodes it will be clear that the initial Roman mission was by no means an immediate and unqualified success, and its course was precarious and perilous. Pope Gregory (died 604), 'apostle of the English', had not lived to see his masterplan implemented, although significant headway had been made. During his thirteen years in office Gregory made a crucial contibution to the rise of the papacy, creating a western sphere of authority upon which its power rested. The wealthy son of a Roman senator, he entered the civil service, but in 573 decided to sell his properties in order to found seven monasteries, six in Sicily and the seventh in Rome – St Andrew's on the Celian Hill, where he himself became a monk. Gregory's own inclination was towards an austere monastic lifestyle, but he was pulled out of the cloister to serve within the church hierarchy and spent several years as papal ambassador to Byzantium. His disillusionment with the Eastern empire may have contributed to his viewing monasticism as the solution to social reform and organization within the West. His interest in the conversion of the English was personal. Bede recounted the oft cited story of Gregory being entranced by the beauty of some Anglo-Saxon slaves offered for sale, whom he described as 'Non Angli, sed angeli' ('Not Angles, but angels') and freed them, conceiving a plan to liberate their race from paganism. He had intended to lead the mission himself, conducting much of the preliminary correspondence and preparing the way, but was called upon to become pope and was immediately confronted by a host of challenges, from plague and famine to Lombardic invasion and Byzantine ecclesiastical dominance. As a result he became the de facto heir of imperial authority in the West, installing governors in the ancient Italian towns and concluding a treaty with the Lombards that excluded the representative of Byzantium in Italy, the exarch of Ravenna. His continued interest ensured that the newborn English Church enjoyed a particularly close relationship with the papacy – and that its affairs remained under close scrutiny.

Gregory's influential and prolific writings notably include: his extensive correspondence (of which an incredible 854 letters survive); homilies on the Gospels; his *Moralia in Job* (a commentary on the Book of Job, which he wrote whilst in Constantinople at the suggestion of Leander, brother of the influential Visigothic Christian scholar Isidore of Seville); his *Dialogues* recounting the lives of the saints; and his *Cura Pastoralis* ('Pastoral Care'). This last became the blueprint for the pastoral outreach of the western episcopate, and was translated into Old English by King Alfred the Great as part of his attempt to resuscitate English church and society in the aftermath of pagan Viking invasion. He became the hero of leading English scholars such as Aldhelm and Bede, whose own work he influenced and who proclaimed him 'apostle of the English' and their special patron. His first biography was written in England at Whitby. Gregory himself, however, preferred the title of 'servant of the servants of God'. Through his accessible work the young western churches became increasingly familiar with the theology of Church Fathers such as Origen, Augustine of Hippo and Ambrose of Milan. They were also introduced to coenobitic (communal) monasticism (with a tinge of nascent Benedictine influence from Benedict of Nursia's 'Little Rule for beginners') and a coherent Catholic doctrine and liturgy. He also pointed the way towards the western contribution to the beauty of worship, fostering church music, especially the form of chant that has become known as Gregorian plainsong (adapted from at least four earlier forms of liturgical chant).

Moreover, Gregory contributed to the international debate on idolatry, in favour of the use of images. Within the Judaic, Christian and Islamic faiths there was hot debate over whether it was acceptable to depict the divine in human form. Emperor Charlemagne and his advisors would still be discussing it at the opening of the ninth century, whilst Byzantium lapsed into a period of iconoclasm throughout much of the seventh and eighth centuries in which many wonderful works of art were destroyed. Gregory countered the iconoclastic tendencies of Serenus, bishop of Marseilles when he wrote to him around 600 , censuring his destruction of images on the basis that:

It is one thing to adore a picture, another to learn what is to be adored through the history told by the picture. What Scripture presents to readers, a picture presents to the gaze of the unlearned. For in it even the ignorant see what they ought to follow, in it the illiterate read.

This effectively opened the way for the amazing didactic art of the early Middle Ages, which made such a contribution to stimulating Christian worship and to deepening people's familiarity and understanding of the Old and New Testament and their messages.

Gregory was also celebrated in the East and in Ireland, where he was given a royal pedigree and attributed with authoring the apocryphal *Liber de Gradibus Coeli* – this despite his championing of papal authority over their divergent traditions. On another front, he supported Leander of Seville in his successful attempts to convert the Visigoths and Suevi from Arianism to Catholic orthodoxy, also importing into Rome Leander's practice of singing the affirming Nicene Creed during the mass. Columbanus must have hit a nerve when he wrote to Popes Gregory and Boniface IV, and his letter may have strengthened the papal resolve to ally the Anglo-Saxon mission as closely as possible to the orthodox churches of Gaul, rather than allowing it to become contaminated by the irregular practices of the Irish and British churches.

RELATIONS BETWEEN THE BRITISH AND THE ANGLO-SAXONS

The early British Penitentials of Wales include stringent penances to be performed for the treachery of consorting with the Germanic invaders, and especially for serving as their guide within British territory. It has therefore been assumed that the British church shunned any attempt to evangelize the Anglo-Saxons. This impression was reinforced by English, largely pro-Roman, accounts of the conversion in sources such as the works of Bede, composed in Northumbria during the early eighth century, and the Anglo-Saxon Chronicle, initially compiled partly from earlier annals in Wessex in the late ninth century. In 731 Bede wrote in his *Historia Ecclesiastica*:

The Britons for the most part have a national hatred for the English, and uphold their own bad customs against the true Easter of the Catholic Church; however, they are opposed by the power of God and man alike, and are powerless to obtain what they want. For, although in part they are independent, they have been brought in part under subjection to the English.

Therein lies the key to Anglo-British relations. They were uncomfortable neighbours who could not overthrow one another and had not found a workable *modus vivendi*. As is so often the case in such circumstances, faith became a convenient cloak for other differences.

This was probably not inevitably the case, however. There is evidence indicating a measure of intermarriage, crossing the geo-political boundaries of faith and ethnicity. And by no means all of the indigenous populace of Britain emigrated or perished in the face of Germanic incursions: some British kingdoms such as Strathclyde, Rheged and Elmet survived into the seventh century and preserved their faith alongside their voracious pagan Germanic neighbours. The introduction of Christianity to Northumbria is usually attributed to a member of the Roman mission, St Paulinus of York (died 644), but an alternative legend ascribes the conversion of King Edwin of Northumbria and his court to the British bishop Rum/Rhun.

The letter that Pope Gregory sent to Augustine along with the pallium in 601 made provision for the creation of two Metropolitans, their archdioceses based on London and York. After Augustine's death their order of precedence was to fluctuate, depending upon seniority of consecration, and they were to make joint decisions. Augustine was initially to exercise overall authority over the bishops to be consecrated by the Metropolitans and over the British bishops – hence Canterbury's rise to primacy. There was evidently no intention of perpetuating any racial divides, so what went wrong? Augustine's words and example were to encourage them all in 'a pattern of right belief and holy life' (Bede, *Historia Ecclesiastica*). The British church, as we have seen, had been steadfast in preserving and nurturing the Christian faith it had originally received under Roman rule. It had been abandoned by the imperial and ecclesiastical authorities and was left to look to its own survival. It had flourished, despite all the odds, and had played an important role in the conversion of Ireland, Pictland and Brittany, providing training, learning and worthy role models. Some of its representatives are likely to have transgressed secular legal rulings concerning non-fraternization with the Germanic enemy, in order to attempt to save their souls. Reunion with Rome was by no means out of the question. Sadly the collision of cultures and personalities prevailed.

In 603, with King Ethelberht's help, Augustine summoned the British bishops of the nearest province to a conference at 'Augustine's Oak' on the border of the Mercian kingdom of the Hwicce (of Worcestershire and Herefordshire) and Wessex, probably in Gloucestershire. This 'lengthy and fruitless' encounter began with Augustine inviting them to join him in Catholic unity and assist in the conversion of the English. When neither 'the advice nor the censures' of he or his companions immediately persuaded them to abandon their ancient and learned customs, Augustine assumed something of the role of magician that Ethelberht had first suspected him of. He demanded combat by miracle, arranging for a blind Englishman to be brought in (was this, perhaps, part and parcel of Ethelberht's assistance in the matter?). Augustine then healed him after the prayers of the British bishops had failed. They accordingly acknowledged that his was the way of righteousness, but requested permission to consult with their people before relinquishing their traditions and independence. This would, of course, have been tantamount to placing themselves politically under Ethelberht's sway, becoming at best tributary provinces. There was much at stake, and they would need the support of their rulers and people, as well as religious consent. Their suggestion of a fuller second conference was, under such circumstances, remarkably conciliatory.

Before the conference, the seven bishops and many sages were sent as the British delegates, mostly from the monastery of Bangor in north Wales, then governed by Abbot Dinoot. Bede relates that the monastery was so large that it was divided into seven sections under individual heads, comprising 300 monks each who supported themselves by manual labour – a monastic university with over 2,000 students. The British delegates had sought the counsel of a hermit venerated for his wisdom, who advised 'If he is a man of God, follow him.' But how might this be gauged on so short an acquaintance? Celtic etiquette was an ancient and well-regulated affair, so they decided to trust to the tried and tested indicator of good manners – surely not too much to ask of a newcomer to their land, the place where they had tended the flame of faith in the face of pagan occupation – the same pagan forces with whom Augustine had now allied himself. The hermit counselled:

Our Lord says, Take My yoke upon you and learn from Me, for I am meek and lowly in heart; therefore if Augustine is meek and lowly in heart, it shows that he bears the yoke of Christ himself, and offers it to you. But if he is haughty and unbending, then he is not of God, and we should not listen to him.

Bede, *Historia Ecclesiastica*

They therefore agreed to arrive after Augustine's party, to see whether he would courteously rise to greet them. He did not.

Things went downhill fast. Augustine advanced three sticking points necessary for conciliation to occur: that the British should keep Easter at the correct time, determined by Rome; that baptism should be conducted according to Rome's rites; and that they should participate in the evangelization of their Germanic aggressors. They refused to acknowledge his archiepiscopal authority, fearing that if he so slighted them now he would have even less regard for them once they submitted to him. The Roman patrician thereupon offered them an ultimatum: peace with fellow-Christians or war with enemies. This was an astute observation, but one that would have appeared a threat, backed as he was by the Kentish king and thegns. The pattern of Anglo-British relations over the next three centuries was determined by warfare and border raids, as the kingdoms of Mercia (the Marches, or borderlands) and Northumbria encroached ever deeper into British territory.

The level of racial and sectarian animosity between British and English was high (recalling many twentieth-century geo-political conflicts, in which differences of faith became a convenient rallying point for ethnic and territorial rivalries). It is woefully revealed by the usually benign Englishman, Bede, when he went on from his account of the conference to relate how Augustine's prophecy came to pass. At the Battle of Chester in 615, King Ethelfrith of Northumbria ordered the slaughter of some 1,200 unarmed monks from Bangor who had assembled to pray for a

The Britons, who had refused to share their own knowledge of the Christian faith with the English, continue even now, when the English nation believes rightly and is fully instructed in the doctrines of the Catholic Faith, to be obdurate and crippled by their errors, going about with their head improperly tonsured, and keeping Christ's solemnity without fellowship with the Christian Church.

BEDE, *HISTORIA ECCLESIASTICA*, BOOK V

British victory, declaring that their prayers represented militant aggression. The morale of their army collapsed, enabling a decisive English victory (Bede, *Historia Ecclesiastica*).

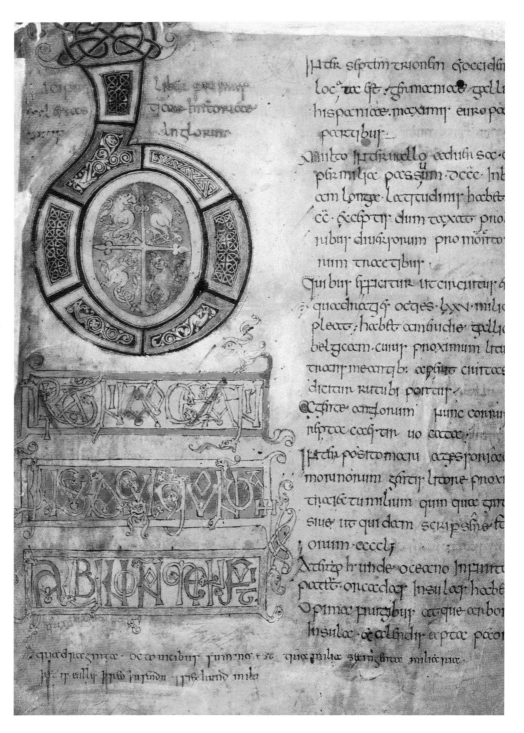

Opening of Book I of Bede's *Historia Ecclesiastica*. From a copy made at Canterbury during the early ninth century – the 'Tiberius Bede', from which the Tiberius group of Southern English manuscripts takes its name.

The Battle for Orthodoxy – the Start of the Easter Controversy

After Augustine had failed to win the British, his successor as archbishop, Laurence, turned his attention to their partners in unorthodoxy, the Irish. He, along with bishops Mellitus of London and Justus of Rochester, wrote them a letter in 605. This is worth quoting, to appreciate its tone (he wrote a similar letter of 'dignified' tone to the British, to no avail):

To our dear brothers the bishops and abbots throughout Irish lands:
from Laurence, Mellitus and Justus, servants of the servants of God.

When, in accordance with its custom, which holds good throughout the world, the apostolic see sent us to the western lands to preach the gospel to the heathen peoples, we came to the island of Britain. Until we realized the true situation, we had a high regard for the devotion both of the Britons and of the Irish, believing that they followed the customs of the universal Church. On further acquaintance with the Britons, we imagined that the Irish must be better. We have now, however, learned through Bishop Dagan on his visit to this island, and through Abbot Columbanus in Gaul, that the Irish are no different from the Britons in their practices. For when Bishop Dagan visited us, he refused not only to eat with us but even to take his meal in the same house as ourselves.

Bishop Dagan's conduct was probably not a mere *faux pas* or intended slight. This sticking point was symptomatic of a growing recognition of the role of monasticism within the organizational structure of the church, and of the implications of the distinction between communal and eremitic modes of life. His practice would not have been to join in a communal meal, but to consume his meagre rations in the solitude of the hermit-monk. The Roman party cannot have been ignorant of this, but probably seized on a useful counter-claim of lack of courtesy to balance Augustine's lapse. In 610 Mellitus attended and subscribed, on behalf of England, to an important council in Rome, convened to draw up regulations for monastic life and discipline. This was a powerful instrument for extending papal authority and regularizing the relationship between the monastic and diocesan structures. Bishops were to exert pastoral and temporal authority from their urban dioceses, whilst monasteries served as powerhouses of prayer and study and managed potentially extensive networks of estates.

Celtic rural, pastoral society had its penchant for eastern-style eremitic monasticism: monasteries were essentially minster churches of the local *tuath*, each governed by an abbot (or abbess) according to their own preferred rule of life, and hosting a bishop in their midst who was subject to the abbot. This would have been a bureaucratic anomaly to the ecclesiastical hierarchies of Rome and Gaul: far too

> *For the northern province of the Irish and all the Picts still observed these customs, believing that they were following the teachings of the holy and praiseworthy father Anatolius, although the true facts are evident to any scholar.*
>
> BEDE, *HISTORIA ECCLESIASTICA*, BOOK III

difficult to control. The Celtic monastic federation (*parochia*), as Columbanus's mission had demonstrated, could extend its tentacles from Ireland, through Gaul and the precious Alpine passes to Italy itself. This made it a potential threat to the control of international diplomacy, which was conducted largely through the offices of the church until governmental ambassadages were established at the Reformation. It also circumvented the church hierarchy and its territorial jurisdiction, blurring the authority of the local bishops. The subsequent solution applied in Columban foundations such as Lindisfarne of sometimes vesting abbatial and episcopal authority in one person, the bishop-abbot, was one answer to this. But it was not one guaranteed to appeal to Rome.

Columbanus's well-meant but inflammatory letters to Pope Gregory and his successor, Boniface IV, may have helped to move such matters up the agenda of the 'Bishop of Rome'. Augustine's mission was not launched solely to achieve the conversion of the English, but to ensure that they should not be converted by the British and Irish, whose dangerous influence already showed signs of spreading to the continent. The papacy was a new concept, exerting the apostolic primacy of St Peter who had founded the church in Rome in order to win its own area of jurisdiction over the 'barbarian' successor states that had replaced Roman imperial authority.

The leading player in championing the military containment and conversion of such peoples to date had been the heir to Rome's power in the East – the Byzantine emperor, Justinian (527–69). The remarkable Christian basilicas, baptisteries and mausolea, with their astoundingly beautiful and didactic mosaics built during the sixth and seventh centuries by Justinian and his successors in the Byzantine exarchate of Ravenna in north-east Italy, bear witness to the abilities and ambitions of the Byzantine empire and its church. It was running its own missionary programme, Ulfilas converting the Goths and others working to combat the Arian and Nestorian heresies in the East, and it would later dispatch Cyril to evangelize the Slavs. With the coronation of Charlemagne in Rome on Christmas Day in the year 800, the West would finally achieve a comparable collaboration (if an often volatile one) between church and state, as the Carolingian empire revived the concept of a western Roman *imperium* that would become the Holy Roman empire. This however was a long way off. Gregory the Great had to rely upon a motley succession of warleaders-cum-kings to help him implement his vision. His natural allies in this – the churches of the Atlantic seaboard – were an unruly lot, with their own flourishing lives and track-records of achievement, and they were by no means convinced by his assertions of the primacy of Roman practices and traditions. The Byzantine empire, powerful as it was, suffered from numerous local and ethnic bids for independence, whilst its vibrant intellectual debates had generated numerous heresies and schisms. Gregory had no intention of allowing the British, Irish and Visigothic churches to engender a similar situation in the West, nor of allowing them to join forces with the Eastern empire, with which their monastic, liturgical and devotional tastes were already exhibiting signs of dalliance.

Letters to representatives of the Irish church from Pope Honorius in 634 and from Pope John took issue with them over their practices for the dating of Easter, and added a note of censure at attempts to revive the Pelagian heresy. Independence and separatism were in danger of fragmenting the illusion of Catholic unity and uniformity that Gregory and his successors sought to construct.

However, the issue that emerged as the crux of the tension in which all of the foregoing considerations were involved was the dating of Easter. It can be difficult for modern secularists to understand why this should have caused such heated debate. Agreement over the celebration of the major festival of the Christian year – the commemoration of the death and resurrection of Christ – was fundamental to the unity of the church, and to the need to present a united front when explaining Christian beliefs and practices to potential pagan converts. At a purely pragmatic level such differences in observance could cause difficulties. By way of illustration, when Greece was admitted to the European Union in the late twentieth century it was given only three years to abandon nearly two millennia of adherence to its own calendrical tradition for the dating of Easter (in accordance with Greek Orthodox practice) and to adopt the western dating. This was because of the Bank Holiday and the disruption to trading. As the Irish-trained King Oswy of Northumbria was to find, it could be highly inconvenient trying to celebrate Easter at a different time to his queen, Eanfled, who had been given a Roman training in Kent, as he would be feasting whilst she was in the penitential season of Lent and could not attend. This bizarre situation of two Easters being celebrated within the same household was tolerated, Bede notes (*Historia Ecclesiastica*, Book III), because of the affection and esteem in which their Irish mentor, St Aidan, was held by royalty, common people and Honorius, archbishop of Canterbury, alike. Domestic and international relations were evidently also relevant issues. The result, in England, was the debate that Oswy convened in 664 at the monastery of Streanaeshalch (Whitby, the 'Bay of the Beacon', perhaps a reference to a Roman lighthouse which was ruled by his daughter, the saintly Abbess Hild) to determine which traditions were to be favoured, those of Ireland or Rome. This was known as the Synod of Whitby.

Some Roman authorities were of the mistaken opinion that the Irish argued that Easter should be observed with the Hebrew Passover, on the fourteenth day of the moon, on whichever day of the week that fell. However, Bede points out that the Irish knew that it was a moveable feast which had to fall on a Sunday (the day after the Sabbath, which is when the Gospels said Christ arose from the tomb). They recognized that its date therefore varied from year to year and, because of the lunar cycle, fell between the fourteenth and twentieth days of the moon within a cycle of 84 years. Speaking of one of his beloved heroes, Aidan, the saintly Irish founder of Lindisfarne, Bede wrote:

I greatly admire and love all these things about Aidan, because I have no doubt that they are pleasing to God; but I cannot approve or commend his failure to observe Easter at the proper time, whether he did it through ignorance of the

> But the Irish in the south of Ireland had already conformed to the injunctions of the Bishops of the apostolic see, and learnt to observe Easter at the canonical time.
>
> BEDE, *HISTORIA ECCLESIASTICA*, BOOK III.

canonical times or in deference to the customs of his own nation. But this in him I do approve, that in keeping his Easter he believed, worshipped and taught exactly what we do, namely the redemption of the human race through the Passion, Resurrection, and Ascension into heaven of the Man Jesus Christ, the Mediator between God and man. He always kept Easter, not as some mistakenly suppose, on the fourteenth moon whatever the day was, as the Jews do, but on the Lord's day falling between the fourteenth and twentieth days of the moon. He did so because he held that the Resurrection of our Lord took place on the day following the Sabbath and because, like the rest of Holy Church, he rightly expected our own resurrection to take place on the same day after the Sabbath, which we now call the Lord's Day.

Bede, *Historia Ecclesiastica*, Book III

Taken out of context and in isolation, as they have been above, Bede's comments on the whole controversy present him in a light that in no way does justice to his work as a whole, or to the man. The *Historia Ecclesiastica* was intended, above all, to create a sense of unity and identity amongst the Germanic tribes who had settled in Britain. Indeed, it effectively gave birth to the concept of 'England', which was only to be realized politically during the tenth century. The issue is therefore central to his theme. In the extract above, however, he overcomes even this when he reminds himself that the spirit of the law is greater than its letter. Details of religious observance were by no means as important as the essence of belief, and the ecclesiastical establishment was not of itself more important than the believer. Christ and living out his teaching was ultimately what mattered.

Was the British and Irish divergent tradition born of isolation from the rest of Christendom? This is often argued and Bede claimed it to be the case, but it seems highly unlikely given the amount of interaction that had already been discussed. Or did it arise from an innate conservatism and a pride in their own traditions and scholarship, which meant that they did not adopt new developments? How widespread was their distinctive calendrical practice? We have already seen that the conversion of Ireland was a multi-faceted affair, conducted under the influence of Britain, Gaul and Rome. Bede, speaking of the foundation of the monastery of Lindisfarne in 635, notes that not all of the Irish were 'in error':

For the northern province of the Irish and all the Picts still observed these customs, believing that they were following the teachings of the holy and praiseworthy father Anatolius, although the true facts are evident to any scholar. But the Irish in the south of Ireland had already conformed to the injunctions of the Bishop of the apostolic see, and learnt to observe Easter at the canonical time.

Bede, *Historia Ecclesiastica*, Book III

Had the southern part of Ireland in fact recently conformed, or had it always adhered to Roman practices from the time that Palladius was first sent there in the early fifth century? We do not know, but what is noteworthy is that the earliest extant Latin literature from Ireland should be devoted to the subject. It is of further interest that, within a couple of generations, its scholars could conduct an informed debate with those of the Mediterranean world, in which they showed themselves to be the heirs of the rhetoric and literary style of the late Roman world. This did not, alas, lead them to be any more measured or conciliatory in their tone than their Roman counterparts where the Easter controversy was concerned. Around 633 the Irish scholar Cummian wrote to Abbot Ségéne of Iona that all the churches of East and West were mistaken and that 'the Irish and British alone know what is right'. His own writings on the subject include his *Paschal Letter*, which drew on no less than forty earlier texts by the Church Fathers and previous Irish scholars, and which gives an indication of the range of reading matter available within Irish monastic schools. It joined the writings of other Irish authors, notably those known as Pseudo-Anatolius (*De Pascha*), Pseudo-Athanasius and Pseudo-Theophilus (termed collectively by some scholars the Irish Paschal Forgeries), all of which were in circulation by the early sixth century. These were based on the Irish 84-year cycle that is thought to have derived from the observances of the church in Gaul during the fourth and fifth centuries. Since the second century, churches had devised mathematical tables to calculate in advance the dates on which Easter would fall. Many variant and rival tables came into existence, as mathematical calculations proved unequal to the task. One of the best displays of scientific knowledge on mathematics, computus and the nature of time, rivaling that of Bede whom it influenced, was the *De ratione conputandi* ('On the method of reckoning time'), composed by an anonymous Irish author who may have been Cummian himself. In around 600, Columbanus wrote to Pope Gregory that the table then being promoted by Rome as the one authoritative table was not 'accepted by our teachers, by the former scholars of Ireland, by the mathematicians most skilled in reckoning chronology, but has been deemed more worthy of ridicule or pity than of authority'. This was possibly correct, but was hardly expressed in a tone designed to recommend itself to the aspirant head of Christendom.

I wish, Holy Father (do not think it excessive of me) to ask about Easter... when an unworthy man like me writes to an illustrious one like yourself, my insignificance makes applicable to me the striking remark which a certain philosopher is said to have once made on seeing a painted harlot: 'I do not admire the art, but I admire the cheek.'

St Columbanus, letter to Pope Gregory the Great, 600

CHAPTER 7

The 'Insular' Church

NORTHUMBRIA'S 'GOLDEN AGE'

The term 'Insular' is a convenient shorthand term for the Christian culture that emerged in the British Isles and Ireland from around 600 to 850. Despite the differences discussed in the previous chapters, this culture was often collaborative. The meeting ground for this collaboration – as well as much conflict and its resolution – was Northumbria in north-eastern England and southern Scotland. Its first Christian ruler was the saintly King Edwin (584–633). Bede portrays his reign as a golden age in which a woman carrying a newborn child could walk unmolested from coast to coast, pausing to refresh herself at the wayside wells which the king had furnished with hanging bowls for travellers to drink from. The course of the conversion process was initially entwined with that of Kent, Essex and East Anglia. The Deiran Prince Edwin was forced into exile in Wales (a curious choice given the alleged animosity of the British), and then at the East Anglian court of King Redwald. Here, however, he was alerted to Redwald's intention of betraying him to his Bernician rival, King Ethelfrith. A mysterious figure warned him of the plot, which was averted by the queen's pleas for honorable conduct. This figure also told him that he should listen to the person who would one day remind him of his deliverance. That person was St Paulinus.

With Redwald's help, Edwin defeated his rival at the River Idle in 616 and gained the Northumbrian throne. During his exile he had married a pagan Mercian princess, Cwenburg/Coenburg, who bore him two sons. We do not know what became of her, but she had presumably died by the time that Edwin petitioned King Eadbald of Kent for the hand of his sister, Ethelberga (or 'Tata', the daughter of King Ethelberht), for polygamy was not tolerated in Christian circles. Consent was only given on the understanding that she should be allowed freedom of worship, and that Edwin himself would give serious consideration to converting – along with his people. Accordingly, she journeyed to York in 625 with her chaplain, Paulinus, who had been consecrated as bishop for the purpose of his mission. Bede related an eye-witness verbal portrait of Paulinus by Deda, abbot of Partney, as 'a tall man having a slight stoop, with black hair, an ascetic face, a thin hooked nose, and a venerable and awe-inspiring presence'. He had been one of the band of reinforcements sent to Canterbury from Rome in 601. For several years they tried to convert the king, who

> *When we compare the present life of man on earth with that time of which we have no knowledge, it seems to me like the swift flight of a single sparrow through the banqueting-hall.*
>
> BEDE, *HISTORIA ECCLESIASTICA*, BOOK II

pondered long and hard which religion to follow, taking very seriously both the wishes of and the implications for his people. Papal correspondence to Ethelberga urged her on in her task, hinting at the impuned legitimacy of their union should she fail, and quoting the scriptural saying 'the unbelieving husband shall be saved through the believing wife'. She must have been under tremendous pressure, surrounded by an alien Anglian territory with a husband who still publicly worshipped idols and who had pagan offspring from a former marriage to threaten the future of her own children, as well has having the eyes of Rome and Christian Kent upon her. The silver mirror and gold and ivory comb that accompanied Pope Boniface's letter of encouragement can have been little consolation.

Three things seem to have finally persuaded Edwin to convert in 627. Firstly an assassination attempt against him was foiled by the self-sacrifice of his close friend and thegn, Lilla. Secondly a daughter, Eanfled, was born to himself and Queen Ethelberga; she was given to Paulinus to serve as a nun and was the first Northumbrian to be baptized. Thirdly Paulinus reminded him of his deliverance at Redwald's court and his promise to obey whomsoever should reveal knowledge of the event, having discovered it by some means. Edwin summoned his council and asked each in turn his opinion of 'the strange doctrine and this new way of worshipping the godhead'. The first to signal his acceptance – with alacrity – was the chief Priest, Coifi, who was quick to point out that the old gods must be worthless, for his devoted service of them had not led to the royal preferment he thought he deserved. Like their Celtic druidic counterparts, many Germanic priests were probably quick to read the runes and to preserve their status by embracing the new faith, some probably becoming Christian priests themselves. Another of the king's chief men made a more profound observation about the attraction of Christian belief, which has become the favourite motif for the conversion of the English:

Your Majesty, when we compare the present life of man on earth with that time of which we have no knowledge, it seems to me like the swift flight of a single sparrow through the banqueting-hall where you are sitting at dinner on a winter's day with your thegns and counsellors. In the middle is a comforting fire to warm the hall; outside, the storms of winter rain or snow are raging. This sparrow flies swiftly in through one door of the hall, and out through another. While he is inside, he is safe from the winter storms; but after a few moments of comfort, he vanishes from sight into the wintry world from which he came. Even so, man appears on earth for a little while; but of what went before this life or of what follows, we know nothing. Therefore, if this new teaching has brought any more certain knowledge, it seems only right that we should follow it.

Bede, *Historia Ecclesiastica*

Upon hearing Paulinus's teaching, Coifi was the first to propose and undertake the destruction of their pagan temples and altars. He rode a stallion and carried arms which were taboo to a pagan Germanic priest, and he cast his spear into the precinct of an important shrine at Goodmanham to the East of York and burned it down. A wooden church dedicated to St Peter was hastily constructed in York, so that Edwin could receive instruction and baptism. Soon afterwards, Paulinus persuaded him to replace it with a basilica of stone, as the centre of his See, and the little wooden oratory was then enshrined inside it. A later example of a timber church, possibly of eleventh-century date, survives at Greenstead in Essex.

Both courtiers and ordinary folk were baptized – Edwin and Paulinus subsequently conducted mass baptisms in Bernicia in the River Glen, near the royal palace of Yeavering. In Deira he likewise baptized in the River Swale, near Catterick, the heart of earlier British resistance, and with the king's support he built a basilica at the royal residence of Campodunum (Doncaster or Slake). This was later burned down by an invading alliance and replaced by one at Leeds, though the altar of the original church was preserved to Bede's day in a monastery in Elmet Wood, which may be Ledsham in Elmet. Ledsham itself retains important fabric from as early as the seventh to eighth century (Bede, *Historia Ecclesiastica*, Book II). Bede only mentions those places that are of significance to his structured narrative. He does not seem to touch on one of the most complete

BELOW: Timber church, dating from the eleventh century but giving a flavour of earlier wooden churches which generally preceded stone ones on most early sites. Greenstead Church, Essex.

ABOVE: Ledsham-in-Elmet, perhaps the church in Elmet Wood mentioned by Bede; eighth-century doorway.

RIGHT: Escomb Church, County Durham, seen from the south. The fabric is seventh- to eighth-century with porch and larger windows inserted later.

late seventh- to early eighth-century buildings in Northumbria – the little church at Escomb, Durham, which must once have been part of a major monastery.

Edwin successfully expanded Northumbrian territory and influence, becoming the first northern bretwalda. He annexed much Pictish, Cumbrian and Welsh territory, including the Menavian Isles of Anglesey and the Isle of Man, and the British kingdom of Elmet around Leeds. His overlordship even extended into southern England. This success made the rulers of surrounding kingdoms fearful. As a result, an alliance was constructed between the equally ambitious pagan King Penda of Mercia and the Christian King Cadwalla/Cadwallon of North Wales. Ethnic antagonism could evidently be put aside in the face of a common threat. Their combined forces defeated Edwin who was killed at the Battle of Hatfield Chase in around 632.

LINDISFARNE, THE HOLY ISLAND

According to Bede, the foundation of Lindisfarne in 635 came about as a direct result of the ensuing contest for the Northumbrian kingship. Edwin was killed some six years after his baptism by Paulinus at York. There is an alternative account of his conversion in the *Historia Brittonum*, which claims he was converted at the hands of Rum (Rhun) – son of the British King Urien of Catreath (Catterick) – and Rheged, and that the whole Bernician race was baptized too. The existence of this account alerts us to early competing claims between the various churches, and clearly signals the political considerations underpinning much of the work of conversion. That Paulinus' centre of operations remained south, at York, may also imply that the reintroduction of Christianity to north-eastern England had not significantly advanced by the time of Edwin's death.

Paulinus and the royal family fled to Kent and the reins of power in Northumbria soon passed to the northern Bernician house, whose members returned from exile in the Christian enclaves of Irish and Pictish Scotland. The affiliations that they had acquired whilst in exile were to exert a profound effect on the history of Northumbria. With the eventual victory of Oswald over Cadwalla at the Battle of Heavenfield in 633, the Celtic (or, more precisely, Columban) tradition of Christianity achieved a foothold in the region. In Bede's account of events (*Historia Ecclesiastica*, Book III), Oswald emerges as a new Constantine, assured of victory over the unholy alliance of the pagan Mercians and the Christian Cadwalla of Wales by his adoption of faith, symbolized by the wooden cross which became his standard and which he set up on the site of his victory at Heavenfield. Oswald's cross was thereby sowing the seeds for the great Old English epic poem, the 'Dream of the Rood'. This event is presented as mirroring Constantine's victory at the Milvian Bridge, viewed retrospectively as the decisive turning point in the fortunes of early Christianity and the springboard for its becoming the state religion of the late Roman Empire.

It was to Iona, site of his own exile and education, that Oswald turned for spiritual support – no doubt accompanied by the secular political backing of the Irish kingdom of Dalriada. Local resistance is signalled by the initial failure of the Columban mission, its first ambassador, the inflexible Corman, returning to Iona in dismay. Not so its next emissary, Bishop Aidan, who adopted a gentler, more persuasive tone. In 635 Aidan arrived at the island stronghold given to the Columban *parochia* by King Oswald – Lindisfarne. The site is reminiscent in so many ways of Iona itself, save that the Northumbrian Holy Island is tidal: it is subject to the rhythms of ebb and flow, and its causeway is open to the mainland twice a day.

Aidan was to found a Columban monastery as a spiritual powerhouse for the conversion of Oswald's people. The king himself relished interpreting Aidan's teaching from Irish into English for his followers. Lindisfarne's mission was not confined to court and the wealthy, however. Aidan and his disciples were renowned for their austere life of poverty and prayer and for their service of the Lord and his people, great and small, rather than of a purely earthly lord. Each generation has its heroes, its role models and its cults of celebrity. In this age the warriors and royals made way for these teachers, preachers, scholars, labourers and risk-takers, who would place their lives on the line to bring humanitarian aid and a message of hope to the most remote and troubled areas, and who worked for their bread and spent endless hours in intense prayer and study.

Oswald's otherwise successful reign was beset by continued conflict with Penda of Mercia, culminating in Oswald's death at the Battle of Oswestry in 641, upon which Bernicia passed to his brother, Oswiu/Oswy. Oswald's relics were subsequently transported to Bardney in Lindsey by his niece, Osthryd, who was married to King Ethelred of Mercia (Bede, *Historia Ecclesiastica*, Book III). His head-relic was taken to Lindisfarne where it was subsequently interred in Cuthbert's coffin, whilst other of his corporeal relics were taken to the citadel of Bamburgh, reinforcing the close connection between the cult and the royal house.

Holy Island was thus a possession of

the Bernician royal house, bestowed upon the Irish-orientated Columban 'Celtic' church as the chosen vehicle for spiritual validation and support in establishing a stable society. The site of the wooden monastery which Aidan (635–651) and his successor Bishop Finan (651–661) constructed, built in wood of Irish fashion and dedicated to St Peter (no anti-Roman feeling there), is thought to underlie the present remains of the later Norman Lindisfarne Priory rather than the imposing outcrop occupied by the castle at the other end of the island. Some archaeological remains suggest that the latter may have functioned as a defensive or symbolic site during prehistory, and it may have retained some such significance in the Anglo-Saxon period, thereby symbolizing – in however basic a fashion – the alliance of church and state. The donation of royal land, often featuring a defensible site such as a Roman fort – Reculver, Bradwell-on-Sea and Burgh Castle, to name but a few – is a feature of conversion in other Anglo-Saxon kingdoms. The fortunes of the religious community here would remain closely linked to those of its royal sponsors. It may be overstating the case somewhat to present Lindisfarne as the *eigenkirche* of the Bernician royalty, a Northumbrian Aachen or St Denis (the distinction of royal

Lindisfarne, the site of the original monastery, now occupied by the Norman Priory and parish church. View from the ridge known as the Heugh, which once was the site of a high cross and a watchtower.

mausoleum being shared in any case with Whitby). But such royal association undoubtedly played an important role in its subsequent prominence, as of course did the spiritual commitment and integrity of its early leaders. Bishop Aidan was a valued member of the royal household (Bede, *Historia Ecclesiastica*, Book III), and one of the many churches that he and his followers established in the region was that at Bamburgh. It was here, leaning against the outer timber walls of this church in the shadow of the royal citadel, that Aidan eventually died.

St Cuthbert's Isle (Hobthrush), an eremitic retreat in the bay adjacent to Lindisfarne monastery. Some of the work on the Lindisfarne Gospels may have been undertaken by Bishop Eadfrith whilst on retreat here.

Kings needed to be reminded of their Christian duties and encouraged to donate more resources, and Aidan seems to have cultivated close relationships with Oswald's successors, Oswy of Bernicia and Oswin of Deira. In 655, as thanksgiving for divine aid in finally eliminating Penda of Mercia, Oswy made numerous donations of land to Lindisfarne, enabling it to extend the Columban *parochia* with its own network of daughter-houses. Six of these ten-hide donations (a hide being enough land to support a family) fell within Bernician territory and may have included Melrose, Coldingham, Norham, Abercorn and Gilling. Others followed and included: some Pictish houses; Hartlepool; the anonymous monastery (which was perhaps Crayke near York) celebrated in the ninth-century poem by Aethelwulf *De Abbatibus*; Peterborough; Bradwell-on-Sea; and Lichfield.

Lindisfarne Castle is essentially a sixteenth-century Tudor fortress remodelled in the early twentieth century by Sir Edwin Lutyens for the owner of *Country Life* magazine. It formed part of a refortification of the island as a supply base for the English navy, as it occupied a strategic position in respect of northern England, Scotland and the continent. The island would always have been a significant site militarily and economically. It was also spiritually evocative and was associated with a nearby grouping of islands, known as the Farnes, that exerted a powerful and deep-rooted pull on the Celtic imagination. The Farne islands were to become a place of retreat for members of the Lindisfarne community, notably its saintly bishops who would conduct their feats of spiritual and physical endurance on behalf of humankind within direct view of the royal citadel of Bamburgh – like Lazarus at Dives' gate. The small islet, known as St Cuthbert's Isle (or 'Hobthrush', Thrush Island), which lay within the bay adjacent to Lindisfarne Priory, also provided a more immediate retreat within the monastery, which favoured the eastern eremitic tradition of the desert fathers. Another crucial aspect of Celtic monasticism, however, was its outreach to the world through preaching and mission: it presented a mirror to secular society, holding forth an idealized and God-centred image. As such, monasteries were not remote from society and played a variety of roles, from trading and manufacturing centres to open prisons (they were part of the religious penitential component of the legal system in which not only fines and penalties but also an element of public penance were exacted for misdemeanours). They and their associated laypeople were, if you like, the early Christian Celtic equivalent of small

Osgyth name-stone, marking the burial of a woman in the vicinity of Lindisfarne monastery, seventh-eighth century. The name is given in runes and roman capitals. Lindisfarne Priory Museum.

towns. When the monks had to leave the island in the ninth century, the 'people of St Cuthbert' went with them.

A tradition has arisen which implies that, as at Mount Athos, women were not permitted on the island from the time of St Cuthbert. There is no evidence of this in the early record. Indeed there is material evidence that would definitely contradict it, such as the name-stone of the woman Osgyth who was evidently buried within the monastic enclave during the early eighth century. Aidan of Lindisfarne had bestowed the veil upon the first Northumbrian nun, Heiu of Hartlepool, and had persuaded Hild of Whitby to remain in her native region rather than pursuing her vocation in Gaul. Double monasteries of monks and nuns ruled by abbesses were also a feature of the Insular church (as in Gaul and at St Brigid's Kildare). Under

Now we must praise the Guardian of Heaven, The might of the Lord and His purpose of mind, The work of the Glorious Father; for He, God Eternal, established each wonder, He, Holy Creator, first fashioned Heaven as a roof for the sons of men. Then the Guardian of Mankind adorned This middle-earth below, this world for men, Everlasting Lord, Almighty King.

High-cross bearing Pictish 'snake boss' motifs, Iona, c.800.

Hild's patronage, a thegn-turned-cowherd, Cædmon, who was too shy to take his turn at singing in the hall, was divinely inspired to compose one of the first English hymns, around the time of the Synod of Whitby.

The 'Lives' of Cuthbert abound in instances of his friendship with, and ministry to, women. There was evidently no particular antipathy towards women in the Northumbrian church. The tradition may have stemmed from St Cuthbert's condemnation of the monks and nuns of Coldingham for their moral laxity, and from the misogyny of his community at Durham during the Norman and Angevin periods. There, women were not allowed east of a line in the floor at the western end of the nave, even after the Galilee Chapel (where Bede now rests) was built in the late twelfth century to accommodate female pilgrims in response to competition from the cult of Thomas Becket at Canterbury.

Excavations on the probable site of the monastery of Lindisfarne have been limited, owing to the presence of the later priory and church buildings and of the village itself. From clues given in the literary record (Bede's *Historia Ecclesiastica* and the 'Lives' of St Cuthbert), and by analogy with Iona, we can deduce that the monastery is likely to have been contained within an earthwork bank (a *rath* or *vallum*) which may have enclosed the area from the foreshore opposite St Cuthbert's Isle to the marketplace. The layout of the village, and later medieval references to outlying chapels and burial grounds, would suggest that there may also have been an outer boundary earthwork extending further through the village to the line of what is now Marygate. Therefore, the inner sanctum would have been demarcated from the outer enclave, in which more worldly domestic and industrial activities might have been conducted. Bede (*Historia Ecclesiastica*, Book IV) refers to an island hermitage (St Cuthbert's Isle) near to the monastery, within its 'outer precinct', that would tend to confirm such an arrangement: an inner sanctum within a bigger enclosure. The inner enclosure contained two churches, one built by Aidan and another by Finan, of wooden planks and thatch. Bishop Eadbert had the latter covered with lead plaques on its roof and walls, which must have given it an appearance resembling contemporary Insular metalwork house-shaped shrines, such as the Pictish Monymusk reliquary (see page 71) or the Irish Abbadia San Salvatore shrine. It is thought that the Norman Priory and the parish church (which may date from the late Anglo-Saxon period) reflect both the position of the original main church containing Cuthbert's shrine (in what is now the Priory) and copy the double church arrangement of late seventh-century Jarrow (see page 162). Or might Jarrow have copied Lindisfarne's layout for its two stone churches? More likely, perhaps, is that both centres were observing an arrangement already practised in the Christian Orient. The church buildings would have been surrounded by a burial ground, and literary sources refer to a dormitory and a guest-house. Excavations on the Heugh, a ridge sheltering the site from the estuary, have revealed a number of features that have been interpreted as a watchtower and pilgrimage stations, including several cross-bases still to be seen on site.

The marking of areas of a monastic enclave with high-crosses is a feature found in many Irish monasteries, including Iona, from the later eighth and ninth centuries onwards, but the Lindisfarne practice may predate this. Two *Lives* of St Cuthbert refer to the healing of a pilgrim who wore the shoes of the saint and who conducted a pilgrimage around the 'places of the sacred martyrs', or 'holy places'. This recalls traditional Irish practice, and the more recent introduction of Roman stational liturgy. There was a well-established pre-existing Celtic and British tradition of inscribing pillars or slabs with crosses, but the earliest reference in the written record to the raising of a free-standing stone cross is that which Bishop Aethilwald of Lindisfarne

LEFT: High-Cross, Ahenny, County Tipperary, eighth century. Its decoration may recall a wooden and metalwork prototype.

BELOW: base of one of the two high-crosses at Ahenny, depicting a desert scene, with palm tree. Eighth century, Ahenny, County Tipperary.

(died 740) ordered to be made as his memorial. The grave of Bishop Acca of Hexham was likewise marked with tall stone crosses at head and foot (one of which survives at Hexham Abbey). Stylistically there would appear to have been something of an earlier Patrician and Columban context, to judge from the stone slabs at Fahan and Carndonagh in County Donegal (close to Lough Foyle whence Columba set sail for Iona). These slabs feature simple crosses that appear as if struggling to liberate themselves from the stone from which they are carved. Later in the eighth century a full three-dimensionality would be achieved in the dramatic free-standing high-crosses at Ahenny in Munster (see page 147). The County Donegal slabs may date from as early as the seventh century but their artistic conception and carving technique are much simpler, and almost primitive, in comparison with the tall, deeply carved cross shafts from Lindisfarne's northern outpost of Abercorn, near Edinburgh, and Acca's Cross at Hexham. The conception of the free-standing stone crosses may have reached maturity at Lindisfarne as part of the Columban tradition. But it was perhaps also a specific recollection of King Oswald's wooden cross and of the stational liturgy of the cross celebrated in Rome from the first quarter of the seventh century onwards.

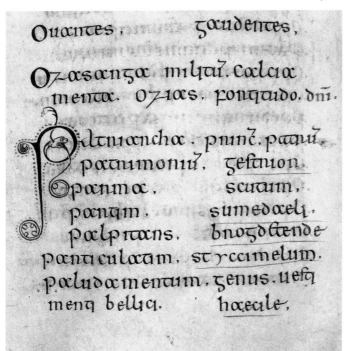

The Corpus Glossary, Corpus Christi College, Cambridge. A schoolroom book, of the sort used in the school established by Archbishop Theodore and Abbot Hadrian at Canterbury. Kent, c.800.

As we have already seen, centres such as these were monastic, but their abbots were generally priested and often exerted authority over the bishops (although recent scholarship is beginning to ascribe more importance to the role of the bishops than was formerly thought). Such an arrangement was geared to overcome the limitations of a non-urban, tribal territorialism and appears to have been indebted to the eastern ecclesiastical tradition. Irish bishops often exercised their diocesan function from monastic seats (or *civitates*, 'cities'), as had Pope Gregory the Great in Rome, who enjoined Augustine to do likewise at Canterbury. This may also be indicative of ultimately eastern influence and such practices continued to feature in the Orthodox church, with the Archbishop of Sinai also serving as abbot of the monastery of St Catherine, for example. At Lindisfarne the abbot was frequently also the bishop.

Their parochial function made Lindisfarne and its daughter-houses a valuable new feature of local government, as well as spiritual powerhouses for Northumbria's rulers. Many key members of these monasteries, both male and female, were increasingly drawn from the ranks of the aristocracy and the royal house itself, further cementing the union. The resumption of harmonious relationships with the other major powers of northern Britain was also highly desirable at this stage in the kingdom's development. During the second half of the seventh century, however, the political stage was changing. Lindisfarne's own *parochia* had spread, with its monks (such as Diuma, Cedd and Chad) contributing to the conversion of Lindsey, Mercia and Essex. However, the extended monastic model was increasingly ill-suited to the territorial and organizational needs of the Anglo-Saxon church and state. The Roman church was making significant headway in establishing the beginnings of a parochial structure, especially under the aegis of Archbishop Theodore from Tarsus in Asia Minor, who arrived at Canterbury in 669 along with Hadrian. Hadrian was a North African who had subsequently been based in Naples. As abbot of St Augustine's Canterbury he assisted Theodore in his ecclesiastical and educational development of the early English Church – a truly cosmopolitan melting-pot of people and influences. Their Canterbury school attracted many English pupils and initiated a tradition of learning in England that produced scholars of the magnitude of Bede, and Aldhelm, abbot of Malmesbury and Bishop of Sherborne (died 709). Theodore and Hadrian taught Latin and Greek, theology and biblical exegesis, computistics (especially calendrical calculations, so crucial to the Paschal controversy), poetry, astronomy, medicine and Gregorian chant. John the papal archcantor was also sent to Monkwearmouth/Jarrow for a time to transmit this art, for musical notation was not written down until the ninth century.

Aldhelm's wordy treatise 'On Virginity' (*De Virginitate*), addressed to Abbess Hildelith and the Barking nuns, exhorted them to chastity and berated them for their vanity in wearing golden embroidered headbands. He is also said, by Bede, to have written a treatise that convinced many Britons under West Saxon jurisdiction to adopt Roman practices, including the dating of Easter. His riddles originated in the need to teach grammar and metrics in the schoolroom, but their gnomic wit no doubt also influenced riddles subsequently written in English, which can be quite saucy:

Riddles

I watched four fair creatures
Travelling together; they left black tracks
Behind them. The support of the bird
Moved swiftly; it flew in the sky,
Dived under the waves. The struggling warrior
Continuously toiled, pointing out the paths
To all four over the fine gold.

I'm a strange creature, for I satisfy women,
A service to the neighbours! No one suffers
At my hands except for my slayer.
I grow very tall, erect in a bed,
I'm hairy underneath. From time to time
A beautiful girl, the brave daughter

Of some churl dares to hold me,
Grips my russet skin, robs me of my head
And puts me in the pantry. At once that girl
With plaited hair who has confined me
Remembers our meeting. Her eye moistens.

The answer to the first is four fingers writing with a quill pen; the second is an onion.

Theodore was also given a remit to ensure the Catholic orthodoxy of England (although Bede hints that his own level of adherence may have been suspect and that Hadrian was in turn to keep a watchful eye on him). He also sought to further Pope Gregory's initial blueprint for the English Church, conducting a thorough visitation on his arrival, reforming abuses, conducting church synods and councils, consecrating more bishops and laying the foundations for ecclesiastical organization and administration. What must this erudite easterner, who was already sixty-five when he left Rome, have made of the English, Irish and British he encountered? He certainly made a tremendous impact during the twenty years he spent here, giving the young English church a sense of unity and identity.

THE EASTER CONTROVERSY AND THE SYNOD OF WHITBY

Following Bede's lead, many historians have crystallized the shifting ideas in the church at this time into a religious controversy between competing Celtic and Roman church traditions, culminating in the famous Synod of Whitby in 664. In attempting to summarize the contentious issues, Bede's emphasis falls upon two main areas. Firstly, the physical appearance of priests (different practices of tonsuring, with the Roman party favouring the corona on the crown of the head, whilst the Celts shaved across the brow from ear to ear, leaving a mane of hair behind). Secondly, Bede notes the different observances in the dating of Easter as being in one sense symbolic of the fundamental issue of whether the English church (and indeed Anglo-Saxon England itself) should favour an increasingly regional stance or should embrace and help to develop the European tradition. Such matters were of vital import in the development of the early Christian church. The First Paschal Controversy had been one of the key issues addressed at the First Ecumenical Council of Nicaea in 325, as it had raised the threat of schism. At even a purely pragmatic level such divergent practices carried greater political as well as theological and liturgical import than a modern audience might immediately perceive. For example, a royal couple might not be able to celebrate the greatest holy day in the Christian calendar together because they hailed from different church traditions. Striking differences of clerical appearance may not have helped to engender a spirit of ecumenism, but the far-reaching cultural and social impacts can only be guessed at.

The Columban tradition was championed in the debate by Bishop Colman of Lindisfarne, whilst that of Rome was defended by Wilfrid, an eloquent Northumbrian nobleman-turned-priest who had initially trained at Lindisfarne and was granted permission to travel to Italy and Gaul to study. We can imagine the impact that standing in the great early Christian churches of Rome made upon this imaginative and dynamic young man, who determined to play his part in reconstructing Rome in his native land. The church he later built at Hexham was the largest stone basilica north of the Alps, and was adorned with much Roman sculpture and pieces of Insular carving inspired by the Roman model. At its heart was a crypt modelled on Christ's tomb, the Holy Sepulchre, in which he placed some of the many relics of the saints which he brought home with him. He built another crypt at his other major church of Ripon and both are still places of prayer today (see page 153). Reused Roman masonry and inscriptions can be discerned in their walls and the approach passages have been designed to maximize the flow of pilgrims.

Inhabited vine-scroll (symbolizing the Tree of Life and the Eucharist). Jarrow, late seventh-century.

Wilfrid's pro-Roman, pro-European arguments gave Oswy the opening he needed in order to try to save the face of the Celts, whilst opting for a unified English church and for English participation in the European mainstream. His ruling was that, much as he respected the traditions of the venerable St Columba, it was St Peter who held the keys to heaven and so offending him was not an option.

Establishing a common observance for the dating of Easter carried many implications for the clerics of the day. The avoidance of schism was, as we have seen, a particularly vibrant concern. One of the factors which coloured English relations with Rome during this period was the Monothelete controversy, which held that Jesus had only one will (rather than a human will and a divine will). In 679, Archbishop Theodore convened the Council of Hatfield which affirmed the faith of the English church – that Christ had a fully human will, accompanied by human courage – thereby rejecting the Monothelete heresy (which denied him any such will, as this would have brought him into conflict with the perfect divine will, in which he shared). Pope Agatho sent a senior member of his household, John the Archcantor, to represent him at this council. John accompanied Benedict Biscop and Ceolfrith on the return journey from Rome to Northumbria, spending some time at Biscop's new foundation of Monkwearmouth instructing its brethren in the liturgy and chant of Rome. Hatfield was one of a number of European councils that prepared the way for the Sixth Ecumenical Council, held in Constantinople in 681, which was

Vine-scroll inhabited by an archer, from Hexham Abbey (now at Durham Cathedral), late seventh century.

Travel and Cultural Transmission

Eastern influences have long been recognized in Insular religion, transmitted through the writings of Church Fathers such as St John Cassian and St Pachomios, and through liturgical and devotional practices, thought perhaps to have been transmitted via post-Roman Gaul and Iberia. There are also intriguing artistic influences, and perhaps transmission of techniques, such as the eastern 'Coptic' form of sewing and binding preserved in the St Cuthbert Gospel, which is suggestive of an actual face-to-face learning/teaching process. People travelled more at this time than we are inclined to think, and there are elusive but intriguing indications of visits to and from the East. There are references to Coptic and Armenian monks preserved in the Irish litanies, and of western pilgrims visiting Jerusalem, the Levant and Egypt. Travel guides were in circulation describing not only the holy places of Jerusalem, but also the Egyptian monasteries of Nitria and Scetis. One such guidebook was allegedly dictated to Abbot Adomnán (who initially recorded it on wax tablets and then transcribed it) by Arculf, a Frankish bishop returning from pilgrimage. On the way his ship was blown off course, causing him to seek shelter on Iona. The resulting account is known as Adomnán's *De Locis Sanctis* ('On the Holy Places') and was subsequently paraphrased by Bede. The frequent visits paid to Rome by Northumbrian clerical noblemen such as Benedict Biscop, Ceolfrith and Wilfrid, are ample testimony of links there – and with parts of France, Switzerland and northern Italy en route. Nor were such travels confined to men. The leader of the Anglo-Saxon mission to Germany, St Boniface (died 754), wrote a letter in 747 to Archbishop Cuthbert of Canterbury advocating that he 'forbid matrons and nuns to make their frequent journeys back and forth to Rome. A great part of them perish and few keep their virtue. There are many towns in Lombardy and Gaul where there is not a courtesan or a harlot but is of English stock.'

Alliance and trade with southern England, Frankia/Gaul, Rome itself and other cosmopolitan centres was also becoming increasingly important. Along with royal centres such as Bamburgh, monastic sites such as Monkwearmouth, Jarrow, Whitby and Lindisfarne are likely to have been the major focuses of communications and trade. Coin hoards, including one deposited on Holy Island, are evidence of probable mercantile activity. St Willibrord (died 739), 'apostle of Frisia', trained at Lindisfarne and Ripon before spending a number of years in Ireland and then travelling to the Germanic homelands. There he founded Echternach in Luxembourg as part of his mission, and certainly permitted at least one of his monks to visit Holy Island (Bede, *Vita Cuthberti*). In the other direction Wilfrid and Acca of Hexham also visited Willibrord in Frisia, and trade between Frisia and Northumbria is likely to have cemented the missionary links – as did family ties, with Wilfrid, Willibrord and Alcuin all having relatives on both sides of the North Sea.

The Cult of St Columba

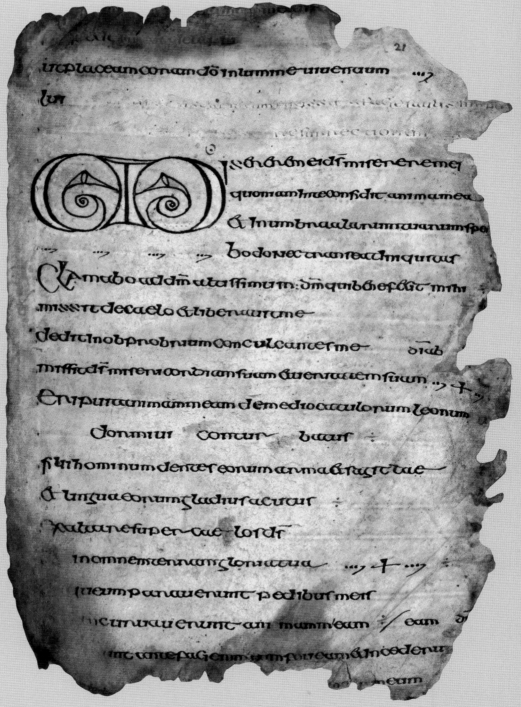

The Cathach of Columcille (Dublin, Royal Irish Academy, s.n., f. 21r). Psalter, traditionally associated with St Columba (d. 597), and sometimes thought to be by his own hand. Ireland, late sixth or early seventh century.

The Book of Kells
A Columban cult-book, Iona, c.800?

(Dublin, Trinity College Library MS 58 f. 34r)
The Chi-rho page from the Book of Kells..

The Book of Durrow

A Columban cult-book, Iona, late seventh century.

LEFT: The Book of Durrow (Dublin, Trinity College Library MS 57 f. 20v). Matthew miniature, resembling a belt-buckle on legs.

RIGHT: The Book of Durrow (Dublin, Trinity College Library MS 57 f. 191v). John miniature, depicted here as a lion, rather than the usual eagle, in accordance with a pre-Jerome ordering of the symbols proposed by St Irenaeus.

convened to resolve this crisis that had divided the church into East and West and had led to the martyrdom of Pope Martin I (649–655) and his advisor, Maximus Confessor. The Council proclaimed that in Christ the divine and human wills were coherently united and that as Christ was incorruptible he never conflicted with the divine will. It was stressed that this incorruptibility lay in his conception, without sin, from the Virgin Mary by the Holy Spirit. From the 650s on we find the cult of the Virgin, and the veneration of the cross upon which Christ displayed his will and courage, developing in Rome (from earlier eastern roots) and influencing its liturgy and art. It also became important to stress the unity of Christ's incarnation, from conception to crucifixion. Both of these events were thought to have taken place on the same date – 25 March. This meant that Christ's conception and death occurred at the Spring equinox and his birth at the winter solstice (25 December), in accordance with the solar cycle upon which the Roman calendar was based. Calendrical niceties carried significant connotations.

Wilfrid's late seventh-century crypt in Ripon Abbey. It was a pilgrim focus, based on the Holy Sepulchre in Jerusalem.

The beginnings of controversy over the Easter dating in Northumbria appear to have been initiated not by the English Wilfrid, however, but by Ronan, an Irish scholar who had studied in Gaul and Italy. He began, with the backing of the queen and Alchfrith the king's son, to persuade his fellows to accept the Roman dating, bringing him into dispute with Bishop Finan of Lindisfarne (died 661). In Ireland itself, a mixed practice prevailed before the Synod of Whitby. This may be deduced from the mixed career of the Frankish Bishop Agilbert, missionary to Wessex in the mid-seventh century, who had earlier trained in the southern part of Ireland with teachers who followed the Roman reckoning of Easter. He came to Wessex in 650 when King Cenwalh gave him the See of Dorchester-on-Thames, previously founded by St Birinus, a Lombard sent by the papacy to participate in the conversion of the English. Agilbert's failure to learn English is said to have alienated the king, who split the diocese, appointing Bishop Wine to Winchester. The disgruntled Agilbert left Wessex and later became the senior prelate representing the Roman cause at the Synod of Whitby at which he appointed the promising young priest Wilfrid to present their case. Agilbert subsequently returned to Gaul and became bishop of Paris, briefing Theodore of Tarsus during his journey to take up the archiepiscopal See of Canterbury. He died around 690 and was buried in the crypt of Jouarre, where his sister was abbess and where a finely carved sarcophagus survives.

Similarly, around 630 a convention of Irish abbots at Columba's own foundation of Durrow had opted to follow the Roman Easter, and soon after, delegates from an Irish synod travelled to Rome to participate in the Paschal celebrations. Henceforth the southern areas of Ireland observed what was perceived to be an international Christian convention. The background to, and the resolution of, the conflict was evidently a complex one. It certainly was not, as so much scholarship suggests, a simple matter of 'Celtic' versus 'Roman', in which 'Roman' won.

Colman and some other representatives of the 'Celtic' church in England (Celt and Anglo-Saxon alike) subsequently withdrew to Scotland and Ireland. They and others, such as the influential English Bishop Ecgbert, who had travelled to Ireland on *peregrinatio* before the Synod of Whitby, founded 'English' centres such as 'Mayo of the English' and Inishbofin. These subsequently conformed to Roman usage, attracting further English recruits and numbering English bishops amongst their visitors during the eighth century. The Irish welcomed all such foreign visitors and accommodated and educated them free of charge. As late as the twelfth century, there was an 'English Quarter' at the monastery of Armagh. Such figures may also have been involved with other centres associated with English names, such as Tullylease, County Cork, which includes, as part of a group of sculptures, a slab with a cross and inscription in Insular script. The inscription commemorates Berechtuine (Old English, Beorhtwine), the Englishman who founded the

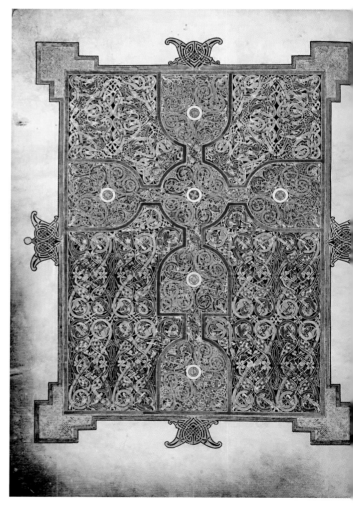

monastery there, which is thought to date to the eighth or ninth century. Its decoration, which features a cross with chalice-shaped terminals, is similar to that encountered on some of the Lindisfarne name-stones and on the Matthew carpet-page of the Lindisfarne Gospels. This need not imply any direct relationship, and certainly does not establish Tullylease as an English foundation; but it does indicate, once again, a shared cultural context. Such a blend is also likely to have prevailed at another important Irish monastery mentioned by Bede – Rath Melsigi (thought to be in County Carlow). Here, English monks such as Bishop Ecgbert and Willibrord came from Northumbria to study during the second half of the seventh century. And from here, along with Irish and Northumbrian personnel, Willibrord launched his mission to convert Frisia, founding monasteries such as Echternach and Utrecht. Other centres have dedications to Colman, Bishop of Lindisfarne. These include Tarbat (Ross and Cromarty) in Pictland, where recent excavations have revealed an important monastery with a wealth of high-quality sculpture incorporating Pictish, Irish and Northumbrian influences, and where there is also evidence of book production. Could this have been one of the places where Colman spent time after he had lost the debate at the Synod of Whitby in 664?

Nonetheless, those parts of the 'Celtic' church that had not already done so also gradually adopted the Roman dating of Easter, renewing their missionary efforts on the continent and conducting internal spiritual reforms. In 686 the abbot of Iona and biographer of St Columba, Adomnán, visited Jarrow where he accepted the Roman Easter and subsequently persuaded many Irish houses to do likewise (Bede, *Historia Ecclesiastica*, Book V). His own community of Iona remained obdurate, however, only finally coming into line in 715/716 following the dedicated persuasion of Ecgbert, an English bishop in Ireland. Ecgbert was also instrumental in motivating Willibrord's mission to the continent (*Historia Ecclesiastica*, Book III and Book V) and may have been crucial in encouraging the Pictish Church to align itself with Northumbria. He may also have composed the letter from King Nechtan to Abbot Ceolfrith of Jarrow in 713–14. It has been argued that, as Ecgbert was based in Ireland, his initiatives (at least in relation to Willibrord's mission) should be viewed as Irish. That may be so, but Ecgbert evidently did not perceive this as restricting his relations with England. Perhaps the English foundations in Ireland, post-Whitby, should be viewed less as 'protest votes' and more as link mechanisms. By 772 the remainder of the Columban church had adopted the Roman Easter and the potential schism was over. From the end of the seventh century onwards there are signs of a new 'eirenic' atmosphere of reconciliation and collaboration pervading the thought of many of the leading ecclesiastical figures of Northumbria and Ireland, as they sought to celebrate their combined Roman, Eastern and Celtic legacies. The leadership of the Lindisfarne community passed into the hands of members of the *parochia* of English birth, such as Eata (an original English pupil of Aidan's) and Cuthbert, formerly of the daughter-house of Melrose.

St Wilfrid of York (died 709/710) is often seen as the champion of *romanitas* in England, closely followed in Northumbria by Benedict Biscop and Ceolfrith. Wilfrid's vision for the English church was dynamic and outward-looking, but it did not take account of the needs and sensitivities of those who might not fully concur. He represented a threat to the royal and aristocratic property-owning interest groups of the North, as well as to the religious foundations that were forced to keep him friendly by subsuming their land-holdings within his own. If ever there was a 'troublesome priest' this was he, and we know too well the fate that was later to befall another – Thomas Becket. From 681–86 Wilfrid evangelized Sussex, with the aid of a large band of armed monks, similar to the one which had accompanied him in his missionary endeavours in Frisia. In Sussex he encountered the Irish abbot Dicul/Deicola of Bosham and his little party of monks, but rapidly eclipsed their work, claiming the region's conversion as his own initiative. The last part of England to be formally evangelized was the Isle of Wight, which was forcibly converted in 686 as part of the subjection and ethnic cleansing of the island by the pagan King Cadwalla of the Gewissae in Wessex, with the connivance of Wilfrid. In 687–88, following Cuthbert's death, Wilfrid administered the See of Lindisfarne, engendering a period of bitterness of which Bede can scarcely bring himself to speak. Wilfrid was expelled from office in 691 and excommunicated in 703, causing him to travel to Rome to appeal, and from where he returned, vindicated, in 705. He died around 709/10, and by the 720s, when his 'Life' was penned by Stephen (sometimes known as Eddius Stephanus, a cantor at Ripon), his cult was being actively promoted at Ripon as a rival to that of another of the delegates at the Synod of Whitby, St Cuthbert (died 687), who came to represent the subsequent reconciliation movement.

St Cuthbert and Reconciliation After Whitby

Cuthbert came to Lindisfarne in 664 with his abbot, Eata, from Melrose, presumably as a direct consequence of the Synod of Whitby. Colman's initial replacement – Tuda, an Englishman trained in the Roman tradition in the south of Ireland – was made bishop at Colman's request (*Historia Ecclesiastica*, Book III) but died very soon after his appointment, with the result that for fourteen years, 664–78, the bishopric was vested in Hexham rather than Lindisfarne. The abbacy, however, remained (again at Colman's request) within the Columban orbit, with Eata's transfer from Melrose. He and Cuthbert were stalwart representatives of the local Columban tradition, having been forced to leave Ripon shortly before 663 to make way for Wilfrid and his followers. They were, however, more inclined than Colman and his party to work towards a resumption of harmonious relationships with the Roman mainstream. The post-Whitby solution, in the case of the monastery at Lindisfarne, therefore seems initially to have been a constructive compromise, allowing it and other key Columban houses such as Melrose and Whitby to retain something of their earlier allegiances whilst actively promoting the new order in Northumbria. The hand of Archbishop Theodore can perhaps be detected behind the subsequent shaping of the Lindisfarne bishopric. He is known to have visited the island on at least one occasion, at which time he dedicated the wooden church built by Bishop Finan to St Peter (Bede, *Historia Ecclesiastica*, Book III). Lindisfarne's relationship with Canterbury, and with York, should therefore be kept in mind as another source of 'romanizing' influence, alongside that of Monkwearmouth/Jarrow.

Aidan's work had been perpetuated by a worthy Irish successor, Bishop Finan. The most influential of Holy Island's saints, however, was the Northumbrian St Cuthbert, whose cult was established there from around 698. It continued to grow during the early eighth century, and came to embody the spirit of the Insular church after the upheavals surrounding the Synod of Whitby. In the first of his early 'Lives', composed around 705 by an anonymous monk at Lindisfarne and reworked into prose and verse lives by Bede, Cuthbert is presented as an eloquent and charismatic preacher who was not afraid to get his hands dirty, travelling to the most remote and hostile places to spread the Word and to heal the sick. He loved the life of the hermit and would retreat to solitude whenever possible to replenish his energy to commit to work in the world. He was also a canny politico to whom Christ's injunction to the apostles to be 'wise as serpents and gentle as doves' must have been a touchstone. For he was dealing not with the benign Oswald but with King Ecgfrith of Northumbria, a difficult and troubled man whose wife, the beautiful Etheldreda (foundress of Ely, died 679), would not consummate their marriage, preferring to leave it at St Wilfrid's behest to become a nun at St Ebbe's monastery of Coldingham. His father had left a formidable military reputation for him to transcend; he was intent upon territorial aggrandisement and was not averse to a little genocide, believing that the ends justify the means. Ecgfrith accordingly embarked upon a policy of subjugating neighbouring British kingdoms and even invaded both Scotland and Ireland – all of them by then Christian territories. The Columban tradition required its key members to urge restraint and morality upon secular leaders, and this was the man whom Cuthbert had to keep on the straight and narrow. Ecgfrith insisted that Cuthbert become bishop of Lindisfarne, a powerful role that he reluctantly accepted. He was fully aware of the tensions and

Bede's Prose *Life of St Cuthbert*. St Cuthbert building his cell with the help of an angel, Durham, late twelfth century.

compromises of working for the eternal kingdom of God in the worldy present. Lindisfarne would become a victim of its own success, as its properties and authority grew. Cuthbert is reported to have said the if only he could build an oratory with walls so high that all he could see was the sky, he would still be afraid that the love of money and the cares of the world would snatch him away. This is exactly what he did build on his Inner Farne hermitage. The island he chose was not one of the more remote, however, but the one closest to the beach beneath the royal citadel of Bamburgh. Every time Egcfrith and his courtiers looked out to sea they were presented with the symbolic presence of Cuthbert – an emaciated, vulnerable, indomitable Gandhi-like figure, reminding them both of the responsibilities that accompanied wealth and power and of spiritual as well as material concerns. It is worth remembering that, in accordance with contemporary Irish law, the means of obtaining ultimate legal redress for an injustice was to fast outside the offender's door. Such an eremitic 'hunger-strike' could be a powerful tool in achieving social justice.

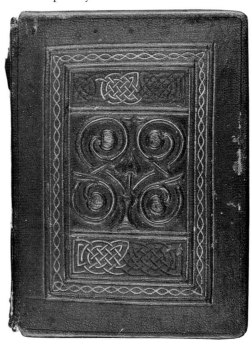

It is Cuthbert however who, following Eata's example, emerges in Bede's narrative as the leading figure in the process of reconciliation. It was this role – along with his ability to combine the best of the Celtic ascetic tradition of spirituality, roving ministry and perceptible sanctity with the administrative tasks of the ecclesiastical infrastructure – which featured in the posthumous development of his early cult. Having trained at Melrose, Cuthbert held the posts of guest-master at Ripon and prior of Melrose and subsequently of Lindisfarne, where Bede tells us he instructed the brethren in the observance of regular discipline (*Historia Ecclesiastica*, Book IV). In the prose *Vita Cuthberti* however, he also says that up to the time of writing the monastic constitution of Lindisfarne remained, with Cuthbert's aid, in the same form as that established under Aidan – indicating that any reform was far from extreme and that the Columban tradition continued to be respected into the eighth century.

Binding of the Cuthbert Gospel of St John (formerly known as the Stonyhurst Gospel), late seventh century. The book was found in the coffin of St Cuthbert in 1104 and retains its binding, the earliest to survive in the West, bound in 'Coptic' fashion. It was made at Monkwearmouth/ Jarrow, perhaps as a gift to Cuthbert's shrine.

Cuthbert became bishop of Lindisfarne in 685, under royal pressure, and died alone on his Farne hermitage in 687. His body was brought back to Holy Island, despite his own wish to remain on his place of retreat – his 'gateway to resurrection' – and his reservations concerning the implications for his community of establishing a major cult. In 698 Bishop Eadbert ordered his relics, along with those of other saintly members of the community, to be moved from the stone sarcophagus to the right of the altar at Lindisfarne and gathered up for greater veneration. Upon opening Cuthbert's tomb his remains were found to be miraculously incorrupt, and plans were rapidly drawn up to make a greater event of the translation and to place his body in a wooden coffin occupying a central focal point on the floor of the sanctuary above the original tomb. Bede (*Historia Ecclesiastica*, Book IV) tells us that eleven years after Cuthbert's death:

Divine Providence guided the community to exhume his bones... When they informed Bishop Eadbert of their wish, he gave approval and directed that it should be carried out on the anniversary of his burial... and when they opened the grave, they found the body whole and incorrupt... the brothers were awestruck, and hastened to inform the bishop of their discovery. At that time he was living alone at some distance from the church in a place surrounded by the sea... it was here that his venerable predecessor Cuthbert had served God in solitude for a period before he went to the Farne Island... having clothed the body in fresh garments, they laid it in a new coffin which they placed on the floor of the sanctuary.

No sign here of a major celebration of the translation, conducted during the penitential season of Lent and in the bishop's absence. It is, nonetheless, the translation of 698 that has come to be associated with the manufacture of the Lindisfarne Gospels, as another visible focus of the cult of St Cuthbert. This conclusion was reached partly on the basis of the attempts of scholars during the twentieth century to make sense of the cultural relationships and the production of artistic monuments of the period. It relied largely upon the later history of the book, notably the colophon added around 950–70 by Aldred, a member of the community after it had moved to Chester-le-Street. This says that the book was made in honour of God and St Cuthbert by Bishop Eadfrith (698–721), bound by his successor Bishop Aethilwald (721–40) and adorned with metalwork by Billfrith the anchorite. Such a statement, made over 200 years after the event, cannot be taken as absolute fact, and Aldred had his own agenda; but it is likely to preserve earlier community lore and may be correct. Other evidence would indicate that this remarkable book was probably made on Holy Island around 715–20.

The Lindisfarne Gospels, like the Book of Durrow and the Book of Kells, have been the subject of a great deal of debate, centering on whether they were made in England or Ireland. Similarly, the perceived opposition of the Celtic and Roman camps has dominated historical, theological and art historical debate relating to the period, and has led to an overly-polarized stance aggravated by modern nationalism. Whitby did not occasion a wholesale English rejection of the Celtic Christian past per se, or a complete breakdown in communications. Neither did Celtdom harbour a pre-existing antipathy to the Roman tradition or a spirit of introverted isolationism from which England had to assert its independence; rather the contrary. In correcting such preconceptions the pendulum of scholarly debate has swung too far in both directions, and only now is it steadying to a more measured, balanced middleground.

Colman and Wilfrid, the key protagonists in the debate, may not have seen it this way, of course. Colman felt obliged to withdraw his labours, and Wilfrid seems to have viewed his victory as bestowing a *carte blanche* to trample over the feelings and rights of those who stood in the path of his ambitious personal vision for the English church. This was to bring him into conflict not only with the remaining representatives of the Columban tradition but also with the kings of Northumbria, Archbishop Theodore and the ecclesiastical establishment. Nor was his area of activities confined to northern England or even to Sussex, Frisia, Gaul and Rome. His intervention in the succession crisis of the Frankish Prince Dagobert has also recently emerged, with Wilfrid negotiating the young prince's safe exile in Ireland and subsequently working for his return to power. That Irish influence continued to be exerted in England is indicated by the Synod of Hertford in 672, at which enactments were passed concerning wandering clergy and the 'orthodox' celebration of Easter; and by the Council of Celchyth (Chelsea) which as late as 810 still considered it necessary to deny Irish clergy the right to exercise any spiritual authority in England. The need for such prohibitions showed that they were still active there.

The Northumbrian conflict with the forces of Mercia and of North Wales, and its incursion into the territories of its British, Pictish and Celtic neighbours, had escalated throughout the reigns of Oswald, Oswy and Ecgfrith. In 679 Archbishop Theodore negotiated a peace that acknowledged the independence of the kingdoms of Northumbria and Mercia. Henceforth Northumbrian ambitions south of the Humber were curtailed, forcing Ecgfrith to concentrate his attentions upon expansion northwards. He raided Dalriada and Pictland, and the latter led to his death in battle in 685. He even launched hostilities in Ireland, but relations seem to have improved under his successors, notably Aldfrith (Oswy's son by an Irish wife) who reigned from 685–705. Aldfrith had been educated in Wessex, Ireland and Iona and was renowned for his learning. He seems to have adopted a more tolerant stance in respect of Northumbria's Celtic, Pictish and British neighbours and their religious traditions. From then on, Northumbrian ambitions generally concentrated upon maintaining the status quo in respect of their neighbours and retaining control of what is now the Scottish Lowlands and Cumbria. They were largely successful in this, and the area between Forth and Tweed remained in Northumbrian hands until Lothian was finally ceded to Kenneth II of Scotland by the English king, Edgar, in the 970s. This deal was facilitated by the community of St Cuthbert, and members of this order, including Aldred, accompanied the Scottish ruler to negotiations in Wessex. The River Tweed finally came to demarcate the Anglo-Scottish border following Malcolm of Scotland's victory at Carham in 1018.

With the accession of the Pictish King Nechtan in 706, Pictland had entered a new phase in its relations with Northumbria. It began conforming to the Roman Easter dating and sought Northumbrian support in 'modernizing' the Pictish Church (*Historia Ecclesiastica*, Book V). Columban influence in Pictland seems to have suffered as a result. The eleventh-century Irish Annals of Tighernach record that in 717 the family of Iona was expelled 'across the back of Britain' by King Nechtan. In this he may have been assisted by Bishop Ecgbert. The letter which Ecgbert may have helped Nechtan to compose included a request to Abbot Ceolfrith of Monkwearmouth/Jarrow for stonemasons to instruct in church construction. This indicates that by this time, the essentially Iron-Age timber

St Peter's, Monkwearmouth; porch with zoomorphic carvings, from Benedict Biscop's original foundation of 674.

construction techniques of hewn oak and reed thatch initially employed on Holy Island and its other foundations were being augmented, if not replaced, by the late Roman tradition of masonry. This had been reintroduced to England via Augustine's mission to Kent, and to Northumbria via Gaulish masons imported to construct two important new linked monasteries – Monkwearmouth and Jarrow, further south on Wear and Tyne. When the Northumbrian nobleman Benedict Biscop (died 689) founded these two houses in the 670s–80s it was with the assistance of a royal land grant of ninety hides; some rate of inflation on the ten hides initially given to Lindisfarne and its satellites. Wilfrid likewise employed impressive stone construction techniques, *more Romanum*, at his key holdings such as Hexham and Ripon.

Throughout the last quarter of the seventh century and the first half of the eighth, the Northumbrian landscape became increasingly populated with worship sites – some, as Bede warns, sadly little more than the 'tax breaks' of the Northumbrian aristocracy. That there was some pagan resistance is indicated by an episode recorded by Bede in his prose *Life of St Cuthbert*, in which the monks of the monastery of Tynemouth were buffeted by a storm whilst making for home and were jeered at from the shore by the newly Christianized populace, who resented the loss of some of their earlier pagan ways. Fortunately Cuthbert's prayers prevailed and they made safe harbour. The impact of the initial apostatization after the withdrawal of Paulinus's mission can also be detected when Bede tells of a church founded in Lincoln by his first convert, Blaecca, Reeve of that

ABOVE: stained glass windows by glaziers imported from Gaul in 681. St Paul's, Jarrow.

RIGHT: The chancel of the present church (to the right of the later Anglo-Saxon tower) is comprised of the masonry and stained glass windows originally constructed in 681 as the easternmost of two aligned churches. The present medieval nave replaces the other. St Paul's, Jarrow.

city. This church, despite being built of stone and displaying fine workmanship, 'today, either through neglect or enemy damage, has lost its roof, although the walls are still standing' (Bede, *Historia Eccleasiastica*, Book II).

Lindisfarne's land-holdings also grew dramatically during this period. Ecgfrith's donations included Carlisle and adjacent land, the Bowmont Valley and Cartmel. Under the auspices of King Ecgfrith of Northumbria and Archbishop Theodore of Canterbury, the church structure of Bernicia became organized around three key bishoprics: Lindisfarne, Hexham and the newly-refounded Whithorn. From its heartland of 'Islandshire', and adjacent 'Norhamshire', Lindisfarne controlled the Bernician coast. Its lands and foundations (such as Coldingham and Aberlady) lined the northern English seaboard as far as Abercorn, near Edinburgh on the Forth Estuary. Abercorn is dedicated to St Serf, a follower of Ninian, and it is thought that the church there may have been refounded from Lindisfarne in the seventh century. As part of the reforms following the Synod of Whitby, Archbishop Theodore had established Trumwine at Abercorn as bishop of the Picts, but following Trumwine's flight south following the Battle of Nechtanesmere in 685 (at which the Pictish King Brude defeated the Northumbrians), administration of the former See is thought to have passed to Lindisfarne and thence to Durham.

Other major houses of Lindisfarne, including Norham and Melrose, lined the strategic Tweed Valley. This line may well have marked a traditional route of communication with the western coast of Scotland and with Iona itself. The rivers Tweed and Clyde come within around five miles of each other in the interior and would have provided a valuable riverine communications route, along with the Forth-Clyde line. The ancient Roman road network also seems to have featured in the planning, with the early monastery of Melrose lying adjacent to a major Roman fort – Trimontium, at what is now Newstead – and near a Roman bridge carrying the region's main north-south road. Nor were Lindisfarne's holdings confined to the North. Some, such as Chester-le-Street, Gilling and Crayke, lay southwards and may have marked staging posts, or *mansios*, en route to York, where the Bishop of Lindisfarne seems to have owned a residence from at least the late seventh century. The area to the north east of York emerged as an important meeting place for the intellectual and ecclesiastical traditions of Lindisfarne and Monkwearmouth/Jarrow, which all held important daughter-houses or other connections around Ryedale and Rosedale from Crayke to Lastingham, including Gilling East, Stonegrave, Hovingham and Kirkdale.

Lindisfarne was a crucial lynchpin in Northumbria's political game-plan, not only in ensuring its physical control of the northern half of the kingdom, but in winning the hearts and minds of its multi-ethnic population. The visible remains of this northern Northumbrian spiritual hegemony survive in the sculptured monuments to be found from Abercorn, Aberlady and Jedburgh to Ruthwell, Bewcastle, Lowther and Hoddom. They also find an echo in the Pictish Class II stones, their crosses and iconographies of Northumbrian derivation merging with the enigmatic ancient Pictish symbols. With its Celtic antecedents and its prominent role within the English establishment, the community of St Cuthbert was ideally placed to act as the regent of the North. Herein lay the roots of the later medieval development of the medieval palatinate – the prince-bishops of Durham.

Such grandeur was yet to be fully realized. At the time that Bede was writing his *Ecclesiastical History of the English People* – which was completed in 731 and dedicated to King Ceolwulf who was about to enter Lindisfarne as a monk – Northumbria's 'Golden Age' was already past and the focus of attention and power had shifted southwards. But temporal power is not always a prerequisite of cultural achievement, and it is in the period of comparative political ebbtide that Northumbria seems to have produced some of the greatest cultural statements of its legacy and identity. These came to embody that of early 'England' as a whole and

RIGHT: The Ruthwell Cross. Mid-eighth-century, of Northumbrian workmanship, but lying within the British kingdom of Rheged which had recently been annexed by Northumbria. Part of the 'Dream of the Rood' is carved on its borders.

FAR RIGHT: The Bewcastle Cross, mid-eighth-century, Northumbrian. Christ is shown adored by the beasts. A runic inscription (now illegible) is thought to name a king of Northumbria, who may be depicted below with his falcon. Alternatively this carving could represent St John with his eagle.

included Bede's remarkable attempt to create a national history, the *Historia Ecclesiastica*, and the work of his literary patron, Bishop Eadfrith of Lindisfarne, in creating the Lindisfarne Gospels.

BEDE AND MONKWEARMOUTH/JARROW

In acting as the chronicler of the conversion, Bede (died 735) is assuming the role of a latter-day Eusebius, Constantine's court bishop and chronicler of the early Church – and also perhaps of St Jerome. In so doing Bede became a Church Father for the new Insular church. He had been presented by his relatives at the age of seven to serve as a novice in one of the most important monasteries in Northumbria. He left the monastery on only a few occasions during his life, and then merely to travel locally, and there he wrote works that encompassed a vision of the world and that allowed others to travel, literally and in the imagination, to the Holy Land. The twin house of Monkwearmouth/Jarrow had two physical locations, one at the mouth of the River Wear and the other of the River Tyne, but they were united under the rule of one abbot. They were founded by Benedict Biscop in 673/4 and 681 and dedicated to Sts Peter and Paul respectively, and were amongst the most romanizing centres in England. Biscop travelled widely on the continent and employed masons and glaziers from Gaul to construct Monkwearmouth and to teach Anglo-Saxons their crafts. Their work can still be seen at both sites, where the current churches incorporate part of their fabric and where stained glass windows, sculptural ornaments and fragments of furniture have been found.

Monkwearmouth/Jarrow were both coenobitic monasteries, their rules of life guided by that of St Benedict of Nursia, and their layout communal. Each had two stone churches in alignment, the smaller and easternmost for the sole use of the brethren. The church at Monkwearmouth preserves its original two-storey porch, with portals open to the elements, carved with long-billed Germanic animal motifs. Beside them were buildings where the monks lived (Jarrow had a refectory on the ground floor and a dormitory above) and an abbot's house. At Jarrow the scriptorium seems to have been in the upper room of the abbot's house and at Monkwearmouth it was upstairs in the two-storey church. Even these magnificent houses nearly died out, however, in the face of plague. At one point only one small boy (probably Bede) and Biscop's friend Ceolfrith (died 716), who succeeded him as abbot, remained alive to intone the Psalms, lections and prayers of the Divine Office at Jarrow. Standing inside the chancel of St Paul's, Jarrow, which effectively embodies the easternmost of the two churches that Biscop built on the site, one can almost hear them still. Biscop and Ceolfrith adorned their churches with images, icons and books gathered on their travels, as Bede tells us in the *Lives of the Abbots of Monkwearmouth and Jarrow*.

Benedict Biscop 'brought back a large number of books on all branches of sacred knowledge, some bought at a favourable price, others the gift of well-wishers. At Vienne on the journey home he picked up the books he had left there in the care of his friends.'

BEDE, *LIVES OF THE ABBOTS*

He brought back many holy pictures of the saints to adorn the church of St Peter he had built: a painting of the Mother of God, the Blessed Mary Ever-Virgin, and one of each of the twelve apostles which he fixed round the central arch on a wooden entablature reaching from wall to wall; pictures of incidents in the Gospels with which he decorated the south wall, and scenes from St John's vision of the apocalypse for the north wall. Thus all who entered the church, even those who could not read, were able, whichever way they looked, to contemplate the dear face of Christ and His saints, even if only in a picture, to put themselves more firmly in mind of the Lord's Incarnation and, as they saw the decisive moment of the Last Judgement before their very eyes be brought to examine their conscience with all due severity.

These images, which Benedict brought back from Rome in 679-80 to adorn the church at Monkwearmouth, may be recollected in the figures engraved on the wooden coffin of St Cuthbert (see page 38), with its virgin and child, its apostles and the angels and evangelist symbols of the Last Judgement. He also came back with 'a great mass of books of every sort', the first and foremost of the benefits that Bede records that he bestowed upon his foundation. In his *Lives of the Abbots*, Bede records that on his next and fifth journey to the eternal city, around 685, Benedict returned with:

… a large supply of sacred books and no less a stock of sacred pictures than on previous journeys. He brought back paintings of the life of Our Lord for the chapel of the Holy Mother of God which he had built within the main monastery, setting them, as its crowning glory, all the way round the walls. His treasures included a set of pictures for the monastery and church of the blessed apostle Paul, consisting of scenes, very skilfully arranged, to show how the Old Testament foreshadowed the New. In one set, for instance, the picture of Isaac carrying the wood on which he was to be burnt as a sacrifice was placed immediately below that of Christ carrying the cross on which He was about to suffer. Similarly the Son of Man up on the cross was paired with the serpent raised up by Moses in the desert.

Thus the images that covered the walls of the churches at Monkwearmouth and Jarrow served as visual summaries of aspects of Scripture and of the relationship between the Old and New Testaments, illustrated by means of didactic typology in which an episode or figure in one prefigured the other.

Benedict collected books from Italy (where he may also have acquired Byzantine tomes), from Gaul, and presumably also from southern England, bearing in mind that he served for a time as abbot of St Augustine's Abbey in Canterbury where the school of Theodore and Hadrian flourished. On one of his first journeys to Rome, Biscop accompanied Wilfrid, and on one of his subsequent Italian trips Biscop took with him Ceolfrith, whom he later commissioned to found Jarrow. Benedict had decreed that, following his death, the library he had amassed for the instruction of the two communities should be conserved and kept as a whole. Upon assuming the abbacy of both foundations, bringing them ever closer as a unit, Ceolfrith not only observed this behest but set about expanding the libraries of both houses (Bede, *Lives of the Abbots*).

He doubled the number of books in the libraries of both monasteries with an ardour equal to that which Benedict had shown in founding them. He added three copies of the new translation of the Bible to the one copy of the old translation which he had brought back from Rome. One of these he took with him as a present when he went back to Rome in his old age, and the other two he bequeathed to his monasteries. For eight hides of land by the River Fresca he exchanged with King Aldfrid, who was very learned in the scriptures, the magnificently worked copy of the Cosmographers which Benedict had bought in Rome.

The Codex Amiatinus. Ezra miniature, from one of the Ceolfrith Bibles. It was made at Monkwearmouth/Jarrow, before 716, the year that Ceolfrith set off for Rome to present it to the pope. Until the 1880s it was thought to have been made in Italy. Along with the Lindisfarne Gospels, it preserves the most reliable version of St Jerome's Vulgate text.

This passage gives some insight into the value of books as commodities at the time: the land exchanged represented the livelihoods of at least eight families, and its riverside location probably rendered it even more valuable. The total land-holdings of the combined communites of Sts Peter and Paul at the time when Ceolfrith set off for Rome in 716 was 150 hides – the value of some nineteen such books. The libraries of Monkwearmouth/Jarrow may have represented their most valuable financial asset, as well as their spiritual and intellectual mainstay.

We can only speculate on the comparative value of the three massive single volume Bibles (pandects) produced for the abbot, which were known as the Ceolfrith Bibles and were formed of some 1,550 calfskins each. These were the result of a major editorial and scribal campaign that must have occupied a number of years sometime during Ceolfrith's abbacy of both houses (689–716). Bede would have played a leading role in this programme, and was probably one of the scribes. One of these pandects accompanied Ceolfrith on this final journey to Rome on retirement in 716 and has survived in the form of the famous Codex Amiatinus (now in the Biblioteca

Medicea-Laurenziana in Florence). Fragments of one of the others have resurfaced and are now in the British Library. This seems to have been donated by King Offa later in the eighth century to Worcester, where it was already thought that it had been made in Rome. The dedication inscription of the Codex Amiatinus had been tampered with and Ceolfrith's name replaced by that of a local Italian saint, and it was only recognized as the work of English rather than Italo-Byzantine artists and scribes in the late nineteenth century, so 'romanizing' is its style. One of the Ceolfrith Bibles was seen by Alcuin of York in the late eighth century, who refers to it in verse. It may have stimulated his own influential edition, which resulted in the single-volume Alcuin Bibles produced by the Tours scriptorium during the second quarter of the ninth century for dissemination throughout the Carolingian Empire. These proved highly influential in the western later medieval transmission of Scripture.

Ceolfrith died en route in Burgundy, but his companions carried his Bible to Rome. This was a visible statement of conformity with the ideas and taste of the Mediterranean world, and elicited a letter of thanks from the Pope which was sent to Ceolfrith's successor, Hwaetberht. It also brought about the entry of the communities into the 'comitatus' (companions) of St Peter, with all the attendant diplomatic benefits. However, there was another – and for Ceolfrith and his brethren, deeper – meaning to such a gesture. Ceolfrith's pandects do not merely represent a culturally and politically motivated attempt to copy a book or books made in early Christian Italy (namely the Codex Grandior and the Novem Codices, written at Cassiodorus's monastery of the Vivarium during the sixth century, and perhaps a Neapolitan Gospelbook that the maker of the Lindisfarne Gospels also used as his textual model. These are thought to have formed part of the Monkwearmouth/Jarrow libraries. The Neapolitan Gospelbook may have been sent to Lindisfarne on inter-library loan through Bishop Eadfrith's friendship with Bede, or the Monkwearmouth/Jarrow copy may have been provided.) Rather, such books represent a further contribution to the complex processes of translation and editing which extend from the first translation of the Old Testament into Greek – the Septuagint – through the translations into Latin from Hebrew and Greek by St Jerome, to Cassiodorus's own editions of the pre-Vulgate Old Latin (his Codex Grandior, which Ceolfrith brought back from Rome) and Jerome's Vulgate (Cassiodorus's Novem Codices). For Ceolfrith desired to create a monumental single volume that stressed the integral, complementary nature of the Old and New Testaments. When Ceolfrith, self-styled in his dedication page as 'abbot from the ends of the earth', set off for Rome with his tribute to the papacy, he was proclaiming his people's role in the apostolic mission. Not only had the holy Word been preached in the farthest corners of the earth; the newly won people of God were able to make an active contribution to its dissemination, worthy of the traditions of the Church Fathers. This essay in book production was no antiquarian feat, designed merely to impress and to gain status (although these were probably welcome bonuses): it symbolized the fulfilment in the West of

Christ's commission to his disciples to take the Good News throughout the world, an achievement which was to herald the very coming of the kingdom of God.

Another welcome by-product of Ceolfrith's embassy, which he so sadly did not live to complete in person, would perhaps have been an *apologia* on behalf of the people of England – and Northumbria in particular – for the persistent squabbles and recalcitrance in enacting papal *dicta* which had accompanied the turbulent career of Wilfrid, and his expulsions from office by king and prelate alike. In recent years the papacy had been forced time and again to listen to the complaints of both parties. England was in need of some powerful PR if the phenomenal achievements of the preceding century and more were not to be tarnished. It transpired that a book served, and served well, as the ambassador of the English nation.

The Making of the Lindisfarne Gospels

The romanizing influence of Monkwearmouth/Jarrow is one of the ingredients in the complex cultural mixture that went into producing one of the greatest and most distinctive symbols of Insular Christianity – the Lindisfarne Gospels (see pages 170–71). It is encyclopaedic in its cultural references and various scholars have claimed that it may have been made at Monkwearmouth/Jarrow, in Ireland at Rath Melsigi where Bishop Ecgbert and Willibrord spent some time, or in the monastery founded by the latter at Echternach in Luxembourg. However, taking all of the evidence on balance, Lindisfarne remains the most likely venue for such a fusion of influences. The exceptional care and resources lavished upon its production reinforce the idea that it was conceived as a cult object – most probably as a focal point at the shrine of the leading Northumbrian saint, Cuthbert. This is likely to have occurred during the first quarter of the eighth century, when St Cuthbert's community on Holy Island is known to have been engaged in collaboration with Monkwearmouth/Jarrow and was in direct communication with Bede, rather than in preparation for the translation of Cuthbert's relics in 698 as traditionally thought.

Considerable time and resource would have had to be allocated to the project and this does not accord with the account of the translation, the celebrations surrounding which seem to have been stepped up only after the discovery of the incorrupt status of Cuthbert's exhumed body. Other factors also tend to support a probable date of production during the second decade of the eighth century. From 710 there were attempts to establish a rival cult of St Wilfrid at Ripon, with a book that he had obtained on the continent, written in gold on purple pages – an overt statement of romanization – as a major focal point. This may have signalled the need for an even greater book for Cuthbert's shrine: one that visually embodied the contribution of the peoples of Britain and Ireland to the international Christian tradition. Its highly gifted maker is likely to have been a very important member of the monastic community, in accordance with Columban tradition in which the scribes transmitting Scripture had to be from amongst the *seniores* – the most experienced, gifted and senior members of the community. There is reason to suspect that it may have been Bishop Eadfrith, who died in 721. His death may explain the unfinished nature of the work, which was about a month short of completion.

What might it actually have meant to those who dedicated their lives to God's service to be entrusted with the transmission of his Word, as preachers and as scribes? In a letter to Bishop Acca of Hexham concerning his commentary on Luke, Bede says that 'I have subjected myself to that burden of work in which, as in innumerable bonds of monastic servitude which I shall pass over, I was myself at once dictator, notary, and scribe' (Bede, *Expositio in Lucam*). This revealing passage shows that he regarded such work as an expression of monastic humility, an *opus dei*, and that he differentiated between the functions of author, note-taker and formal scribal transmitter. Cassiodorus (the founder of an influential Italian monastery, the Vivarium or 'Fishponds', devoted to learning and dissemination of Scripture) wrote in his *Institutiones* that each word written by the monastic scribe was 'a wound on Satan's body', thereby implying that the scribe could be a 'soldier of Christ'. In the

same work he says that the Spirit continues to work in those who translate, expand or humbly copy Scripture, as in the biblical authors who were first inspired to write them. Indeed, Scripture lends the scribal analogy to the Lord himself (see Jeremiah 31:33; Hebrews 10:16; Psalm 45:1-2). Cassiodorus also says (in his commentary on Psalm 45:1-2 and in the *Institutiones*) that the scribe could preach with the hand alone and 'unleash tongues with the fingers', imitating the action of the Lord, who wrote the Law with his all-powerful finger. Bede pursues this theme in relation to Ezra the Scribe, who fulfilled the Law by rewriting its destroyed books, thereby opening his mouth to interpret Scripture and teach others. The act of writing is therefore presented as an essential, personal act for the scribe or teacher.

Such scriptural resonances have a bearing upon the circumstances of production of the Lindisfarne Gospels. For this amazingly complex and elegant book is surprisingly the work of a single artist-scribe who, from the evidence of his preparatory designs, intended to undertake all of the work himself, but who was prevented, probably by illness or death, from completing the final stages. The textual aspects were completed by the rubricator to make the book usable, but the final touches to the artwork remained unfinished. Modern scribes estimate that at least two years of full-time work in optimum physical conditions would be required to produce such a work and that, given the physical demands of the task, only three hours or so of good-quality work is likely to have been sustained each day. An assessment of the time needed to undertake such a task alongside the other monastic duties of the Divine Office, prayer, study and manual labour, would suggest that something more like five to ten years would actually have been required, depending on how much exemption was granted from other duties. This may have represented a recollection of a distinctive Celtic scribal response to injunctions to *meditatio/contemplatio*. The act

The Lindisfarne Gospels, British Library. Carpet-page and incipit-page of Luke's Gospel with a cat at the foot of the lower right border. In early Christian lore, the cat symbolized the threat of evil waiting to pounce on the unwary, such as the solemn, preoccupied procession of birds that march across the lower border towards the cat's mouth. It has already devoured a string of them that fill its stomach. The cat, Cruithne, was also the ancient equivalent of Cerberus, the guardian of the underworld. Lindisfarne, c.715–20.

of copying and transmitting the Gospels was to glimpse the divine and to place oneself in its service, and this may have been seen as a solitary undertaking on behalf of the community rather than a communal collaboration, as with many aspects of Celtic eremitic monasticism. As such these books are portals of prayer – the work of the scribe, like that of the icon painter, forming an act of prayer in which those who later read the book could participate. The physical endurance and deprivation and the levels of meditation and prayer required to produce a book such as the Lindisfarne Gospels equated it to the hermit's 'desert'. Just as St Cuthbert struggled with his demons on the Inner Farne hermitage on behalf of all humanity, so the monk who produced the Gospelbook which was to serve as a focus of his cult may also have seen his work as a sustained feat of spiritual and physical endurance, and as part of the apostolic mission of bringing the Word of God to the furthest outposts of the known world, enshrining it there within the new Temple of the Word and the embodiment of Christ – the Book.

The Insular illuminated copies of Scripture represent a sophisticated response to the patristic concept of the 'inner library' and the necessity for each believer to make him or herself a library of the divine Word. This was a sacred responsibility which Cummian referred to as 'entering the Sanctuary of God' by studying and transmitting Scripture (Cummian's Letter *De Controversia Paschale*). Books are the vessels from which the believer's ark, or inner library, is filled. They are the enablers of direct, contemporary Christian action, channels of the Spirit, and gateways to revelation, for 'In the beginning was the Word, and the Word was with God, and the Word was God' (John 1:1).

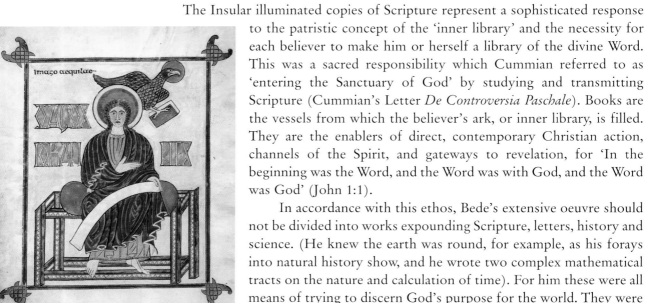

John miniature from the Lindisfarne Gospels, Lindisfarne, c.715–20.

In accordance with this ethos, Bede's extensive oeuvre should not be divided into works expounding Scripture, letters, history and science. (He knew the earth was round, for example, as his forays into natural history show, and he wrote two complex mathematical tracts on the nature and calculation of time). For him these were all means of trying to discern God's purpose for the world. They were ways of asking the questions 'how' and 'why', pre-empting the later quest to reconcile faith and science during the Age of Enlightenment – a different approach to the artificial post-Darwinian dichotomy between the two that still besets much current thinking.

Connections with Bede's commentaries written during the early eighth century and the influence of the three great pandects made at Monkwearmouth/Jarrow for Ceolfrith would also suggest a somewhat later date than the traditional 698 for the production of the Lindisfarne Gospels. So too would the inclusion of those lections that are marked within its carefully planned decorative programme, along with some from the Columban, Aquileiagian and Neapolitan traditions, which were papal additions to the Roman liturgy in 715. These may, of course, have enjoyed an earlier circulation, but their prominence in papal liturgical initiatives is likely to have drawn significant attention to them. Those planning the Lindisfarne Gospels were evidently taking pains to devise a layout in which lections from several sources were synthesized into a new decorative programme, designed to articulate the text and to enshrine not only an authoritative version of Jerome's Vulgate rescension of the Gospels but also the liturgy – including some of the most up-to-date papal thought on the subject. Unity and the avoidance of schism seem to have been a major consideration, not only textually but in the careful balancing within the decoration of iconic and non-figural decorative features. This was an impressive feat of tightrope walking at a time when iconoclasm and the whole question of idolatry (whether it is acceptable to depict the divine in human form) was definitely a live issue in both East and West.

When the opening words of the Gospels explode across the page they become an icon in their own right. They are the manifestation of the Word which is God (John 1:1), thereby avoiding the issue of idolatry, their maker reaching the same solution to the dilemma as that explored by Islamic scribes in their sacred lettering several centuries later. A similar solution is embodied in the great cross-carpet-pages (see pages 170-71) that introduce each of its Gospels. Their stylistic metalwork consciously alludes to the *Crux Gemmata*, the jewelled cross which for early Christians was a symbol of the Second Coming, also embodied in the metalwork processional crosses which were carried before the Gospelbook in the liturgy. This motif, of Coptic derivation, was termed a 'carpet-page' by art historians because it resembles an oriental rug, but references in books from Monkwearmouth/Jarrow to an Ordo for the celebration of Good Friday indicate that prayer mats were used in Europe at this time. If you were venerating the cross on Holy Island on Good Friday around the year 720 you would have spent part of the day praying in an easterly direction on a prayer mat: an indication of the dissemination of the shared rituals and culture of the eastern Mediterranean and its various faith groups during the early Middle Ages.

The fear of idolatry, enshrined in the Second Commandment, was bequeathed by Judaism to the other monotheistic religions of the Word. From its inception, Islam fostered the use of sacred calligraphy in a religious context to avoid such dangers. In the early Christian Church images had already assumed an iconic status as focuses of veneration which might be misinterpreted as the objects of worship. Yet, even during the state-sponsored iconoclasm in eighth-century Byzantium under Leo the Isaurian, certain symbols could be used as an alternative to figural representation. Thus the cross and the book became acceptable symbols of orthodox Christianity. In the 720s the iconoclast party erected a tablet above the great gate of the imperial palace, recording the substitution of a cross with the figure of Christ.

The Council of Nicaea of 787, however, supported attempts by the Empress Irene to restore images and stated that:

We therefore follow the pious customs of antiquity and pay these icons the honour of incense and lights just as we do the holy gospels and the venerable and life-giving cross.

Thus the practice of portraying the Godhead by means of abstract or symbolic images was reinforced within the Christian tradition from an early date. In the magnificent cross-carpet-page and decorated introduction to the Lindisfarne Gospels, the crosses and adorned words embody the Godhead and we are presented with the physical embodiment of the Word made flesh – or rather, the Word made word.

We therefore follow the pious customs of antiquity and pay these icons the honour of incense and lights just as we do the holy gospels and the venerable and life-giving cross.

THE COUNCIL OF NICAEA, 787

All of this complex cultural symbolism was assisted in the Lindisfarne Gospels by their maker's probable invention of new methods and materials of design. This included the following: chemical experimentation with pigments to provide an extensive palette (which achieved the range available to Mediterranean artists but using local materials); the pioneering of the lead-point (forerunner of the pencil) to achieve flexibility of layout and complexity of design; and the introduction of backlighting. This involved using a glass or horn writing slope with a strong light source behind it as well as a weaker light source behind the artist's shoulder to achieve the effect of a lightbox, so that the designs could be drawn on the back of the leaf of vellum. This meant that their fine detail was not obscured when the first layers of pigment were applied to the side of the leaf actually painted (a technique similar to that employed by modern cartoon animators prior to computerization). Such innovative techniques were well ahead of their time, and were developed by the artist to achieve the maximum integration of word and image. A scientific and technical knowledge of God's world was thereby utilized in his praise.

The resulting volume, the Lindisfarne Gospels, was a stunning object and a faithful textual embodiment of the Word of God as transmitted by the evangelists and St Jerome in his Vulgate Latin edition text. It was adapted for contemporary use in the liturgy – the public prayer life of the community – but it appears to have been consulted and used only on special occasions. It was a focal point, an enshrinement of ideals and a tabernacle of the Word which is divinity itself, designed to be seen. The viewer was to contemplate it as a portal of prayer, just as its creator, immersed in meditation in his eremitic desert, was rewarded with a glimpse of revelation – that all-consuming, all-transforming glimpse of the presence of God, and the awesome profundity of the sense of joy and completion to come. Its presence on the altar, or in its metalwork shrine, symbolically evoked the very presence of God and celebrated the tradition of the transmission of the Gospels and their use in preaching and prayer. It evoked the relationship between God, those who spread his Word in written and oral form throughout the ages and the nations, and those who had eyes to see and ears to hear. This was a Gospelbook to be seen, to celebrate, to enshrine and to inspire. This outstanding book has been the meeting place of faith and politics since its inception and it continues to fulfil that delicate role today. It was made in an age which had no perception of an imposed division between spiritual and secular, between work and prayer, as still remains the case in many modern societies. In its making it was conceived as an intercessory endeavour on behalf of all creation, celebrating its reconciliation and union with its creator. It remains a powerful, energized symbol of that perpetual human quest.

The picture which emerges shows the Lindisfarne Gospels being made in a centre which valued its Columban origins and which remained in communcation with the parochia. But this was also a centre that was textually independent, open to the influence of 'romanizing' centres such as Monkwearmouth/Jarrow and to contemporary papal innovations to the liturgy. It was also sensitive to 'live' ecclesiastical debates on matters which threatened schism. The cult of St Cuthbert was being shaped by Bishop Eadfrith, the probable maker of the Lindisfarne Gospels around 715–21, with the assistance of the greatest scholar of the day, Bede. Their aim was to present the saint as a focus of reconciliation, and to emphasize the collaborative nature of the Insular church which had been formed with the cultural input of Rome, the Celts, Gaul and the Middle East. Its decorated pages formed a visual statement of reconciliation in the post-Whitby Insular church and signalled its place in a wider Christian ecumen. They combine motifs from Celtic Iron-Age art, the animal interlace of the Germanic world, evangelist portraits akin to the frescoes of the early Roman churches, Coptic carpet-pages and a Latin text which preserves one of the purest versions of the Vulgate and in which Greek and runic-style letters are introduced. Pilgrims to the shrine of St Cuthbert – whether they had travelled from nearby, from Celtdom, from southern England, from the continent or the Middle East – would all have seen something on the pages of the Lindisfarne Gospels to make them feel welcome in this vision of cultural collaboration and ecumenical unity.

Around 950–70, Aldred also added an Old English word-by-word translation as a gloss between the lines, making it the oldest surviving translation of the Gospels into English. Such an initiative had however started earlier, for on his death bed in 735 Bede was translating the 'little Gospel that treats of the workings of love' – John's Gospel – into English. Unlike their later medieval counterparts who condemned Wycliffe and Tyndale as heretics, the Anglo-Saxons and the Celts did not suppress scholars who demystified Scripture by making it accessible to ordinary people in their own tongue. Instead they used whatever was helpful in imparting the 'Good News'.

THE IMPORTANCE OF THE BOOK IN INSULAR SOCIETY

Under such circumstances it is not surprising that every book should be an intensely personal work, reflecting the training and influences operating upon the individual as much as that of the community. People travelled as well as books and other stylistic models. When considering the relationships between the tiny proportion of books that have survived it is unwise to adopt a magnet-theory, grouping them all around known centres. The only places in Anglo-Saxon England to which extant books can be securely ascribed in any number are Monkwearmouth/Jarrow and Canterbury. That does not mean that they were all made there. In each case, the subtle balance of similarities and dissimilarities have to be carefully assessed and the possibility that artists and scribes from different backgrounds operated in the same place at the same time needs to be considered – especially in centres that are less inclined by their rules of life to favour coenobitic scriptorium practices, such as Lindisfarne. Books that are closely related stylistically (such as the Durham Cassiodorus) could have been made in Lindisfarne, Melrose, Norham, Hartlepool, or further south in Rosedale and Ryedale close to York, to name but a few candidates within the *parochia*.

Secular authorities were quick to avail themselves of the potent symbolism of word and image. Constantine stressed that his authority was based upon the sign of the cross, in the name of which he triumphed at the Milvian Bridge (echoed in the Jarrow cross-slab with its 'hoc signum' inscription). The mosaics portraying the Emperor Justinian and his entourage at San Vitale, Ravenna, feature a shield (the shield of faith) bearing a chi-rho-headed cross and a Gospelbook in a jewelled cover. Christ of the Last Judgement is likewise depicted at Sant Apollinare in Classe, and elsewhere, holding the book. The church was quick to represent the advantages of such tools to the aspirational dynasties encountered in north-western Europe. A major achievement accredited to St Augustine, following his conversion of King Ethelberht of Kent and his court, was the commital of the ruler's lawcode to the 'safe-keeping of writing' (preserved in the twelfth century Textus Roffensis). Augustine is even said, by Bede, to have devised written Old English especially for that purpose. A newly converted Anglo-Saxon ruler could thereby have sought to associate himself with Christian culture, and the ultimate Judge, and to have used writing to bolster his role as an heir to the authority of his late Roman precursors.

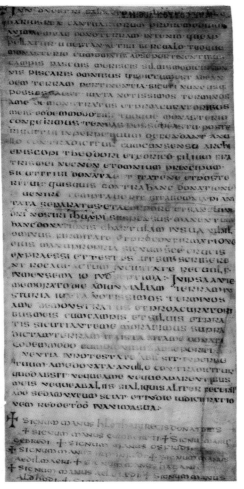

Charter of King Hlothere of Kent. The earliest dated surviving example of Anglo-Saxon handwriting, in high-grade uncial script. Hlothere granted land on the Isle of Thanet to Berhtwald, Bishop of Reculver in the presence of Archbishop Theodore. Reculver, Kent, 679.

Such developments are likely to have been indebted to heightened perceptions of the authority of the written word in the context of conversion and liturgy. The earliest extant Anglo-Saxon charters are written not in late Roman handwriting as seen on the continent, but in stately, high-grade lettering, of the sort usually reserved for religious texts. In 735 St Boniface sent a letter from the Germanic mission-fields to Abbess Eadburh of Minster-in-Thanet in Kent, requesting that she have written for him a copy of the Petrine Epistles, penned in gold (which he sent her for that purpose as it was such a valuable commodity) to impress the natives. The impact of such symbols may have saved him from a hostile audience of potential converts on many occasions. Alas, the book that he held above his head to try to fend off a sword-blow (which still survives in Fulda as Codex Bonifatianus 1, and bears a painful gash in its original binding) could not save him from his martyrdom on the river bank at Dokkum in 754. Boniface was the Devon-born son of peasant ceorls, who in 716 launched a mission to convert the pagan Germanic homelands. He built on the earlier work of Wilfrid and Willibrord, and earned the titles of apostle of Frisia and Germany and Archbishop of Mainz. His key foundations included Fulda and Eichstatt and his influential followers included Lull, Leoba, Wigbert, Tecla, Walburga, Eoban, Burchard, Winnibald and Willibald, the latter even reforming St Benedict's monastery of Monte Cassino.

To the Celtic and Germanic peoples of north-western Europe, with their sophisticated oral societies, their abstract and symbolic art, their love of words and their limited writing systems (ogham and runes), the book presented itself as the new symbol of ultimate, divine authority. It was therefore natural that they should seek to adorn it with the ornaments that for centuries had conveyed signals of wealth, status and power through elaborate metalwork. In Byzantium, honour had been paid to the Word of God by writing it in letters of gold and silver upon purple-stained parchment. In Insular books the word assumes iconic status, as the decorated opening words of its Gospelbooks grow to occupy the entire page. They became vehicles of contemplation, intimately combining word and image. The modest initials of sixth- and seventh-century Italy and of Merovingian Gaul, with their crosses, birds and fishes, do not begin to approach the level of adornment accorded to the Word in an Insular context. Nor is it surprising that the story-telling 'historiated' initial should have made its first known appearance in Insular books: the Vespasian Psalter, a Kentish work of around 730, and the St Petersburg Bede, written at Monkwearmouth/Jarrow around 746. What more intimate visual symbiosis of text and image could there be, and what greater mutual validation? The intimacy between word and image extends in far subtler ways throughout Insular Christian texts, revealing a level of cross-referencing founded upon a wealth of Scriptural sources. It shows too the many-layered levels of 'reading' employed in Scriptural interpretation, from which our sophisticated electronic age might well learn.

The Vespasian Psalter, King David and his musicians; opening of Psalm 26, with historiated initial 'D' depicting David and Jonathan, Kent, c.720–30, with Old English gloss added at Canterbury in the mid-ninth century. This may be the sort of work produced by nuns at Minster-in-Thanet under Abbess Eadburh.

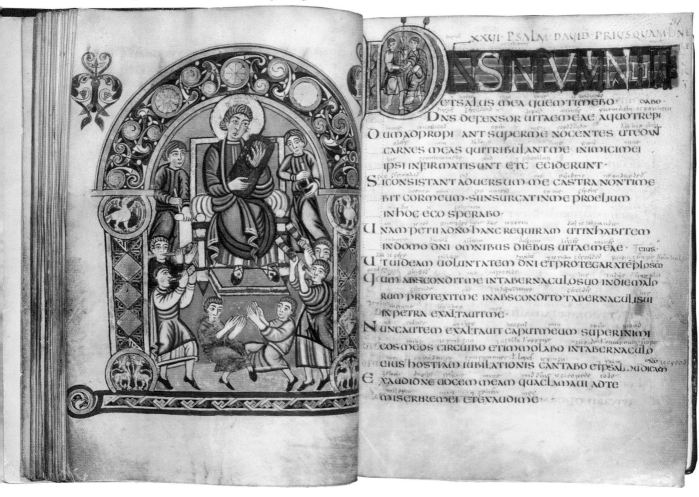

THE RISE OF MERCIA

During the eighth century the pre-eminence of Northumbria gave way to that of the kingdom of Mercia, a conglomerate of peoples and territories centred upon the Midlands and the borders with Wales. Under its most prominent rulers, Aethelbald (716–57), Offa (757–96) and Coenwulf (796–821), Mercia extended its authority over the other Anglo-Saxon kingdoms. It came to govern the whole of Southumbria as, in effect, 'Greater Mercia' via sub-reguli (under-kings), and even held sway over Northumbria, to which it owed the start of its conversion.

Since its foundation Lindisfarne had continued to produce a number of important missionaries who carried the Gospel abroad and who helped to complete the conversion of Southumbria. Peada, son of Penda, had been baptized under Northumbrian influence in 652/3 and founded an important cathedral/monastery at Peterborough (Medeshamstede). When Penda finally died in 654, King Oswy of Northumbria ruled Mercia himself for a few years. With Peada, he allowed Bishop Finan to send four monks from Lindisfarne to evangelize this turbulent kingdom, which occupied the Midlands and was pushing westwards into British territory, along with the Middle Angles and the people of Lindsey (around Lincoln and the Wash) whom it embraced. These missionary monks were Diuma, the first bishop of the Mercians and Middle Angles, Betti, Adda and Cedd.

SAINTS CEDD AND CHAD

Bede relates the missionary endeavours of four famous priests of the day – all brothers: Cedd, Chad, Cynibil and Caelin (*Historia Ecclesiastica*, Book III). Cedd (died 664) moved on from Mercia to become the bishop of the East Saxons who, despite the earlier endeavours of St Mellitus, had apostatized. Their king, Sigebert, had just been baptized under the sponsorship of his overlord, King Oswy. Cedd founded monasteries at Tilbury and Bradwell-on-Sea (where his church survives, built in Roman fashion) and baptized new converts in East Anglia at Rendlesham, seat of the kings formerly buried at Sutton Hoo (see feature on Sutton Hoo between pages 120 and 121). Cedd liked to return to his native Northumbria periodically to renew his spirit and here he founded another important spiritual focus at Lastingham. His brother, Cealin, had become the chaplain of King Oswald's son, Ethelwald, who ruled Deira. Through him Ethelwald came to know Cedd and offered him a donation of land on which to found a monastery in Yorkshire. This was to be a place of spiritual succour for the king himself and became his own royal mausoleum. It must have come as a shock to him when the ascetic Cedd did not chose one of the more lucrative, hospitable farmlands of Yorkshire but a dimple in the wild moors – Lastingham, an English wilderness in the tradition of the desert fathers. Bede hints that this was a place of brigandage, a lair of murderous cut-throats outside of the reach of the law, which needed to be cleansed, physically and spiritually, before it could be reclaimed for God. On a little grassy mound in the centre of the village stands the church, the churchyard wall reflecting the line of the original monastic *rath*. Beneath it lies a crypt, largely dating from the rebuilding of the church in 1078, undertaken by monks from Whitby as part of a Norman revival of venerated earlier Insular sites, incorporating some earlier Anglo-Saxon fabric, and housing a fine collection of carved cross-heads and door jambs which indicate the architectural importance of the earlier church here. The atmosphere in Lastingham crypt certainly speaks eloquently of the spirituality of its founders.

Cedd's foundation of Lastingham is usually dated to 654. We do not know if his patron, King Ethelwald of Deira, was ever buried there. Does he lie in its crypt alongside Cedd? It is highly unlikely, for he subsequently turned against his uncle, Oswy, in an alliance led by the pagan Penda of Mercia, to whom he served as guide. This act of treachery probably led to his downfall after Oswy's victory at the Battle of Winwaed in 655, and would not have found him favour in ecclesiastical circles, scuppering his ambitions to achieve royal sanctity.

St Peter's Church, Bradwell-on-Sea, Essex. It was built by St Cedd in the mid-seventh century in the style of the Augustinian mission in the old Roman fort of Othona.

Cedd himself was carried off in 659 by one of a series of plague epidemics that swept across Europe from the East, during a century that must have been as apocalyptic as the notorious fourteenth century, with its Black Death and associated famine, demographic decline and social unrest. Bede's narration of his interment seems to prefigure that of St Cuthbert; for Cedd was, likewise, initially buried outside the first church, which must have been made of wood, and his remains were translated to the right of the high altar upon the building of a new stone church.

Bede also tells how Cedd's brother, Chad, succeeded him as abbot of Lastingham but was sent to Canterbury in 665 by King Oswy to be consecrated as bishop of York (*Historia Ecclesiastica*, Book III). Finding that the Archbishop, Deusdedit, the first native Anglo-Saxon to hold that office, had died of plague, Chad proceeded to Wessex where he was installed by Bishop Wini/Wine. Wini was at that point the only canonically consecrated bishop in Britain. Because of this he was assisted by two bishops of the British church – another valuable piece of evidence counteracting the view of a complete stand-off between the British and English churches. This meant that Chad's consecration was subsequently successfully challenged and overturned as uncanonical by Wilfrid, who seized the bishopric of York for himself. Chad retired to his monastery of Lastingham in relief and may have remained there contentedly had he not been instructed in 669, by the influential new Archbishop of Canterbury Theodore of Tarsus, to become bishop of the Mercians.

Chad was much respected for living out the Christian message, even by Wilfrid. His humility is recounted by Bede, who relates a touching passage in which he refused to accept a horse, preferring to walk on his arduous pastoral travels, but was made to ride it by Archbishop Theodore, who personally helped him to mount it

(*Historia Ecclesiastica*, Book III and Book IV). The image of the dignified, elderly intellectual who represented the highest learning and authority of the Mediterranean world, bending down to help the self-effacing, late-middle-aged Celtic bishop onto his steed is a moving one. The earlier breaches of etiquette and assumptions of superiority on the part of those sent from Rome were past.

Chad established his *cathedra* at Lichfield, near the Mercian royal centre of Tamworth. There he died of disease in 672 and was buried. Bede's account gives some details that may also reflect something of the arrangement of Lastingham at the time. At Lichfield, Chad 'built himself a house near the church, where he used to retire privately with seven or eight brethren in order to pray or study whenever his work and preaching permitted' (*Historia Ecclesiastica*, Book IV). Further on in Bede's chapter, this house is referred to as his 'oratory'. This blurring of the distinction between the episcopal and monastic life recalls that of the Columban federation, notably Lindisfarne. Membership of such a spiritual elite attracted the powerful and wealthy, but as Bede's account of the case of Owini (Ovin)

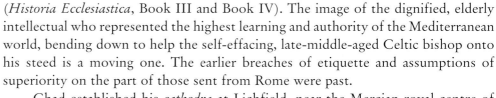

Lastingham Church, North Yorkshire, founded by St Cedd in 654. It was rebuilt in 1078 and later, incorporating earlier Anglo-Saxon fabric. The crypt houses an assembly of Insular sculpture, such as the cross-head (BOTTOM). This originally had a metalwork relic-boss which was later prised out of it and is now missing.

illustrates, this need not entail recreating the monastery in the image of the court. Owini, an influential Northumbrian nobleman who also helped St Etheldreda to establish her community at Ely, gave up his wealth and status and came to Lastingham carrying only an axe and an adze. His background did not incline him to intellectual pursuits and he preferred to devote his time to hard manual labour whilst his brethren studied. The value system of those who served an eternal kingdom and its agendas could evidently be different to that of the transitory world. Whatever one's gifts, they had a role to play.

Chad was initially buried beside the little church he built and dedicated to the Virgin at what is now Stowe in Lichfield. By the time that Bede was writing, this had been replaced in stone nearby, on the site of the current cathedral, and was dedicated to St Peter. Chad's remains were translated to this new church and covered by a wooden house-shaped shrine that became a focus of miracles of healing (Bede, *Historia Ecclesiastica*, Book IV). Might the early church and shrine of Cedd at Lastingham have been similar to these? By the second half of the tenth century the Chad Gospelbook had become a focal point of the shrine of Chad at Lichfield. It was made in the mid-eighth century by an artist who had studied the major decorated pages of the Lindisfarne Gospels. It may even originally have been made to commemorate Chad and have been restored to Lichfield. This would have followed a sojourn in Wales where, as an inscription in the volume records, it was exchanged during the mid-ninth century by the Welshman Gelhi for his horse and presented to the altar of St Teilo (Llandeilo Fawr). Border raids were common, although many of them may have been launched from the English side of the great Dyke built by King Offa to define the border, rather than primarily from the Welsh side.

MERCIAN CULTURE

Other important monasteries in Mercia included Repton, site of Diuma's first *cathedra* in Mercia, which became a royal mausoleum and which preserves an impressive early ninth-century crypt (see page 186), and Breedon-on-the-hill where there is a remarkable array of architectural sculpture and figural panels from altarpieces (see page 182). These feature an exotic mix of eastern Mediterranean and Italianate influences and motifs, with friezes incorporating mythical beasts and lions reminiscent of Syrian hunting scenes. The figure-style is related to that of an important series of sculptures in the vicinity of Peterborough (Medeshamstede) – the Hedda shrine in Peterborough Cathedral, Castor (a major nunnery) and Fletton. Although on the borders of East Anglia, this important cathedral was a major Mercian centre. One of the finest Insular manuscripts of the early ninth century, the Barberini Gospels, may have been made for its archdeacon, Wigbald. It incorporates designs of Mercian fashion, resembling the sculpture and metalwork of the region, and Byzantine-influenced evangelist portraits.

Other significant Mercian books include a series of four prayerbooks made in western Mercia, in the vicinity of Lichfield and Worcester, during the first quarter of the ninth century. These seem to represent the first attempts to order private devotional material around central themes, such as Christ as the healer and health of humanity and the Communion of Saints. At least two of these, the Book of Nunnaminster and the Royal Prayerbook were made for, and probably by, women (see feature on Mercian Book Culture between pages 184 and 185). The most elaborate, the Book of Cerne, was probably made for Bishop Aethelwald of Lichfield (818–30), and features evangelist miniatures in which the individual Gospel writers are equated with different aspects of the nature of Christ. It also includes the earliest example of western liturgical drama, relating the 'Harrowing of Hell'. This, along with an abbreviated Psalter and an acrostic poem, may originally have been composed by an earlier Bishop Aethilwald of Lindisfarne (died 740) – the probable binder of the Lindisfarne Gospels – and were probably adapted for use by his later Mercian namesake. The image of Luke in this prayerbook echoes that of a more sumptuous volume made at a similar period in Kent, perhaps for Archbishop Wulfred – the fragmentary remains of a magnificent single volume Bible known as the Royal Bible (see feature on Mercian Book Culture). This exhibits up-to-date Carolingian influence in its painterly figures and its major pages, written in gold and silver on imperial purple grounds. At the end of the Insular age, with the Viking invaders at the door, its Christian culture was evidently still flourishing and responding to new stimuli.

THE MERCIAN HEGEMONY

Historically a scenario emerges of the construction of a 'Greater Mercia', in which the core territories were supplemented by the acquisition of tributary regions.

These formed an inner zone of what is known overall as the Mercian 'hegemony'. The overlordship of other Southumbrian kingdoms then formed its outer zone. These were often vigorously contended, as in the case of Kent. A cultural reflection of such zones and their interaction can be seen in the pages of books written and illuminated in Southumbria and it is similarly signalled in other aspects of visual and material culture – church archaeology and architecture, sculpture, carving and metalwork. These include such Mercian masterworks as the Gandersheim Casket, the Pentney brooches, the Witham pins, the Ormside bowl and perhaps the St Ninian's Isle chapes and sword pommel.

The preconditioning factor in the rise of both the Mercian and Pictish

Mercian Women

The Mercian double monastery at Breedon-on-the-Hill in Leicestershire housed many important sculptures. This image, from an altarpiece carved around 800, is thought to represent either the Virgin or an abbess.

Mercia displays an unusually high level of politically significant women, even in the depleted historical record. Offa's wife, Cynethryth, not only witnessed his crucial documents, but had coinage struck in her name. Not surprisingly, Anglo-Saxon women also played a leading role in church life. We have already heard of Northumbrian abbesses who oversaw important double monasteries, such as Hild of Whity, St Ethedreda foundress of Ely, and Ebbe of Coldingham, the latter criticized by Cuthbert for its lax sexual morality. Their counterparts in southern England featured the learned Abbess Cuthswith of Inkberrow, Abbess Hildelith of Barking, Abbess Aelfrith of Repton, Abbess Cyneburga of Castor, the abbesses of Breedon-on-the-Hill and the abbesses of Minster-in-Thanet. The latter included St Mildred (died c.700) and her sisters Milburga of Wenlock and Mildryth of Eastry, daughters of its foundress, Princess Ermenburga of Kent and King Merewald of Mercia. Mildred had trained at the Merovingian double monastery of Chelles and Wenlock that was founded by a nun from Chelles, Liobsynde. Under Abbess Eadburh, a close friend and correspondent of St Boniface's, the Minster-in-Thanet scriptorium produced de luxe liturgical and scriptural manuscripts during the mid-eighth century. It supplied the German missionfields and perhaps even Canterbury Cathedral and Abbey; the nuns' work perhaps even included the resplendent Vespasian Psalter and the Stockholm Codex Aureus.

Boniface's assistants in his mission included his kinswoman St Leofgyth/Leoba/ Lioba (died 782), abbess of Tauberbischofsheim, who studied at Thanet under Abbess Tetta of Wimborne and won renown as one of the most learned teachers and poets in Europe.

Abbess Cwoenthryth, daughter of King Coenwulf, was politically active in the affairs of church and state during the early ninth century and was acknowledged as his heir. She was simultaneously abbess of Minster-in-Thanet in Kent and of Winchcombe in western Mercia, the repository of the royal archives.

The ending of an independent kingdom of Mercia in the early tenth century even culminated with two unique early medieval instances of female rule – Aethelflaed, Lady of the Mercians and her daughter, Aelfwyn. The latter was removed by her uncle, King Edward of Wessex, to prevent her from serving as an alternative focus of loyalty and of resistance to the Danes.

hegemonies was their struggle with Bernicia in the 670s and the failure of King Ecgfrith to maintain the dominant position inherited from his father, King Oswy of Northumbria. Study of contemporary Ireland also reveals a number of intriguing similarities to developments in Mercia. For example, a number of core dynasties were created and then expanded by attracting other groups claiming a common ancestry. There was also a corresponding growth of royal and ecclesiastical authority and alliances between kings and clerics. At the same time, cults were created and promoted, especially those with dynastic overtones, and the role of women was also changing. The entry of royal personages into monasteries, voluntarily or otherwise, was a further development common to both Mercia and Ireland, as was its use as a means of eliminating dynastic competitors – perhaps of the sort employed in the case of the 'pretender' to the throne of Kent, Eadberht Praen. Both Charlemagne and the Pope intervened in his case, but his opposition to King Coenwulf nonetheless led to his mutilation (his hands were severed and his eyes put out) and his imprisonment in a monastery. The historical record may retain little evidence of direct connections between Ireland and Mercia, but similarities in general political and social trends, coupled with the discovery of links in the art historical, devotional and archaeological material, raise some intriguing possibilities.

THE CHRISTIANIZATION OF MERCIA

In addition to military campaigns, alliances and the politics of the marriage-bed, the church played a fundamental role in the cohesion of this extended hegemony. The traditional date for Peada's conversion, 653, is taken to mark the commencement of the conversion of Mercia, with the royal foundation of Medeshamstede (Peterborough) in 657, and St Chad's mission to Lichfield and the Mercian heartland around 670. Evidence for the early stages of the Christianization of Mercia hints, intriguingly, at the possibility of interaction with the post Romano-British church in western Mercia. It also suggests pre-Anglo-Saxon origins for the foundation of Worcester, the focus of an independent Hwiccan bishopric. Lichfield likewise has traditions indicating an earlier Romano-British church, with rumours of many Christian martyrdoms during the Roman period at nearby Letocetum (Wall), where an early Christian bronze bowl inscribed with a chi-rho was found.

The remains of other important Mercian churches also survive. At Brixworth there remains an extraordinarily impressive, large eighth-century building reusing Roman material and featuring a royal viewing gallery, in Byzantine fashion, at its west end. It was the probable site of some major church councils (perhaps being the important centre of 'Clofesho' mentioned in the charters) and the resting place of a relic of the missionary St Boniface, venerated by pilgrims to its crypt. Similar churches survive elsewhere: Deerhurst, with its similar ring-crypt and royal gallery and its polygonal pilaster-faced apse; Britford, with its carved arch soffits; and Repton and Wing, both of which incorporate important, well-preserved crypts. The significance of others, such as Barking and Flixborough, is attested by the important excavated finds, including evidence of scriptoria.

A thriving hagiographic tradition evolved, notably that surrounding the most significant Mercian cult of St Guthlac of Crowland (died 714). Felix's 'Life of St Guthlac' contains an important early example of the visionary genre, relating the torments endured by the saint at the hands of numerous fiends. But it also serves a political end, promoting the future King Aethelbald of Mercia and Guthlac's links with Repton, site of the royal mausoleum. Guthlac was a Mercian prince who

Brixworth, Northamptonshire. An imposing seventh–eighth century church which reused Roman materials. The triple opening inserted in the west wall may have formed a royal gallery. The building could possibly have possessed a relic of St Boniface, and may have been the venue for important synods.

became a warrior at fifteen but left his secular life to become a monk at Repton under Abbess Aelfrith when he was twenty-four. He subsequently became a hermit in the swamps of the Fenlands at Crowland in Lincolnshire. Mercian literary output continued – even after it had been partially occupied by the Danes – during the Alfredian revival, and included the Old English Bede, the Old English Martyrology and an English translation of Pope Gregory's hagiographical *Dialogues* by Bishop Werferth of Worcester, tutor to King Alfred the Great.

THE MERCIANS, THEIR NEIGHBOURS AND THEIR IDEOLOGY

The *Mierce* or 'Marcher People' were to some extent defined, as their name suggests, by their relationships with their neighbours. Their dealings with the Welsh were complex. Penda allied with them against the Northumbrians, leading to the deaths of King Edwin at the battle of Hatfield (632) and of King Oswald at *Maserfelth* (Oswestry, 641), and setting Mercia on the path towards overlordship. Then came the obscure period of Welsh history from the 670s to 820s, during which Wales may have formed part of the outer zone of Mercian hegemony, as did East Anglia, Kent, Sussex and Wessex. An initial military clientship of mutual convenience may have gradually been transformed into something far more onerous. This was accompanied by a sharper definition of a frontier, in the face of a hardening of attitudes between the two churches, after an initial period of more positive interaction between Britons and 'English'. Subsequently, forceful campaigns to extend Mercian overlordship in Wales were conducted by Coenwulf and, later, Aethelflaed. At the same time, King Alfred the Great of Wessex pursued a policy of 'protection' of the southern Welsh kingdoms against Mercia, the sons of Rhodri Mawr from north Wales and the Vikings. Finally, the Mercian 'third party' was removed from West Saxon/Welsh relations when Edward the Elder forcibly ejected Aelfwyn, the last independent ruler of Mercia, in the early tenth century. This paved the way for the absorption of Wales into a new *imperium*. Offa's Dyke emerges within this complex pattern of relationships as a dynamic source of turbulence, in both directions, connected with English attempts to control Wales through overlordship: it was not only a trade frontier but also a political border.

Mercian book culture

The Book of Cerne (Cambridge, University Library, MS Ll.1.10 f. 31v). John miniature, prefacing Gospel extracts in a prayerbook. Probably made at Lichfield for Bishop Aethelwald (818–830).

The Royal Bible

The Royal Bible (British Library, Royal MS 1.E.vi, f. 43r). Luke Incipit page. Canterbury, c.820-840. A single-volume Bible made in Kent when the Viking raids were beginning. The up-to-date influence of the Carolingian Empire is apparent in its opulent style and purple pages, as is that of Byzantine art.

The Barberini Gospels

The Barberini Gospels, (Vatican, Biblioteca Apostolica
Vaticana, MS lat.570). f. 1r. Canon Table, headed by symbols
of the evangelists and a male mask.

There is a growing body of evidence for direct relations between Offa and Charlemagne (the powerful continental ruler), as well as the broader context of trade and ecclesiastical contacts between their realms. The picture which emerges is one in which Offa may have aspired, and on occasion have been encouraged, to think of himself as 'a contender' upon the bigger stage. This is well illustrated by Charlemagne's proposal of a marriage between Offa's daughter and his son Charles – which was rapidly withdrawn when Offa countered with an over-ambitious request that his son should receive the hand of Charlemagne's daughter, Bertha.

Coin dating from the reign of King Offa of Mercia, modelled on a dinar of the Abbasid Caliph al-Mansur, with Offa's name appearing with that of Allah. It has not been copied correctly, indicating that the script was not fully understood. But it graphically conveys Offa's aspirations as a ruler of international stature.

However, the scale and the nature of their internal achievements and international relations differed: the Mercian 'hegemony' was not of comparable stature to the emergent Carolingian Empire. Offa could be useful to Charlemagne, on occasion, and was accorded due diplomatic regard when being addressed, but this was in no sense a relationship of equals. Nonetheless, the growth of the Mercian supremacy was part of a broader trend of consolidation and extension of regimes and larger territorial areas of overlordship. Pictland, Ireland and Wales were experiencing similar phenomena. The Bernician house had attempted something similar in the North and had, in so doing, occasioned its own eclipse; Mercia was soon to do the same. What its rulers perhaps failed to realize (unlike their West Saxon successors and their Carolingian 'big brothers'), was the fundamental need for strong ideological foundations to underpin political and administrative constructs and to compensate for the animosity and competition that such expansionism aroused. The trappings of such cultural ideology may, nonetheless, be perceived in the quality and the self-conscious exoticism of the visual imagery of Mercia, as seen in its manuscript, metalwork, sculptural and architectural monuments. Some of Offa's coinage was even modelled upon the dinars of the Abbassid Caliphate and featured his name alongside that of Allah, symbolizing the extent of his kingdom's cultural and economic reach – or rather its aspirations.

The value of the spiritual basis for intellectual and cultural achievements, so prized by the circles of Charlemagne and Alfred, may also have been well-recognized by members of the Mercian church. This is demonstrated by the construction of cults, the continued provision of liturgical books and the growth of a vibrant genre of private devotion, expressed in the Mercian prayerbooks, with their emphasis upon spiritual health and the solidarity of the Communion of Saints. The ambitious iconographic programme of the Sandbach crosses in the diocese of Lichfield was formulated as a response to the debate concerning ecclesiastical authority, affirming its divine source. This debate was stimulated by the visits of the papal envoys in 787 and 803 and resulted in the archbishopric of Canterbury and the Mercian episcopate attempting to fend off increasing royal and aristocratic appropriation of their authority. They did this through a concerted campaign of church councils and litigation, represented by the visually impressive charters and forgeries that survive from around 800, and by introducing canons to important cathedrals such as Canterbury and Lichfield.

The Carolingian Empire may have been of similar longevity to Mercia, but it was of a very different order of scale and complexity to that of Mercia: its dynastic longevity was not that much greater but its ideological image was imperishable. That Offa was all too well aware of the crucial importance of ensuring dynastic continuity is demonstrated by his ruthless removal of any potential counter-claimants to the rule of his son, Ecgfrith. Indeed, Offa was determined to have him consecrated as king of the Mercians during his own lifetime. This unorthodox event occurred in 787, but in the process Offa had found it necessary to reorganize the southern English church, obtaining hard-won papal permission to establish a new archbishopric at Lichfield. This proved to be short-lived, as the hapless Ecgfrith died some four and a half months after his father, in 796. However, it served to harden the attitude of churchmen such as Archbishops Jaenberht of Lichfield and Wulfred of Canterbury and to further their promotion of solidarity amongst the episcopal ranks in the face of attempts to extend royal and lay control. This assertion of episcopal rights eventually found its most powerful expression in the canons of the Council of Chelsea held in 816. Archbishop Wulfred, himself a wealthy Mercian nobleman, successfully opposed King Coenwulf in the courts and at Rome, reclaiming Canterbury's rights and primacy and the relegation of Lichfield to the status of bishopric in 803. Offa may have absorbed the lessons of Aethelbald's reign concerning the subjugation of men, but neither fully grasped the longer-term need to touch their hearts and minds. From his vantage point in Charlemagne's kingdom Alcuin lamented such dangerous times in his homeland, concurring with the psalmist, 'Except the Lord build the house, they labour in vain that build it; except the Lord keep the city, the watchmen waketh but in vain' (Psalm 127:1).

The Anglo-Saxon crypt at Repton, a Mercian royal mausoleum of the eighth and ninth centuries.

THE MERCIAN LANDSCAPE AND ECONOMY

A study of landscape and environment gives an impression of the tremendous regional diversity of Greater Mercia, from the Peaks and the Welsh Marches to the coastal and riverine trading centres – access to which was a compelling factor in Mercian expansion, especially towards London and the Thames. Supplementation of the Roman road system suggests that this was still at least partially in use, although probably primarily for military use as the term 'highway' ('army-way') implies. Saltways also served to disseminate the products of the brine extraction industry at centres such as Droitwich. Other industries, such as lead mining at Wirksworth, would similarly have benefitted from a communications network. The water mill at Tamworth and the fish weirs at Chelsea and Colwick on the Trent also indicate advances in food provision. Settlement and economy were essentially rural in character, with 'central places', such as the estate centres of royal vills and minsters, nonetheless serving as foci for economic redistribution. Multiple estate units focused upon such centres were gradually subject to fragmentation into smaller estates and parishes, with tribute simultaneously taking the form of services and money renders.

There seems to have been a hierarchy of settlement, from single farms to larger settlements, with some indications of continuous occupation from the Roman to the medieval periods. An element of post-Roman continuity may be indicated by burial practices at sites such as Wasperton and Blacklow Hill, whilst the transfer of a Roman farm unit to an Anglo-Saxon one may be preserved at Orton Hall Farm (west of Peterborough). The Roman town of Wroxeter may have continued as a settlement until replaced as a focus by the nearby Atcham Hall. Regional centres, some with royal connections, feature at places like Tamworth, Flixborough and Northampton, where a possible royal hall may have formed part of a monastery, as in Carolingian Paderborn. Some, such as Newark, subsequently became market towns. Mid-Saxon urbanization is easier to demonstrate in eastern Mercia, at centres such as Northampton, Bedford and Nottingham, than in the more rural interior. Major urban development would have to wait for the Anglo-Saxon *burhs* and Danish boroughs of the late ninth and tenth centuries. However, the purely archaeological record may be misleading: potential sites have been located and there is significant evidence in the form of traded goods to indicate commercial development. It is instructive that the commercial heart of London – Lundenwic – remained undiscovered until the mid-1980s. Exciting recent archaeological work, especially in the vicinity of Aldwych and Covent Garden, indicates the complexity of this industrial and international trading centre, which lay close to the ecclesiastical focus within the old Roman town at St Paul's, a major pilgrim focus with its shrine to St Erkenwald. Above all, there is the eloquent witness of the coinage which provides evidence not only of trade and of a monetary economy, but also of the aspirations and the governmental capabilities of Mercia's rulers at different points in its history.

THE DECLINE OF MERCIA AND THE RISE OF WESSEX

The overlordship so energetically forged and wielded by a series of powerful Mercian rulers was not supported by dynastic continuity, despite Offa's labours and the promotion of a perception of ultimate common ancestry. Different kin groups vied for prominence, not unlike their Irish contemporaries the Ui Neill. The collapse of the Mercian supremacy and the passing of the mantle of power to Wessex may be viewed from a number of perspectives. For some scholars it occurs in the 820s as an almost inevitable result of the overbearing methods employed in its construction – the Mercian iron gauntlet giving way to the West Saxon velvet glove. This led to a dynastic crisis provoked by the absence of an individual strong enough to seize and retain personal rule. Coenwulf stepped forcefully into the breach in 796, but there was apparently no such leader to hold things together following his death during a military campaign in Wales. This, coupled with ongoing disputes in Kent, undoubtedly assisted Ecgberht of Wessex both in his defeat of one of the hapless and rapidly ousted successors to the Mercian throne, Beornwulf, at Ellendun in 825, and his subsequent conquest of Mercia in 829. Yet by 830 the kingdom had been regained by Wiglaf, whether in his own right or as a client of Wessex – Mercia was not yet dead.

Pressure from Viking attack brought Mercia into even closer contact with Wessex. King Burgred's immediate response to the invasion of Mercia in 867-68 was to appeal to the West Saxons for help, before finally departing for Rome with his wife and intimates in 874. Hostile West Saxon sources, and many modern historians, might write off Mercia at this point and refer disparagingly to the Viking puppet-ruler, Ceolwulf II (874–c.879) as a 'foolish king's thegn'. Yet even at this stage the charter and coinage evidence presents a picture of some continuity of rule and identity within the kingdom. Then, as earlier, the ealdormen of its component regions may have preserved some stability, and the system of mutual dependence and extension of royal control ensured by the Mercian promotion of bookland (land granted by charter, rather than held by heredition or tradition) may also have stood the kingdom in good stead. The early basis for Mercian military success, based on the personal bond between lord and follower, was retained, along with responsibility for the construction and maintenance of roads, bridges and fortresses. Wessex built on these foundations and extended such obligations to the construction of an effective network consolidated through documented property tenure. And while aggressive warfare was probably limited to an elite, defensive warfare may have involved a wider section of society. The people also built more of the defensive settlements known as *burhs*, but their use of the Danelaw as part of a campaign of reconquest was significantly furthered by Alfred's daughter, Aethelflæd, 'Lady of the Mercians'. The 'kingdom of the Mercians' retained its identity and played an often crucial role in the power-balance which sustained the 'kingdom of the English' forged by Alfred and his successors as a response to the Viking raids and settlements which beset Britain from the end of the eighth century onwards.

Thor's Hammer and Christ's Cross: The Impact of the Vikings

In 793 the monks of Holy Island became the first of the Christian flock to fall prey to the ravening wolfish attacks of a new force in European history: the Vikings. The island was an undefended smorgasbord of ecclesiastical treasures, conveniently located in one of the greatest super-highways of the day, the North Sea. It was an easy target for these early piratical raiders, on the lookout for opportunity. Many of the brethren were brutally slain and the community did incredibly well to hide the leading relics of the shrine, including the coffin of St Cuthbert with its precious contents and the Lindisfarne Gospels. The event sent shock waves throughout the West. From the Carolingian court at Aachen the scholar Alcuin of York, who had been head-hunted by Charlemagne to assist in the educational, spiritual and ideological shaping of his expanding empire, wrote a letter of condolence to one of the Lindisfarne monks, Cuthbert. He could not resist pointing out that such awesome retribution must have been provoked, in part, by the laxity of the community there and its departure from the ascetic spiritual precepts and lifestyle of its founding fathers, Aidan, Finan and Cuthbert. For the latter's fears had proven to be justified. The community had become the wealthy victim of its own success. Its territories were extensive and over-stretched. Its role as a pilgrim focus had brought people flocking to a place prized for quietness and contemplation. It had become involved in secular disputes, with the right of sanctuary playing a part in this. This is shown in one instance from the late eighth century, when a prince claimed sanctuary at its high altar but was dragged out for punishment, along with the abbot who sought to defend his rights. Royal monkish recruits had imported aspects of their former lifestyle – King Ceolwulf (to whom Bede dedicated the *Historia*

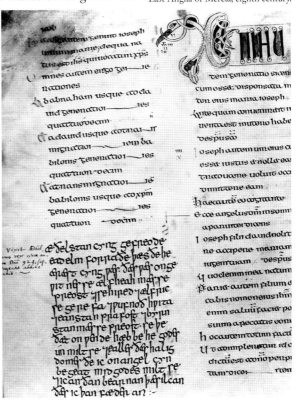

Gospelbook, copied from the same sixth-century Neapolitan model as the Lindisfarne Gospels. The earliest extant English manumission was added (BOTTOM LEFT), by which King Athelstan freed slaves in 924 to celebrate his accession, having presented the book to Christ Church, Canterbury. Northumbria, East Anglia or Mercia, eighth century.

Ecclesiastica) refusing to let the brethren continue drinking water as he preferred wine.

Writing from the immense luxury of the Carolingian court, it was perhaps somewhat churlish of Alcuin to point this out, but it is indicative of a contemporary awareness that the growth of Christianity and its ecclesiastical formalization – its establishment, in effect – could bring disadvantages as well as benefits to the shaping of a regulated society. What was in danger of being lost, then as in subsequent ages, was teaching by example and the actual living out of Christ's teachings.

Sages at the courts of Charlemagne, and later of Alfred the Great, King of Wessex, came to the same conclusion as the woman who compiled her little prayerbook in Mercia at the beginning of the ninth century: what most needed to be addressed was the spiritual health of the Christian state and of the individuals who comprised it. Christ's healing ministry was required for the soul as well as for the bodily ills that caused pilgrims to flock to the newly established shrines of Christian saints (as they had to those of minor pagan deities for centuries before). To help achieve this spiritual wellbeing, society could help itself by adhering to Christian morality and behaviour, and by study and prayer. This became the reforming agenda that underpinned the creation of the cohesive Christian states of Europe, including a unified England and unified Celtic kingdoms. Each came under the ultimate authority of a supreme ruler who governed with the support of the church, within which each person played their part and was answerable for their actions in the present – both for their impact upon the collective whole and upon the welfare of their own eternal soul.

The ninth century was a time of upheaval in which Viking raids escalated around the western seaboard and gradually coalesced into more structured invasions and settlements. Initially, the attacks were carried out by war-bands, then by larger armies and later, in the tenth to eleventh centuries, by Scandinavian monarchs intent on conquest and on incorporating whole kingdoms within their expanding trade empire, which stretched from Byzantium to Newfoundland. These vigorous newcomers, who proved such a catalyst in the development of the newly Christianized West, were pagan Germanic peoples. In some respects they were latecomers to the Migration period, during which those outside of the old

Roman Empire flocked into its territories as ideological opponents or economic migrants. They were land-hungry and were looking for new markets. Some may have been additionally prompted by animosity to Christianity and by pagan zeal, as were Turgesius and his wife when they desecrated the altar at Clonmacnoise.

What was markedly different to the early Germanic migrations, however, was that this time the pagan influx did not expunge Christianity from any of the regions seized or settled. The seed sown by the men and women who had devoted their lives to sharing the Christian

The Stockholm Codex Aureus, mid-eighth century. Matthew miniature and incipit with mid-ninth-century inscription recording its ransom from Vikings and donation to Christ Church, Canterbury, Kent.

teaching had fallen upon fertile ground, and their example helped to sustain those who followed and who felt themselves to be in continued communion with their predecessors. The foundations of the house were built on rock and stood firm, even at the darkest moments, when the Christian flame flickered and seemed about to be extinguished along with the lives of the secular and religious leaders who defended it. Those who rallied, despite all the odds, to Alfred of Wessex (871–99) – who had been reduced to hiding out as a guerrilla in the inhospitable fastness of the Athelney Marshes during the 870s – or to Brian Boru at the Battle of Clontarf in 1014, fought their ferocious Viking adversaries not primarily in the name of nationalism or regionalism (for such allegiances often ran counter to

The Nunburnholme Cross, Yorkshire. Late ninth-century with tenth-century additions. above: A seated king with helmet and sword (a local ruler or King David), with reset panel of the crucifixion below.

traditional group loyalties), but to defend their faith and the civilized societies it had helped to shape.

In these Atlantic islands the pattern of Viking settlement was such that initial raids by Danish and Norse (Norwegian) pirates on coastal areas gave way to inland penetration during the second quarter of the ninth century. The Danes focused upon England, and the Norse upon Scotland and Ireland, where they established the Viking kingdom of Dublin and the earldoms of the Highlands and Islands. They also settled on the Isle of Man, where there is a particularly fine corpus of sculptured cross slabs exhibiting Celtic, Anglo-Saxon and Viking stylistic influence. Wales experienced coastal raids and has yielded a number of Viking age hoards, which were hidden by or from the raiders and remaining unclaimed until they were discovered by accident many centuries later. Cumbria also witnessed settlement by the 'black strangers', as the Norse were known, the Danes being the 'white strangers'. Cornwall seems to have got off relatively lightly, the only tangible signs of a Viking presence being an occasional funerary monument and several hoards of metalwork. The most notable of these is the Trewhiddle Hoard, that contained the hacked remains of a wealth of southern English silver jewellery (characterized by a playful brand of animal ornament) and coins. However, the rise of Wessex as the only credible source of opposition ultimately led to its annexation as part of England during the reign of Athelstan (924–39), Alfred's grandson. Athelstan attempted to assert his overlordship in respect of Wales and Scotland, a process which was consolidated by King Edgar later in the tenth century and laid the foundations of a 'United Kingdom' that was to occasion much conflict over the ensuing millennium.

The general approach of the Vikings to the Christian cultures they encountered was not intrinsically hostile, it seems. They could appreciate the value of its symbols at an economic and artistic level, even if they did not initially subscribe to their meaning. Much Insular metalwork was melted down to form ingots (bars of metal with a bullion value according to weight). But many pieces were used for other purposes: the head of Christ transformed into a weight, or book and shrine mounts converted into jewellery for the girls back home. A particularly splendid Psalter, made in Kent in the mid eighth century, was held hostage and ransomed by a Viking army, as an inscription added in its margins records. It was redeemed for silver by Ealdorman Alfred of Kent and his wife Werburh, who presented it to Canterbury for the good of their souls. It is dripping with gold leaf, of the sort sent by Boniface to Abbess Eadburh of Minster-in-Thanet to fashion such work to 'wow' the pagans, and it must certainly have spellbound its Viking captors in order to have survived. Paying honour to your Lord in such a way was something they could understand, and it may not just have been gain that motivated them in safeguarding and ransoming it – as they might an important and valuable person – but a fear of offending this Christian Lord who could command such tribute.

The Anglo-Saxon Chronicle records under the year 876 that one of the Viking leaders, Halfdan, 'shared out the land of the Northumbrians and they proceeded to plough and support them selves'. The newcomers were here to stay. Despite halting the

Viking incursion at Wessex, King Alfred was forced to negotiate a territorial division between English 'England', south of the Thames-Chiltern line, and the Danelaw to its North (focusing upon the Five Boroughs). This was to enable the Christian Anglo-Saxons living under pagan Danish rule to retain their legal rights and freedom of worship. The treaty, known as Alfred and Guthrum's Frith, was a wise piece of statesmanship and also laid the way in defining the boundaries for transcending them. This occurred in the subsequent English campaign of encroachment and reunification, which was finally achieved under King Edgar later in the tenth century at a time when the English church was blossoming. By this time most of the Scandinavian settlers in the Danelaw had been assimilated into the society that they now led and had conformed to many of its practices – including Christian worship.

The vast body of Anglo-Scandinavian sculpture from central and northern England, along with its counterparts in Celtic areas, is the most tangible expression of this conformity and of the rapid integration and conversion of this incoming population group. Intermarriage must have played a big part in this, for no missionary enterprise was entailed (although missionaries from England later participated in the conversion of Scandinavia, as they had in that of Germany and the Netherlands, wishing to share their faith with the homelands). The people of England were Christian, and not merely superficially so, and they fostered the assimilation of their incoming Germanic cousins, encouraging them to fit into the existing well-woven fabric of society. This did not entail relinquishing their previous beliefs entirely. The early sections of this book have examined the points of synergy between Christianity as expressed in northern Europe, and pre-existing modes of expressing faith. Having discovered these for themselves, the English and their Celtic neighbours were adept at applying the same processes to the newcomers. There was no reticence of the sort experienced by the British church when its existence was initially threatened by a tide of immigrants of other faiths, who threatened to engulf it and who were to some measure racially segregated (although the extent of this is being reassessed). In the fifth century, Christianity had been 'respectable' for less than a century. Many people had probably not even converted, or had only done so superficially for social conformity when it became the state religion. By the mid-ninth century Christian beliefs had been the norm for at least two centuries (and much longer in the Celtic and British regions), and had helped to transform and develop the societies of these islands at a fundamental level.

There was no parish system yet in place – that would have to await the Norman period – and people travelled to monasteries or other focal churches or gathered at wayside crosses or leachts (stone altars). Those living in very remote areas might only see a travelling priest once a year – the minimum requirement for Christian communion was to receive the sacraments at rites of passage and the Eucharist at Easter. Yet these early Christians were strong enough to survive and had a deep-rooted sense of identity that could afford to absorb and adapt aspects of the incoming cultures without relinquishing their own sense of identity. There is much here from which we might usefully learn today. Thus, within a generation of arrival,

The Nunburnholme Cross. A hooded monk or nun above a reset panel showing a priest performing Mass. A scene added below depicts Sigurd and Regin eating the flesh of the dragon Fafnir, equating Christian and pagan Viking symbolism.

Dream of the Rood

…Wondrous was the tree of victory, and I was stained
By sin, stricken by guilt. I saw this glorious tree
Joyfully gleaming, adorned with garments,
Decked in gold; the tree of the Ruler
Was rightly adorned with rich stones;
Yet through that gold I could see the agony
Once suffered by wretches, for it had bled
Down the right hand side. Then I was afflicted,
Frightened at this sight; I saw that sign often change
Its clothing and hue, at times dewy with moisture,
Stained by flowing blood, at times adorned with treasure.
Yet I lay there for a long while
And gazed sadly at the Saviour's cross
Until I heard it utter words;
The finest of trees began to speak:
'I remember the morning a long time ago
That I was felled at the edge of the forest
And severed from my roots. Strong enemies seized me,
Bade me hold up their felons on high,
Made me a spectacle. Men shifted me
On their shoulders and set me on a hill.
Many enemies fastened me there. I saw the Lord of Mankind
Hasten with such courage to climb upon me.
I dared not bow or break there
Against my Lord's wish, when I saw the surface
Of the earth tremble. I could have felled
All my foes, yet I stood firm.
Then the young warrior, God Almighty,
Stripped Himself, firm and unflinching. He climbed
Upon the cross, brave before many, to redeem mankind.
I quivered when the hero clasped me,
Yet I dared not bow to the ground,
Fall to the earth. I had to stand firm.
A rood was I raised up; I bore aloft the mighty King,
The Lord of Heaven. I dared not stoop.
They drove dark nails into me; dire wounds are there to see,
The gaping gashes of malice; I dared not injure them.
They insulted us both together; I was drenched in the blood
That streamed from the Man's side after He set His spirit free.

On that hill I endured many grievous trials;
I saw the God of hosts stretched
On the rack; darkness covered the corpse
Of the Ruler with clouds, His shining radiance.
Shadows swept across the land, dark shapes

Under the clouds. All creation wept,
Wailed for the death of the King; Christ was on the cross.
Yet men hurried to eagerly to the Prince
From afar; I witnessed all that too.
I was oppressed with sorrow, yet humbly bowed to the hands of men,
And willingly. There they lifted him from His heavy torment,
They took Almighty God away. The warriors left me standing there,
Stained with blood; sorely was I wounded by the sharpness of spear-shafts.
They laid him down, limb-weary, they stood at the corpse's head,
They beheld there the Lord of Heaven; and there He rested for a while,
Worn-out after battle. And then they began to build a sepulchre;
Under his slayers' eyes, they carved it from the gleaming stone,
And therein laid the Lord of Victories. Then, sorrowful at dusk,
They sang a dirge before they went, weary,
From their glorious Prince; He rested in the grave alone.
But we still stood there, weeping blood,
Long after the song of the warriors
Had soared to heaven; the corpse grew cold,
The fair human house of the soul. Then our enemies
Began to fell us; that was a terrible fate.
They buried us in a deep pit; but friends
And followers of the Lord found me there
And girded me with gold and shimmering silver...

He sipped the drink of death. Yet the Lord rose
With his great strength to deliver man.
Then he ascended into heaven. The Lord Himself,
Almighty God, with His host of angels,
Will come to the middle-world again
On Domesday to reckon with each man.
Then he who has the power of judgement
Will judge each man just as he deserves
For the way in which he lived this fleeting life.
No-one then will be unafraid
As to what words the Lord will utter.
Before the assembly, He will ask where that man is
Who, in God's name, would undergo the pangs of death,
Just as He did formerly upon the cross.
Then men will be fearful and give
Scant thought to what they say to Christ.
But no-one need be numbed by fear
Who has carried the best of all signs in his breast;
Each soul that has longings to live with the Lord
Must search for a kingdom far beyond the frontiers of this world...'

Scandinavians were adopting Christian burial practices and being commemorated by gravemarkers on which they might appear as Viking warriors (as at Middleton in Yorkshire), but also as *miles Christi*, ready to fight the good fight against evil in the form of the dragon of Satan or the Germanic World Serpent. The Nunburnholme Cross in York (see page 193) carries carvings of Christian iconographies such as the Crucifixion, King David harping, the Virgin and Child and a priest celebrating Mass, executed during the late ninth century. It was carefully recarved during the tenth century to integrate scenes from Germanic mythology, in which Sigurd and Regin devour the flesh of the dragon Fafnir. This was a ritual meal of salvation and the defeat of evil given as a parallel to the scene depicting the Christian Eucharist above. As Pope Gregory had said, 'in images the illiterate read', and drawing such cultural parallels could be a valuable didactic means of explaining to the newly Christianized how their age-old beliefs might be read as part of a new revelation of God's purpose, which was being continually revealed to each generation in its own cultural 'language' and symbolism. The man-made hubbub of the Tower of Babel was giving way to the multi-lingual communication inspired by the Holy Spirit at Pentecost, rather as the Old Testament informed and was reinterpreted by the New Testament. Those who went before would accordingly be resurrected with Christ to eternal life, as well as those to whom his teaching was newly revealed and those who came from a longer background of Christian worship. Difference of faith need not engender rift and separation, for all would ultimately be reconciled and unified.

In the eighth century, at the zenith of the flowering of Northumbrian Christian culture, two carvers had made similar contributions of constructive cultural synthesis that reveal how such a process of integration was possible. One chiselled extracts from the 'Dream of the Rood' in runic and Roman letters onto the frames surrounding scenes from the life of Christ on a lofty and elegant stone cross at Ruthwell (Dumfries). This stood in a monastery that lay just within the ancient British kingdom

The Franks Casket, whalebone casket, perhaps a reliquary or book-shrine. Northumbrian, eighth century. The scenes are drawn from world history and mythology and are identified by inscriptions in Roman capitals and runes. Like Bede's History and the Lindisfarne Gospels it celebrates earlier cultures and assimilates them into a Christian present.

BELOW LEFT: panel depicting the sack of the Temple in Jerusalem by Emperor Titus.

BELOW RIGHT: front panel showing Weyland the Smith (left) and the Adoration of the Magi (right).

of Rheged, recently been annexed by Northumbria. This is one of the greatest and most moving examples of Christian poetry and is couched in the form of the Celto-Germanic epic recitations of the mead hall (Bede himself confessed to a weakness for his people's poetic tradition). Christ is presented as a young warrior and hero, who wins the ultimate victory over Death on behalf of his people. The cross that is forced to bear him aloft speaks, its voice assuming the tone of a woman – a mother or lover – and recalling earlier love poems. But here the genre acquires a new universal poignancy in which all of creation, including its flora, grieves for the loss of its beloved Creator and experiences the sublime joy of reunion. It is in effect an Insular creed.

Another hand carved the panels of a Northumbrian whalebone casket known as the Franks Casket (after a later owner), which was probably made to contain either relics or an important book, either of Scripture or, as has recently been suggested, the genealogy of the Northumbrian kings. Its scenes are again identified by inscriptions in Germanic runes and Roman capitals, themselves a sign of cultural synthesis and affiliation. On one side appear Romulus and Remus, founders of Rome, suckled by the she-wolf; on another is the sack of the Temple in Jerusalem by the Emperor Titus and his troops; on a third is a battle fought by one 'Egil', who may be a figure from Germanic legend, or, as has recently been suggested, the Greek hero Achilles; and on a fourth is the passage from Germanic mythology in which Weyland the Smith magically helps to conceive a hero. Opposite this is a depiction of the Virgin and Christ-child adored by the Magi – Epiphany, the time of revelation.

The Franks Casket, like most other important examples of Insular Christian culture, is a supreme statement of cultural assimilation and transformation: Christian society and belief are sited within the ongoing revelation of world history and the growth of knowledge as God's purpose is revealed. The old heroes of former ages and religions prepare the way for the coming of a new and all-powerful hero and Saviour – Christ.

Glossary

Anglo-Saxon Of/relating to the Germanic invaders/settlers and the kingdoms they established in England following the Roman withdrawal from the fifth century AD onwards.

Apostasy Reversion to a pre-existing form of belief.

Ascetic Of/relating to the practice or practioner of an austere discipline of physical self-denial.

Bard A poet, part of the Celtic class of druids.

Barrow An ancient burial mound.

Beehive hut A dry-stone corbelled hut, shaped like a beehive, often built by Irish monks as their cells.

Bernicia The northernmost of two Anglo-Saxon kingdoms (the other being Deira), centred upon County Durham and Northumberland, which together formed Northumbria.

Britons Name given to the peoples who populated Britain prior to the Roman conquest and who remained there during and after the Roman period.

Broch A defensive stone tower with a double stone skin with passages inside it, built by the Pictish inhabitants of Scotland and the Isles.

Bronze Age Period of Prehistory following the New Stone Age (Neolithic) and preceding the Iron Age, characterized by the production of bronze metalwork made by the smelting of copper and tin. In Britain its duration was c.2000–650 BC.

Brythonic A branch of the Celtic language (Welsh, Cornish, Breton), also known as 'P Celtic' on the basis of distinctive features in its spelling.

Burh Fortified camp built by the Anglo-Saxons to defend England against the Vikings.

Byzantine Of/relating to the Christian kingdom/empire of Byzantium, centred upon Constantinople (modern Istanbul), which succeeded the eastern part of the Roman Empire.

Caim A form of prayer, of Irish derivation, that protected whoever recited it from sin and evil.

Carolingian A Germanic dynasty established by the mayors of the Merovingian royal household, whom they succeeded as rulers of Frankia (the Franco-Bene-Lux countries / Netherlands / Germany).

Caryatid An architectural column or pilaster in the form of a human figure.

Cashel Celtic word for regions of a fortified or walled settlement, derived from the Latin *castellum*, a fort/castle. Also, Rock of Cashel, the focal sacred/royal site of the Irish kingdom of Munster.

Celtic An Indo-European linguistic group which came to prominence during the Iron Age and developed distinctive cultural features, including an intelligentsia known as druids and a rich material culture distinguished by its organic ornament.

Codex An ancient manuscript in book form.

Chi-rho A Christian symbol, formed from a monogram composed of the letters 'x' and 'p', the opening letters of the name of Christ in Greek.

Cœnobitic Of/relating to a monastic community in which monks/nuns observed a rule of communal life.

Colophon A note written in a manuscript saying by who/where/when it was made.

Columban Of/relating to the traditions and monastic federation established by the Irish St Columba in parts of Ireland, Scotland and England.

Coptic Of/relating to the Christian inhabitants and church of Egypt.

Crannóg A fortified dwelling constructed in a lake/marsh, found in the Celtic regions of Ireland/Scotland/Wales. Built on an artificial island formed of stones and wooden pilings or set on wooden stilts.

Cross-carpet-page Decorated page in a manuscript, based on a cross, embedded in a panel of ornament resembling an eastern carpet. Usually found preceding the Gospels.

Crozier The hooked staff carried by a bishop, symbolizing his pastoral care.

Curragh Irish/Scottish word for a hide-covered boat.

Cursive A style of writing which used lower-case (minuscule), joined-up lettering.

Dalriada Irish kingdom in Argyll, western Scotland, established by settlers from the Dal Riata tribe of north-east Ireland. It became the focus of St Columba's mission.

Danelaw The area of central and northern England seized and settled by Danish Vikings during the ninth century. In the late ninth century King Alfred the Great of Wessex agreed a border with them, with Anglo-Saxon law and Danish law observed in their respective areas.

Deira The southernmost of two Anglo-Saxon kingdoms (the other being Bernicia) centred upon Yorkshire, which together formed Northumbria.

Divine Office A series of services consisting of Psalms, bible readings and prayers, recited by priests, monks and nuns eight times throughout every day and night (*see also* the Hours).

Dolmen The large stones forming the central burial chamber in prehistoric barrows. Also known as quoits.

Druid The Celtic intelligentsia, a highly trained/qualified legal class of priests, judges, jurists and bards.

Dun A Celtic Goidelic term for a fort, often a hill with defensive ramparts.

Eirenic Literally, 'aimed at peace'. Used especially to refer to attempts to reconcile different traditions within the Christian church.

Eremitic Of/relating to the life of the hermit and of the desert fathers. Also used of monasteries which favoured a rule of life in which monks/nuns

lived separate lives, coming together for some occasions of worship (as distinct from the usual communal rule of monastic life).

Fogou Celtic Brythonic term (particularly popular in Cornwall) for an underground passageway and chamber(s) found in some Celtic Iron Age and early Christian settlements. Perhaps used for chilled food storage and/or ritual purposes.

Frankia Kingdom ruled by the Franks, a Germanic people whose land expanded in the sixth century to include most of France as well as Belgium, Luxembourg and parts of Germany.

Gaul A Roman province focusing upon France, Belgium and western Switzerland. Also used of Celtic inhabitants of this area, before, during and after the Roman period.

Goidelic A branch of the Celtic language (Irish, Scottish Gaelic, Manx), also known as 'Q Celtic' on the basis of distinctive features in its spelling.

Gyrovagues Irish wandering monks or hermits who could not settle anywhere.

Hagiography The process or product of writing about the life, deeds or martyrdom of a saint.

Half-uncial A style of script, combining some rounded uncial upper-case letters with lower-case (minuscule) cursive letters.

Hallstatt Celtic culture of the early Iron Age (c.650–450 BC), named after a burial site yielding characteristic artefacts in Austria.

Herbals A book containing information on the medicinal and culinary uses of herbs.

Hermit A member of the church who chose to live a solitary life as a form of religious discipline.

Hermitage Dwelling place of a hermit.

Hill-fort A hill fortified by the construction of defensive ramparts. Usually occupied during times of danger during prehistory and sometimes reoccupied after the Roman withdrawal.

Hours, the Collection of services to be said at particular times of the day as part of the Divine Office.

Illumination The decoration or illustrations that 'light up' a manuscript.

Incipit literally, 'here begins'. Used of the opening words of a text which were often distinguished by decoration.

Indo-European Of/relating to the linguistic family of Western Asia and Europe (which include the Romance, Celtic and Germanic languages). Also, the peoples who spoke these languages.

Insular Of/relating to the islands of Britain and Ireland. Often used to denote cultural collaboration during the early Christian period and to avoid imposing a rigid distinction between the cultural products of Ireland, Scotland and northern England.

Iron Age Period of Prehistory following the Bronze Age characterized by the production of iron metalwork. In Britain its duration was c.650 BC to the Roman Invasion of AD 43. In Ireland and parts of Scotland it was c.650 BC until the conversion to

Christianity during the fifth-sixth centuries AD.

La Tène Celts Celtic culture in the later part of the Iron Age, named after a site in Switzerland where much distinctive decorated metalwork was cast into a lake as a votive offering.

Laets A distinct semi-free class, perhaps the Christian inhabitants of post-Roman Britain, provided for within the early seventh-century law-code of the Anglo-Saxon King Ethelberht of Kent.

Life of a saint A written record of the events in the life of a saint, often embellished by the writer. Also known by the Latin term *Vita/uita*.

Litany Invocations of named saints, beseeching their intercessions, used in church services and sometimes in private prayer.

Llan Celtic Brythonic term for a defensive and/or symbolic earth or stone enclosure surrounding a secular or, more usually, a religious settlement.

Lombards Germanic settlers who established a kingdom in northern Italy, one of a number of successor states to the Roman Empire.

Lorica A breastplate, worn as a ritual object by ancient Judaic high-priests and part of the armour of the Roman soldier. The term was adapted by the Irish to describe a prayer that protected whoever recited it from sin.

Manuscript Handwritten book, scroll or document.

Majuscule Upper case, formal script.

Marches Border area between England and Wales.

Megalithic Of/relating to prehistoric monuments made from large stones.

Menhir A single prehistoric standing stone.

Mercia Anglo-Saxon kingdom (from 'Mierce', people of the Marches) centred upon the Midlands of England and the Marches.

Merovingian Germanic dynasty which ruled Frankia and preceded the Carolingians.

Mesolithic Of/relating to the middle period of the Stone Age or Middle Stone Age (c.10,000–4000 BC).

Miniature Small painting in a manuscript.

Minuscule Lower case script.

Minster A large or important church that served as the base for an outreaching mission.

Mithraism Persian cult, particularly popular within the late Roman military, focusing on the redemptive slaying of the bull by Mithras.

Monothelete One who believes Jesus had only one will, rather than united divine and human wills.

Mystic One who seeks to obtain greater experience and knowledge of God through the act of sustained contemplation and heightened spirituality.

Neolithic Of/relating to the later part of the Stone Age, or New Stone Age (c.4000–2000 BC).

Œcumen The Christian ecumen, an eternal fellowship that transcends time, space and varied traditions.

Ogham/Ogam Script consisting of a series of horizontal and diagonal lines arranged around a central, vertical baseline, developed during the Iron Age by the Celts in response to Roman script. Named after the Celtic god Ogma/Ogmios.

Orans Posture of prayer, with the arms upraised.

Oratory A chapel or small building set aside for prayer, and sometimes for study.

Parochiae Monastic federations consisting of a series of monasteries united under the name and traditions of the original founding saint.

Penitential A manual or guidebook giving instruction on the confession of sins and the penances to be imposed on the penitent.

Peregrinatio Pilgrimage/voluntary exile in the name of Christ.

Picts The indigenous prehistoric inhabitants of much of Scotland, known by the Romans as 'picti' (painted ones) due to their practice of adorning their bodies with tattoes or paintings, often using woad.

Promontory fort A cliff-castle in which a headland is fortified by the construction of defensive rampart(s) on the landward side.

Quoit The large stones forming the central burial chamber in prehistoric barrows, now uncovered by the removal of the smaller stones that formed the covering mound. Also known as dolmens.

Rath Celtic Goidelic term for a defensive and/or symbolic earth or stone enclosure, surrounding a secular or, more often, a religious settlement. Known in the Brythonic languages as a *llan*.

Relic The tangible remains or belongings of a saint, usually their bones, which were imbued with the saint's power and were often considered to be capable of working miracles, often of healing.

Reliquary The sacred containers of the relics of saints, often made of decorative metalwork.

Romano-British Of/relating tothe Roman provinces of Britain and their inhabitants.

Rule, monastic A code of practice to guide the monastic life, often composed by a prominent founding saint. In the Insular world the abbot/abbess of a monastery generally formulated their own rule of life for their monks/nuns to follow, often with reference to one or more rules by such prominent monastic founders.

Script Style of handwriting used for a particular book or document.

Scriptorium A room in a monastery that was set apart for the writing and copying of manuscripts.

Secretary A type of cursive script.

Sept A clan or branch of a dynasty.

Sidhe The fairy-folk of Irish legends.

Skete A group of hermits or their hermitages, forming an eremitic monastery in which they followed their own separate lives as monks but came together for some acts of worship.

Stone Age Period of prehistory preceding the Bronze Age, prior to c.2000 BC .

Tír na nÓg The Celtic otherworld, the Land of the Young, which was thought to float as an idyllic island in the Atlantic.

Tuath A Celtic tribe.

Turas Irish word for a pilgrimage 'round', a journey of prayer around the stations of the cross.

Ui Neill An important ancient Irish dynasty, later known as the O'Neills, initially based in Connacht in northern and western Ireland, which traced its descent from Niall of the Nine Hostages.

Uncial A formal, rounded upper-case (majuscule) script used for writing Scripture and some high-grade early Anglo-Saxon charters.

Valkyrie Mythical handmaidens in Germanic/Scandinavian folklore who conducted those slain in battle from the battlefield to Valhalla (the otherworldly feast-hall).

Vikings Scandinavian raiders, traders and settlers who expanded into Europe, taking control of parts of Britain, Ireland, Normandy and Russia (Kiev) from the 790s until the eleventh century.

Wessex An Anglo-Saxon kingdom in south-west England, focusing upon the royal/religious centre of Winchester and the port of Hamwih (Southampton).

Select Bibliography

Chapter 1

Chadwick, N., 1971 *The Celts*, London

Collis, J., 1984 *The European Iron Age*, London

Hawkins, G. S., 1963, *Stonehenge Decoded*, reptd 1982, Glasgow

Joussaume, R., 1985, *Dolmens for the Dead: Megalith Building Throughout the World*, London

MacCulloch, J. A., 1991, *The Religion of the Ancient Celts*, London

Piggott, S., 1977, *The Druids*, Harmondsworth

Powell, T. G. E., 1980, *The Celts*, London

Ross, A., 1967, reptd 1974, *Pagan Celtic Britain*, London

Ross, A., 1970, *Everyday Life of the Pagan Celts*, London

Wait, G. A., 1985, 'Ritual and Religion in Iron Age Britain', *British Archaeological Reports* 149, Oxford

Chapter 2

Cunliffe, B., 1988, *Greeks, Romans and Barbarians. Spheres of Interaction*, London

Green, M. J., 1976, 'The Religions of Civilian Roman Britain', *British Archaeological Reports* 24, Oxford

Henig, M., 1984, *Religion in Roman Britain*, London

Lane Fox, R., 1986, *Pagans and Christians in the Mediterranean World from the Second Century AD to the Conversion of Constantine*, London

Morris, J., 1968, 'The Date of St Alban', *Hertfordshire Archaeology* 1, 1-8

Rodwell, R. J., 1982, 'Temples, Churches and Religion in Roman Britain', *British Archaeological Reports* 77, Oxford

Wacher, J., 1978, *Roman Britain*, London

Woodward, A., 1992, *English Heritage Book of Shrines and Sacrifice*, London

Chapter 3

Alcock, L. 1972, *'By South Cadbury is that Camelot...' The Excavation of Cadbury Castle 1966-1970*, London

Berresford Ellis, P., 1993, *Celt and Saxon. The Struggle for Britain AD 410-937*, London

Brown, P., 1982, *Society and the Holy in Late Antiquity*, London

Carley, J. P., 1988, *Glastonbury Abbey. The Holy House at the Head of the Moors Adventurous*, Woodbridge

Casey, P. J., ed., 1979, 'The End of Roman Britain', *British Archaeological Reports* 71, Oxford

Dark, K., 2000, *Britain and the End of the Roman Empire*, Stroud

Dumville, D. N., ed., 1985, *The Historia Brittonum,* Cambridge

Dumville, D. N., 1993, *St Patrick, AD 493-1993*, Woodbridge

Frend, W. H., 1979, 'Ecclesia Britannica: Prelude or Dead End?', *Journal of Ecclesiastical History* 30:2, April 1979

Higham, N. J., 1994, *The English Conquest. Gildas and Britain in the Fifth Century*, Manchester

Hood, A. B. E., ed., 1978, *St Patrick: His Writings and Muirchu's Life*, Chichester

Hunt, E. D., 1982, *Holy Land Pilgrimage in the Later Roman Empire*, Oxford

Lapidge, M. and Dumville, D. N., 1984, *Gildas: New Approaches*, Woodbridge

Morris, J., 1977, *The Age of Arthur. A History of the British Isles from 350 to 650*, London

Morris, J., ed., 1978, *Gildas*, Arthurian Period Sources vol. 7, London

Powell, T. G. E., 1992, 'Christianity or Solar Monotheism: the Early Religious Beliefs of St Patrick', *Journal of Ecclesiastical History* 43:4, October, 1992

Rees, B. R., 1991, *The Letters of Pelagius and His Followers*, Woodbridge

Sharpe, R., 1982, 'St Patrick and the See of Armagh', *Cambridge Medieval Celtic Studies* 4, 33-59

Thomas, C., 1981, *Christianity in Roman Britain to AD 500*, London

Webster, L. and Brown, M. P., eds, 1997, *The Transformation of the Roman World*, London

Weyer, R. Van de, 1995, *The Letter of Pelagius, Celtic Soul Friend*, Evesham

Chapter 4

Barley, M. W. and Hanson, R. P. C., eds, 1968, *Christianity in Britain, 300-700*, Leicester

Bowen, E. G., 1977, *Saints, Seaways and Settlements*, Cardiff

Chadwick, N., 1961, *The Age of the Saints in the Early Celtic Church*, London

Chadwick, N., 1965, *The Colonization of Brittany from Celtic Britain*, Sir John Rhys Memorial Lecture, British Academy

Cramp, R., 1994, 'Whithorn and the Northumbrian Expansion Westwards', *Third Whithorn Lecture*

Cubbon, A. M., reptd 1994, *The Art of the Manx Crosses*, Douglas

Davies, W., 1982, *Wales in the Early Middle Ages*, Leicester

Deuffic, J. L., 1986, 'La production manuscrite de scriptoria Bretons (VIII-IXe siècles)', in M. Simon, ed., *Landévennec et le monachisme breton dans le haut moyen âge*, Landevennec, pp. 289-321

Driscoll, S. T., 1998, 'Church Archaeology in Glasgow and the Kingdom of Strathclyde', *Innes Review* 49, 95-114

Driscoll, S. T., 2004, *Govan from Cradle to Grave*, Friends of Govan Old, Govan

Dumville, D. N., 1993, *Britons and Anglo-Saxons in the early middle ages*, Aldershot

Evans, J. G. and Rhys, J., 1893, *The Text of the Book of Llan Dâv*, reptd 1979, Aberystwyth

Gill, S., Colwill, S. and Leonard, R., 1986, *The Saints' Way: Forth an Syns*, Wadebridge

Gregory, R., 1989, *Wales Before 1066. A Guide*, Lanrwst

Higgitt, J., Forsyth, K. and Parsons, D. N., eds, 2001, *Roman, Runes and Ogham. Medieval Inscriptions in the Insular World and on the Continent*, Donington

Higham, N. J., 1992, *Rome, Britain and the Anglo-Saxons*, London

Hill, P., 1992, *Whithorn 4. Excavations 1990-1991. Interim Report*, Whithorn

Hill, P., 1994, *The Whithorn Dig*, Whithorn

Jackson, A., 1984, *The Symbol Stones of Scotland*, Kirkwall

Jenkins, D. and Owen, M. E., eds, 1980, *The Welsh Law of Women. Studies Presented to D. A. Binchy*, Cambridge

Kent, A. M., 2000, *The Literature of Cornwall*, Bristol

Laing, L., 1973, 'The Angles in Scotland and the Mote of Mark', *Trans. of the Dumfriesshire and Galloway Natural History and Antiquarian Soc.*, third series, 50, 39-52

Laing, L., 1975, 'The Mote of Mark and the origins of Celtic interlace', *Antiquity* 49, 98-108

Lindsay, W. M., 1912, *Early Welsh Script*, Oxford

Morris, J., ed., 1980, *Nennius. Arthurian Period Sources vol. 8*, London

Redknap, M., 1991, *The Christian Celts. Treasures of Late Celtic Wales*, Cardiff

Rees, A. and B., reptd 1990, *Celtic Heritage: Ancient Tradition in Ireland and Wales*, London

Ritchie, G. and A., 1981, *Scotland, Archaeology and Early History*, London

Romilly Allen, J. 1989, *Celtic Crosses of Wales*, reptd Llanerch, 1989

Romilly Allen, J. and Anderson, J., 1903, *The Early Christian Monuments of Scotland*, 2 vols, reptd Angus, 1993

Sims-Williams, P., 1990, *Religion and Literature in Western England, 600-800*, Cambridge

Small, A., Thomas, C. and Wilson, D. M., 1973, *St Ninian's Isle and its Treasure*, Oxford

Smith, I. M., 1983, 'Brito-Roman and Anglo-Saxon: the unification of the Borders', in P. Clack and J. Ivy, eds, *The Borders*, Durham, 9-48

Smyth, A. P., 1984, *Warlords and Holy Men, Scotland AD 80-1000*, London

Sutherland, E., 1994, *In Search of the Picts*, London

Thomas, C., 1971, *The Early Christian Archaeology of North Britain*, Oxford

Thomas, C., 1986, *Celtic Britain*, London

Thomas, C., 1992, 'Whithorn's Christian Beginnings', *First Whithorn Lecture*

Thomas, C., 1994, *And Shall These Mute Stones Speak?*, Cardiff

Thomas, P., 1993, *Candle in the Darkness: Celtic Spirituality from Wales*, Dyfed

Victory, S., 1977, *The Celtic Church in Wales*, London

Weatherhill, C., 1985, *Cornovia. Ancient Sites of Cornwall and Scilly*, Penzance

Chapter 5

Anderson, A. O. and M. O., 1991, *Adomnan's Life of Columba*, Oxford

Anderson, J., 1992, 'The Voyage of Brendan, an Irish Monastic Expedition to Discover the Wonders of God's World', *American Benedictine Review* 43:3, September, 1992

Armstrong, E. C. R. and R. A. S. Macalister, 1920, 'Wooden book with leaves indented and waxed found near Springmount Bog, Co. Antrim', *Journal of the Royal Soc. of Antiquaries of Ireland* 50 (6th series, 10), 160-6

Bieler, L., 1963, *Ireland, Harbinger of the Middle Ages*, London

Bieler, L., 1963, *The Irish Penitentials*, Dublin

Bieler, L., 1979, *The Patrician Texts in the Book of Armagh*, Dublin

Binchy, D. A., 1936, *Studies in Early Irish Law*, Dublin

Binchy, D. A., 1970, *Celtic and Anglo-Saxon Kingship*, Oxford

Bitel, L., 1986, 'Women's Monastic Enclosures in Early Ireland: a Study of Female Spirituality and Male Monastic Mentalities', *Journal of Medieval History* 12

Bitel, L., 1990, *Isle of the Saints: Monastic Settlement and Christian Community in Early Ireland*, Itaca, NY

Byrne, F. J., 1973, *Irish Kings and High-Kings*, London

Campbell, E. and Lane, A., 1993, 'Celtic and Germanic Interaction in Dalriada: the 7th-Century Metalworking site at Dunadd', in Spearman and Higgitt, 1993, pp. 52-63

Carney, J., 1985, *Medieval Irish Lyrics with the Irish Bardic Poet*, Portlaoise, second edn

Department of the Environment for Northern Ireland, 1983, *Historic Monuments of Northern Ireland*, Belfast, sixth edn

Duke, J. A., 1957, *The Columban Church*, Edinburgh

Edwards, N., 1990, *The Archaeology of Early Medieval Ireland*, London

Farr, C, 1997, *The Book of Kells, its Function and Audience*, London and Toronto

Fox, P., *et al.*, ed., 1990, *The Book of Kells, MS 58, Trinity College Library Dublin*, 2 vols, facsimile and commentary, Luzern

Greene, D. and O'Connor, F., eds, 1990, *A Golden Treasury of Irish Poetry AD 600-1200*, Dingle

Harbison, P., 1970, *Guide to the National Monuments in the Republic of Ireland*, Dublin, second edn 1975

Harbison, P., 1991, *Pilgrimage in Ireland*, London

Henry, F., 1954, *Early Christian Irish Art*, Dublin

Henry, F., 1964, *L'Art Irlandaise*, Yonne

Henry, F., 1974, *The Book of Kells*, London

Herbert, M., 1988, *Iona, Kells and Derry: History and Hagiography of the Monastic Familia of Columba*, Oxford

Herren, M. W., 1981, 'Classical and Secular Learning among the Irish before the Carolingian Renaissance', *Florilegium* 3, 118-57

Howlett, D., 1998, 'Vita I Sanctae Brigitae', *Peritia* 12, 1-23

Hughes, K., 1972, *Early Christian Ireland: Introduction to the Sources*, London

Hughes, K. and Hamlin, A., 1981, *Celtic Monasticism: the Modern Traveller to the Irish Church*, New York

Hughes, K., 1987, *Church and Society in Ireland AD 400-1200*, London

Kenney, J. F., 1979, *The Sources for the Early History of Ireland.*

Ecclesiastical. An Introduction and Guide, Dublin

Lane, A., and E. Campbell, 2000, *Dunadd. An Early Dalriadic Capital*, Cardiff Studies in Archaeology, Oxford

Lindsay, W. M., 1910, *Early Irish Minuscule Script*, Oxford

Luce, A., et al., 1960, *Evangeliorum quattuor Codex Durmachensis*, facsimile and commentary, 2 vols, Olten

MacCarthy, B., ed., 1893, *The Annals of Ulster*, Dublin

Mac Niocaill, G., 1972, *Ireland Before the Vikings*, Dublin

McCone, K., 1982, 'Brigid in the Seventh Century: A Saint with Three Lives', *Peritia* 1, 107-45

McGrath, F., 1979, *Education in Ancient and Medieval Ireland*, Blackrock

Meehan, B., 1994, *The Book of Kells*, London

Meehan, B., 1996, *The Book of Durrow*, Dublin

Murray, P., ed., 1986, *The Deer's Cry: a Treasury of Irish Religious Verse*, Dublin

Ní Chatháin, P. and Richter, M., eds, 1984, *Irland und Europa: Die Kirche im Frümittelalter*, Stuttgart

Ní Chatháin, P. and Richter, M., eds, 1987, *Irland und die Christenheit: Bibelstudien und Mission*, Stuttgart

Ó Cróinín, D., 1984, 'Rath Maelsigi, Willibrord and the Earliest Echternach Manuscripts', *Peritia* 3, 17–49

Ó Cróinín, D., 1995, *Early Medieval Ireland, 400–1200*, London and New York

O'Fiaich, T., 1974, *Columbanus in his own words*, reptd 1990, Dublin

O'Loughlin, T., 2000, *Celtic Theology, Humanity, World and God in Early Irish Writings*, London

O'Mahony, F., ed., 1994, *The Book of Kells. Proceedings of a Conference at Trinity College Dublin*, 6–9 September 1992, Aldershot

O'Neill, T. 1984, *The Irish Hand*, Portlaoise

O'Sullivan, P., 1977, *A World of Stone. The Aran Islands*, Dublin, reptd 1991

Richter, M., 1988, *Medieval Ireland, The Enduring Tradition*, Basingstoke

Ryan, M., ed., 1983, *Treasures of Ireland. Irish Art, 3000 BC–1500 AD*, DublinRyan, M., ed., 1991, *The Illustrated Archaeology of Ireland*, Dublin

Schaumann, B.T., 1978/9, 'Early Irish Manuscripts: the Art of the Scribes', *Expedition* 21, 33–47

Severin, T., 1978, *The Brendan Voyage*, London

Sharpe, R., 1982, 'Vitae S. Brigitae: the Oldest Texts, *Peritia* 1, 81–106

Sharpe, R., 1991, *Medieval Irish Saints Lives*, Oxford

Sharpe, R., 1995, *Adomnan's Life of St Columba*, Harmondsworth

Stalley, R., 1991, *Irish High Crosses*, Dublin

Stalley, R., 1994, 'Scribe and mason: the Book of Kells and the Irish high crosses', in O'Mahony, ed., 1994, pp. 257-65

Walker, G. M. S., reptd 1970, *Sancti Columbani Opera*, Dublin

Youngs, S., ed., 1989, 'The Work of Angels', Masterpieces of Celtic Metalwork, 6th–9th Centuries AD, London and Austin

Chapter 6

Anglo-Saxon Chronicle, ed. and trans. G. N. Garmonsway, London, 1982;

The Anglo-Saxon Chronicle, a Collaborative Edition, ed. D. N. Dumville and S. Keynes, Cambridge, 1995–

Battiscombe, G. F., ed., 1956, *The Relics of St Cuthbert*, Oxford

Bede, *De Templo and De Tabernaculo*, ed. D. Hurst, Corpus Christianorum Series Latina 119A, Bedae Opera, Pars II 'Opera Exegetica', 2A, Turnhout, 1969

Bede, *On the Tabernacle*, Transl. A. G. Holder, Liverpool, 1994

Bede, *On the Temple*, Transl. S. Connolly, with intro. by J. O'Reilly, Liverpool, 1995

Bede, *Expositio in Lucam* ed. D. Hurst, Corpus Christianorum Series Latina 120, Turnhout, 1960

Bede, *Historia Abbatum*, ed. C. Plummer, Oxford, 1896

Bede, *Historia Ecclesiatica* (HE),
ed. D. H. Farmer, transl. L. Sherley-Price, revd R. E. Latham,

Bede, *Ecclesiastical History of the English People*, London, 1990., ed. B. Colgrave and R. A. B. Mynors, *Bede's Ecclesiastical History*, Oxford, 1969.

ed. C. Plummer, *Bedae Opera Historica*, Oxford, 1956.

Bede, *Lives of the Abbots of Wearmouth and Jarrow* ed. D. H. Farmer, *The Age of Bede*, revd edn, Harmondsworth, 1983

Bede, *Homilia Homiletica*, Corpus Christianorum Series Latina 122, ed. and transl. by D. Hurst, Turnhout, 1955

Bede, *Vita*, Bede, Prose *Life of Cuthbert*, ed. and transl. by D. H. Farmer, Harmondsworth, 1983

Blair, P. H., 1977, *An Introduction to Anglo-Saxon England*, Oxford

Brooks, N., 1984, *The Early History of the Church of Canterbury*, Leicester

Brown, G. H., 1987, *Bede the Venerable*, Boston

Brown, G. H., 1996, *Bede the Educator*, Jarrow Lecture 1996, Newcastle-upon-Tyne

Chazelle, C., 1990, 'Pictures, Books and the Illiterate: Pope Gregory I's Letters to Serenus of Marseilles', *Word and Image* 6, no. 2 (1990), 138-153

Dumville, D. N., 1993, *Britons and Anglo-Saxons in the early middle ages*, Aldershot

Gameson, R. G., ed., 1999, *St Augustine and the Conversion of England*, Stroud

Glover, J., Mackie, S. and Magnusson, M., ed. and trans., 1987, *Beowulf*, Stroud

Kiernan, K., 1996, *Beowulf*, Ann Arbor

Kirby, D. P., 1974, *St Wilfrid at Hexham*, Newcastle

Markus, R. A., 1997, *Gregory the Great and His World*, Cambridge

Mayr-Harting, H., 1977, *The Coming of Christianity to Anglo-Saxon England*, Oxford

Speake, G., 1980, *Anglo-Saxon Animal Art and its Germanic Background*, Oxford

Walsh, M., 1986, *Roots of Christianity*, London

Weitzmann, K., 1977, *Late Antique and Early Christian Book Illumination*, London

Wormald, P., 1984, *Bede and the Conversion of England*, Jarrow Lecture 1984, Newcastle-upon-Tyne

Wormald, P., 1993, 'The Venerable Bede and the "Church of the English"', in G. Rowell, ed., *The English Religious Tradition and the Genius of Anglicanism*, Wantage

Chapter 7

Alexander, J. J. G., 1978, *Insular Manuscripts, 6th to the 9th Century*, London

Bischoff, B. and V. Brown, 1985, 'Addenda to Codices Latini Antiquiores', *Mediaeval Studies* 47, 317-366

Blair, J. and Sharpe, R., eds 1992, *Pastoral Care Before the Parish*, Leicester

Bonner, G., et al., eds, 1989, *St Cuthbert, His Cult and His Community to AD 1200*, Woodbridge

Brown, G. H. and Karkov, C., eds, 2003, *Anglo-Saxon Styles*, New York

Brown, M. P. 1990, *A Guide to Western Historical Scripts from Antiquity to 1600*, London and Toronto, 1990, 1994, 2nd edn 1999

Brown, M. P., 1991, *Anglo-Saxon Manuscripts*, London

Brown, M. P., 1996, *The Book of Cerne. Prayer, Patronage and Power in Ninth-Century England*, London and Toronto

Brown, M. P., 2000, '"In the beginning was the Word": books and faith in the age of Bede', *The Jarrow Lecture 2000*, Newcastle-upon-Tyne

Brown, M. P. and Farr, C., eds, 2001, *Mercia: An Anglo-Saxon Kingdom in Europe*, Leicester, esp. M. P. Brown, 'Mercian Manuscripts? The 'Tiberius' Group and its Historical Context', pp. 278-91

Brown, M. P., 2001, 'Female book-ownership and production in Anglo-Saxon England: the Evidence of the Ninth-Century Prayerbooks', in C. Kay & L. Sylvester, eds, *Lexis and Texts in Early English: Papers in Honour of Jane Roberts*, Amsterdam

Brown, M. P., 2001, 'The Life of St Fursey: what we know and why it matters', The Inaugural Fursey Lecture, Diocese of

Norwich, Norwich, 2001

Brown, M. P., 2003, *The Lindisfarne Gospels: Society, Spirituality and the Scribe*, London, Toronto and Luzern; Commentary vol. (published in English / German parallel edition, Luzern; also published as a stand-alone monograph, London & Toronto) to accompany *The Lindisfarne Gospels* facsimile, Faksimile Verlag, Luzern

Brown, M. P., 2003, *Painted Labyrinth: the world of the Lindisfarne Gospels*, London

Brown, M. P., 2005, 'The Tower of Babel: the origins of the early western written vernaculars', in memorial vol. for Leonard Boyle, ed. A. Duggan and B. Bolton, Turnhout

Brown, M. P., 2006, *Manuscripts from the Anglo-Saxon Age*, London

Brown, T. J., See J. Bately, M. P. Brown and J. Roberts, eds, 1993, *A Palaeographer's View: Selected Papers of Julian Brown*, London

Bruce-Mitford, R., 1967, *The Art of the Codex Amiatinus*, Jarrow Lecture 1967, Newcastle-upon-Tyne

Bruckner, A. et al., eds, 1954-, *Chartae Latinae Antiquiores (Olten)*, see esp. III and IV

Bullough, D. A., 2004, *Alcuin*, Leiden, Boston and Brill

Cameron, M. L., 1993, *Anglo-Saxon Medicine*, Cambridge

Clayton, M., 1990, *The Cult of the Virgin Mary in Anglo-Saxon England*, Cambridge

Crossley-Holland, K., 1982, *The Anglo-Saxon World: an Anthology*, Oxford

Deshman, R., 1984, *Anglo-Saxon and Anglo-Scandinavian Art: an Annotated Bibliography*, Toronto

Dodwell, C. R., 1982, *Anglo-Saxon Art, a New Perspective*, Manchester

Dumville, D. N., 1995, 'The importation of Mediterranean manuscripts into Theodore's England', in M. Lapidge, ed., *Archbishop Theodore*, Cambridge, pp. 96–119

Dumville, D. N., 1997, 'The origins and early history of Insular monasticism: aspects of literature, Christianity and society in Britain and Ireland, AD 400-600', Bulletin of the *Institute of Oriental and Occidental Studies*, Kansai University, 30, 85–107

Dumville, D. N., 1999, *A Palaeographer's Review*, Osaka

Fell, C., 1984, *Women in Anglo-Saxon England*, London

Gameson, R. G., ed., forthcoming, *The History of the Book in Britain*, I, Cambridge

Ganz, D., 2002, 'Roman Manuscripts in Francia and Anglo-Saxon England', in *Roma fra Oriente e Occidente, Settimane di Studio del Centro Italiano di Studi sull'Alto Medioevo*, XLIX, Spoleto

Gneuss, H., 1996, *Books and Libraries in Early England*, Aldershot

Gneuss, H., 2003, *A Handlist of Anglo-Saxon Manuscripts, a list of manuscripts and manuscript fragments written or owned in England up to 1100*, Tempe, Arizona (first printed in *Anglo-Saxon England 9*; Supplement in Anglo-Saxon England 32, 2003)

Hawkes, J., 1996, *The Golden Age of Northumbria*, Morpeth

Henderson, G., 1987, *From Durrow to Kells, the Insular Gospel-books 650–800*, London

Herren, M. W., 1981, *Insular Latin Studies: Papers on Latin Texts and Manuscripts of the British Isles, 550-1066*, Toronto

Higham, N. J., 1993, *The Kingdom of Northumbria*, Stroud

Hull, D., 2003, *Celtic and Anglo-Saxon Art, Geometric Aspects*, Liverpool

Kelly, S., 1990, 'Anglo-Saxon Lay Society and the Written Word', in R. McKitterick, ed., *The Uses of Literacy in Early Mediaeval Europe*, Cambridge, pp. 36–62

Kendrick, T. D., 1938, *Anglo-Saxon Art to A.D. 900*, London

Kendrick, T. D., et al., 1956-60, *Evangeliorum Quattuor Codex Lindisfarnensis*, facsimile, 2 vols, Olten and Lausanne

Ker, N. R., 1957, *Catalogue of Manuscripts Containing Anglo-Saxon*, Oxford

Ker, N. and M., 1982, *A Guide to Anglo-Saxon Sites*, London

Knight, S. 1984, *Historical Scripts. A Handbook for Calligraphers*, London

Lapidge, M, 1986, 'The School of Theodore and Hadrian', *Anglo-Saxon England* 15, 45-72

Lapidge, M., 1988, 'The Study of Greek at the School of

Canterbury in the Seventh Century', in M. Herren (ed.), *The Sacred Nectar of the Greeks: The Study of Greek in the West in the Early Middle Ages*, London, 169–94

Lapidge, M. and Herren, M., eds, 1979, *Aldhelm, The Prose Works*, Ipswich

Lapidge, M., 1979, 'Aldhelm's Latin Poetry and Old English Verse', *Comparative Literature* 31

Levison, W. and Tangl, M., eds, 1968. *Bonifatii Epistula*, Darmstadt

Levison, W., 1946, *England and the Continent in the Eighth Century*, Oxford

Lowe, E. A., 1934–1972, *Codices Latini Antiquiores*, 11 vols and suppl., Oxford

See also Bischoff and Brown, supplement, above

Marsden, R., 1995, *The Text of the Old Testament in Anglo-Saxon England*, Cambridge Studies in Anglo-Saxon England 15, Cambridge

McGurk, P., 1961, *Latin gospel books from AD 400 to AD 800*, Les Publications de Scriptorium, V, Paris-Brussels, Anvers-Amsterdam

McGurk, P., 1998, *Gospel Books and Early Latin Manuscripts*, Variorum Collected Studies, Ashgate: Aldershot

McKitterick, R., 1986–1990, 'Anglo-Saxon missionaries in Germany: reflections on the manuscript evidence', *Transactions of the Cambridge Bibliographical Society* 9, 291–329

Meyvaert, P., 1996, 'Bede, Cassiodorus and the Codex Amiatinus', *Speculum* 71, 827–83

Mitchell, B. and Robinson, F. C., 1989, *A Guide to Old English*, London

Netzer, N., 1994, *Cultural Interplay in the Eighth Century, the Trier Gospels and the Making of a Scriptorium at Echternach*, Cambridge

Neuman de Vegvar, C., 1987, *The Northumbrian Renaissance: a Study in the Transmission of Style*, London and Toronto

Nordenfalk, C., 1977, *Celtic and Anglo-Saxon Painting*, London

Ó Carragáin, E., 1994, *The City of Rome and the World of Bede*, Jarrow Lecture 1994, Newcastle-upon-Tyne

Ó Carragáin, E., 2005, *Liturgical Thought And 'The Dream Of The Rood', Communal Rituals And Meditative Reading in Anglo-Saxon England*, London and Toronto

Okasha, E., 1971, *Hand-list of Anglo-Saxon non-runic inscriptions*, Cambridge

Orchard, A. 1994, *The Poetic Art of Aldhelm*, Cambridge

O'Reilly, J., 2001, 'The Library of Scripture: Views from the Vivarium and Wearmouth-Jarrow', in P. Binski and W. G. Noel, eds, *New Offerings, Ancient Treasures. Essays in Medieval Art for George Henderson*, Stroud

Page, R. I., 1995, *Runes and Runic Inscriptions*, Woodbridge

Parkes, M. B., 1982, 'The Scriptorium of Wearmouth-Jarrow', *Jarrow Lecture* 1982, Newcastle-upon-Tyne

Parkes, M. B., 2000, 'Rædan, areccan, smeagan: how the Anglo-Saxons read', *Anglo-Saxon England* 26, 1–22

Pulsiano, P. and Traherne, E., eds, 2001, *Anglo-Saxon Literary Culture*, Oxford

Ridyard, S. J., 1988, *The Royal Saints of Anglo-Saxon England*, Cambridge

Rollason, D., 1990, *Saints and Relics in Anglo-Saxon England*, Oxford

Sawyer, P. H., 1968, Anglo-Saxon Charters, an annotated list and bibliography, London

Stenton, F. M., 1971, *Anglo-Saxon England*, Oxford

Stevick, R., 1994, The Earliest Irish and English Bookarts. Visual and Poetic Forms Before AD 1000, Philadelphia

Taylor, H. M. and Taylor, J., 1965, *Anglo-Saxon Architecture*, Cambridge, reptd 1980

Thacker, A., 2002, *Local Saints and Local Churches in the Early Medieval West*, Oxford

Verey, C. D., et al., 1980, 'The Durham Gospels', *Early English Manuscripts* in Facsimile 20, Copenhagen

Webster, L. and Backhouse, J. M., eds, 1991, *The Making of England: Anglo-Saxon Art and Culture AD 600–900*, London

Whitelock, D., ed., 1979, *English Historical Documents* I, revd edn, London

Wilson, D. M., 1981, *The Anglo-Saxons*, London

Wilson, D. M., 1984, *Anglo-Saxon Art*, London

Wood, I., 1995, *The Most Holy Abbot, Ceolfrid*, Jarrow Lecture, 1995

Wright, D. H., 1967, *The Vespasian Psalter*, Early English Manuscript in Facsimile 14, Copenhagen

Zimmermann, E. H., 1916, *Vorkarolingische Miniaturen*, Berlin

Epilogue

Dumville, D. N., 1992, Wessex and England, from Alfred to Edgar, Woodbridge

Gneuss, H., 1986, 'King Alfred and the history of Anglo-Saxon libraries', in P. R. Brown et al., eds, Modes of Interpretation in Old English Literature, Toronto, pp. 29-49

Keynes, S. and Lapidge, M., 1983, Alfred the Great, Harmondsworth

Lang, J., ed., 1978, Anglo-Saxon and Viking Age Sculpture, BAR Brit. Series, 49

Lang, J., ed., 1991, Corpus of Anglo-Saxon Stone Sculpture, III, York and Eastern Yorkshire, Oxford

Morrish, J., 1982, 'An Examination of Literature and Learning in the 9th Century', unpubl. Ph.D. dissertation, Oxford University

General

Ayerst, D. and A. S. T. Fisher, A. S. T., eds. 1977, *Records of Christianity II*, Oxford

Brown, P., 1981, *The Cult of Saints: Its Rise and Function in Latin Christianity*, Chicago and London

Clanchy, M., 1993, *From Memory to Written Record*, 2nd edn, Cambridge Mass. & Oxford; reptd 1998

De Waal, E., 1988, *The Celtic Vision*, London

Farmer, D. H., 1978, fifth edn 2003, *Oxford Dictionary of Saints*, Oxford

Fischer, Bonifatius, 1988-1991, *Die lateinischen Evangelien bis zum 10. Jahrhundert*, Freiburg im Breisgau, (Aus der Geschichte der lateinischen Bibel, 13, 15, 17, 18, Matthew 1988, Mark 1989, Luke 1990, John 1991)

Gameson, R. G., ed., 1994, *The Early Medieval Bible*, Cambridge

Grabar, A., 1980, *Christian Iconography. A Study of its Origins*, London and Henley

Knowles, D. and Hancock, R. N., 1953, *Medieval Religious Houses: England and Wales*, London

Laing, L., 1975, *The Archaeology of Late Celtic Britain and Ireland c.400-1200 AD*, London

Joyce, T., 1998, *Celtic Christianity*, Maryknoll, NY

Laing, L. and J., 1979, *A Guide to the Dark Age Remains in Britain*, London

Laing, L., 1993, 'A Catalogue of Celtic Ornamental Metalwork in the British Isles c.AD 400-1200', *BAR*, Brit. Ser. 229

Lampe, G. W. H., ed., 1969, *The Cambridge History of the Bible. 2, The West from the Fathers to the Reformation*, Cambridge

Lapidge, M. and Sharpe, R., 1985, *A Bibliography of Celtic-Latin Literature, 400-1200*, Dublin

Larousse, 1979, *The New Larousse Encyclopedia of Mythology*, London, NY, Sydney and Toronto

McKitterick, R., 1990, *The Uses of Literacy in Early Medieval Europe*, Cambridge

McNeill, J. T., 1974, *The Celtic Churches: a History, AD 200-1200*, Chicago

Mitchell, B. and Robinson, F. C., 1989, *A Guide to Old English*, London

Morris, R., 1983, *The Church in British Archaeology*, Council for British Archaeology Res. Rep. 47, London

Morris, R., 1989, *Churches in the Landscape*, London

O'Loughlin, T., 2000, *Journeys on the Edges, the Celtic Tradition*, London

Raby, F. J. E., 1953, *Christian Latin Poetry*, Oxford

Rees, A. and B., reptd 1990, *Celtic Heritage: Ancient Tradition in Ireland and Wales*, London

Reynolds, L. D., ed., 1983, *Texts and Transmission: a Survey of the Latin Classics*, Oxford

Sheldrake, P., London, *Living Between Worlds. Place and Journey in Celtic Spirituality*, 1995

Stansbury, M., 1999, 'Early Medieval Biblical Commentaries, Their Writers and Readers', in K. Hauck, ed., *Frümittelalterliche Studien*, Herausgegeben von H. Keller und C. Meier, Berlin and New York, pp. 50-82

Thomas, C., 1971, *Britain and Ireland in Early Christian Times AD 400-800*, London

Thompson, D. V., 1956, *The Materials and Techniques of Medieval Painting*, New York

Travis, J., 1973, *Early Celtic Versecraft*, Shannon

Wessels, A., 1994, *Europe: Was it Ever Really Christian?*, London

Youngs, S., ed., 1989, 'The Work of Angels', *Masterpieces of Celtic Metalwork, 6th-9th Centuries AD*, London and Austin

Index

Picture Acknowledgments

Picture research by Zooid Pictures Limited.

AKG – Images: pp. 20 (Pietro Baguzzi); 22–23, The Cult of St Columba ii.

Alamy: pp. 90 (David Lyons); 92 (Liam White).

Bridgeman Art Library: pp. 38a, The Cult of St Columba iii (The Board of Trinity College, Dublin, Ireland); 49 (British Museum, London, UK); Early Christian Irish artefacts ii, vi (National Museum of Ireland, Dublin); 126, Early Christian Irish artefacts vii.

British Library: pp. 87, 176.

British Museum: Sutton Hoo iv.

Michelle Brown: pp. 2r, 4 (British Library Board, Cotton MS Nero D.iv, f. 29r, Mt 1.18), 12–13, 13ar, 14, 16, 28, 29a (Chedworth Roman villa), 29b (Chedworth Roman villa), 33 (Durham Cathedral), 44, 46, 50 (Bodleian Library, Oxford, MS Canon. Misc. 378, f. 153), 54 (British Library Board, Cotton MS Vitellius A.vi, f. 16v), 59, 61 (British Library Board, Harley MS 3859, f. 187r), 62, 63, 64, 67 (Trinity College Library, MS 52, f.159v), 71r, 77, 78 (Chapter of Lichfield Cathedral, MS 1, p. 218), 80al (St David's Cathedral), 83a, 83b, 84, 85a, 85b, 86, 96a, 96b, 102a, 102b, 106, 115, 124b (British Museum), 125 (Durham Cathedral), 132 (British Library Board), 140a, 140bl, 140br, 142–143, 144, 146, 147l, 147r, 148 (Corpus Christi College, Cambridge, MS 144, f. 1r), 151a, 154l (British Library Board, Cotton MS Nero D.iv, ff. 26v–27r), 154–155, 158 (British Library Board, BL, Yates Thompson MS 26, f. 39r), 159 (Society of Jesus, (image) formerly the Stonyhurst Gospel, BL Loan MS 74), 162a, 162m, (Bede's World / St Paul's, Jarrow), 162b (Bede's World / St Paul's, Jarrow), 164l, 164r, 170–171 (British Library Board, Cotton MS Nero D.iv, ff. 138v–139r), 172 (British Library Board, Cotton MS Nero D.iv, f. 209v), 177 (British Library Board, Cotton MS Vesp. A.i, ff. 30v–31r), 179, 180a, 180m, 180b, 182, 186, 189 (British Library Board, Royal MS 1.B.vii, f. 15v), 190–191 (Stockholm, Kungl. Biblioteket, Codex Aureus, MS A.135, ff. 9v–11), 192 (St Mary's Church, Nunburnholme), 193 (St Mary's Church, Nunburnholme), The Cult of St Columba iv, v, Mercian book culture i (by permission of the Syndics of Cambridge University Library, Book of Cerne, MS L1.1.10, f. 31v), Mercian book culture ii (British Library Board, Royal MS 1.E.vi, f. 43r), Mercian book culture iii (British Library Board, Royal MS 2.A.xx, ff. 16v–17r), Mercian book culture iv (Biblioteca Apostolica Vaticana, MS lat. 570, f. 1r), Mercian book culture v (Biblioteca Apostolica Vaticana, MS lat. 570, f. 11v), The Picts ii, iii, iv, v, The Picts vii (Historic Scotland), The Picts viii, x, Sutton Hoo v (British Museum).

Cambridge University Library: The Picts vi.

Corbis UK Ltd.: pp. 15 (Adam Woolfitt); 22bl (Werner Forman); 105 (Tom Bean); The Cult of St Columba vi (Archivo Iconografico, S.A.).

Corpus Christi College, Cambridge: p. 120.

Durham Cathedral: pp. 38b, 151b.

English Heritage Photo Library: p. 145 (Jonathan Bailey).

Heritage Image Partnership: pp. 3r, 185, 196, 197 (The British Museum); 36 (© Museum of London).

Horton Design: p. 153.

Manx National Heritage: p. 80br.

Museum of London Archaeology Service: pp. 1, 124a.

National Museum of Ireland: Early Christian Irish artefacts i, Early Christian Irish artefacts iii, Early Christian Irish artefacts iv, Early Christian Irish artefacts v.

National Museums of Scotland: pp. 3l, 71l, 107.

National Trust Photographic Library: Sutton Hoo ii (Joe Cornish).

Zev Radovan, Jerusalem: p. 167.

Royal Irish Academy (© RIA): The Cult of St Columba i.

Martin Sanders (maps): pp. 6–7.

SCRAN IT Ltd.: The Picts ix (Royal Commission on the Ancient and Historical Monuments of Scotland); p. 3m, The Picts i.

Society of Jesus: p. 159.

TopFoto: pp. 2l, 32, 34, 35a, 35b, 184, Sutton Hoo i, iii (Topham Picturepoint); Sutton Hoo vi (The British Museum).

The Board of Trinity College Dublin: The Cult of St Columba vii.

Zooid Pictures: pp. 2m, 42, 43 (British Museum).

(l = left, r = right, m = middle, a = above, b = below)

Lion Hudson

Commissioning editor: Morag Reeve
Project editor: Catherine Giddings
Picture research: Juliet Mozley
Designer: Nick Rous
Production manager: Kylie Ord